Critical Essays on
American Humor

Critical Essays on American Humor

William Bedford Clark
W. Craig Turner

G. K. Hall & Co. • Boston, Massachusetts

Library of Congress Cataloging in Publication Data

Main entry under title:

Critical essays on American humor.

    (Critical essays on American literature)
    Includes index.
    1. American wit and humor—History and criticism—
Addresses, essays, lectures.   I. Clark, William Bedford.
II. Turner, W. Craig.   III. Series.
PS430.C7   1984   817'.009   84–4489
ISBN 0–8161–8684–7 (alk. paper)

This publication is printed on permanent/durable acid-free paper
MANUFACTURED IN THE UNITED STATES OF AMERICA

CRITICAL ESSAYS ON AMERICAN LITERATURE

This series seeks to anthologize the most important criticism on a wide variety of topics and writers in American literature. Our readers will find in various volumes not only a generous selection of reprinted articles and reviews but original essays, bibliographies, manuscript sections, and other materials brought to public attention for the first time. This volume on American humor, edited by William Bedford Clark and W. Craig Turner, is a welcome addition to our list. In addition to an extensive introduction, which surveys the history of criticism on this topic, there are reprinted articles by Constance Rourke, Sculley Bradley, Bernard DeVoto, Louis J. Budd, Arlin Turner, and James M. Cox, among others, as well as seven original essays by Walter Blair, Robert Micklus, Milton Rickels, David B. Kesterson, Sanford Pinsker, Emily Toth, and Hamlin Hill. We are confident that this volume will make a permanent and significant contribution to American literary study.

James Nagel, General Editor

Northeastern University

TO CHARLENE AND ANNETTE,
who know when to laugh.

CONTENTS

INTRODUCTION

At the end of Plato's *Symposium*, perhaps the most influential synthesis of heady philosophy and hearty farce in all of Western literature, the reader is presented with an oblique report of Socrates arguing that "the genius of comedy" is "the same with that of tragedy, and that the true artist in tragedy" is "an artist in comedy also."[1] In one sense, it *is* rather tragic that Aristodemus is too hung over to recall how Socrates arrived at so provocative a conclusion, but any number of thinkers since Plato's time have suggested much the same thing about the intimate link between the comic and tragic spirits, and an American, Henry David Thoreau, in a journal entry for January 24, 1841, seemed to have been close to the source of Socrates' assertions when he observed

> By spells seriousness will be forced to cut capers, and drink a deep and refreshing draught of silliness; to turn this sedate day [Sunday] of Lucifer's and Apollo's, into an all fools' day for Harlequin and Cornwallis. The sun does not grudge his rays to either, but they are alike patronized by the gods. Like over-tasked schoolboys, all my members and nerves and sinews petition Thought for a recess, and my very thigh-bones itch to slip away from under me, and run and join the mêlée. I exult in stark inanity, leering on nature and the soul. We think the gods reveal themselves only to sedate and musing gentlemen. But not so; the buffoon in the midst of his antics catches unobserved glimpses, which he treasures for the lonely hour. When I have been playing tomfool, I have been driven to exchange the old for a more liberal and catholic philosophy.[2]

Be that as it may, the Comic Muse remains not a little suspect. Even in the United States, a nation in which the lachrymose and ludicrous have gone hand-in-hand from the beginning, we often feel an undeniable compulsion to excuse ourselves for laughing. The greatest of America's comic geniuses, Mark Twain, was bitterly stung at suggestions that he might be nothing more than the first among "Phunny Phellows," and he yearned throughout his later career to formulate some serious assessment of man's place in the moral order of things, seemingly unaware that he had done precisely that in *Huckleberry Finn*. Twain's plight is paralleled today by that of Woody Allen, who brought

1

the raw materials of Jewish standup comedy to full dramatic fruition in a succession of brilliant films before giving himself over for a time to Bergmanesque musings for the most part unleavened by the candid awareness of self-absurdity that had given his earlier work its peculiar humanity. If Americans in general, and American writers in particular, have often been a bit self-defensive and apologetic about their laughter, they have continued to laugh, however good-naturedly or bitterly, nonetheless, and it is for this reason that the study of American humor, in all its varied modes and phases, is so valuable a tool for understanding the American character. Students of American humor recognize that when D. H. Lawrence described the "essential American soul" as "hard, isolate, stoic, and a killer,"[3] he uttered a typically Lawrentian half-truth. The aggregate American soul is equally whimsical, gregarious, ironic, and given to laughter, ranging from the snicker to the belly-laugh. Occasionally, the violence and the laughter may manifest themselves concurrently, and the result can be either mayhem or high art, but in either case the Comic Muse steadfastly refuses to abandon American soil. From the beginning, she was here to stay, and her presence accounts for some of the greater glories in our national literature.

Whatever role the Comic Muse has played in shaping the American character and determining the course of American destiny, it is obvious that her own character has been modified and reshaped in the process in response to the novel exigencies of a New World. Even as Emerson urged his countrymen to wean themselves away from "the courtly muses of Europe," an unidentified British reviewer pointed to the work of regional American humorists as evidence "that American literature has ceased to be exclusively imitative." "A few writers" (and by this he meant principally the creators of Sam Slick, Major Jack Downing, and the authors of the Crockett books) had managed to "produce original sounds instead of far-off echoes,—fresh and vigorous pictures instead of comparatively idealess copies."[4] American humor mirrored American experience, and to clinch his point, this early champion of the vitality and uniqueness of that humor felt it sufficient to quote at length and with obvious relish from the material at hand, making what soon would be a commonplace observation about humor in America: that its overriding characteristic was a tendency toward exaggeration. Writing nearly a half-century later, another British commentator, the Reverend Mr. H. R. Haweis, a genteel, pious, but nevertheless mirthful gentleman, attempted to be more specific about the sources of a distinctly "American wit." American humor, he argued, had "three main roots" which "seem part and parcel of the national character, and are inseparably connected with the early history of our American cousins."[5] The first of these had to do with the unavoidable tension arising from Americans' pragmatic devotion to a materialistic success ethic on the one hand and their concommitant religious piety

on the other. The second, and here Haweis seems uncannily, if crypti-
cally modern, had to do with the juxtaposition of Red and White civilizations on the frontier. Finally, the very vastness of the North American
continent had, according to Haweis, left its indelible stamp on American
humor, nurturing an indigenous hyperbolic tendency in the national
imagination. Shortly afterward, the popular Scot lecturer Andrew Lang
similarly observed that "colossal exaggeration is, of course, natural to a
land of ocean-like rivers and almighty tall pumpkins,"[6] but for Lang
the terms "rusticity" and "puritanism" best described the dynamic polar-
ities that had generated a characteristically American humor. For the
most part appreciative of Mark Twain and his contemporaries, Lang
nevertheless felt that the American comic sense was inferior to that of
Thackeray and Dickens in that it was altogether too irreverent and
somewhat wanting in the milk of human kindness (two charges that
would be hard to refute, even if the present editors desired to do so),
but Lang went on to praise American humorists for an intrepid willingness to address controversial issues.

We cite these representative British observers as an indication
that the perennial insistence of critics on this side of the Atlantic that
our humor was a thing apart and the peculiar fruit of American soil was
not simply a manifestation of literary chauvinism.[7] The question of
when and how American humor became distinctly American might be
a point of contention. Was it born by necessity out of a reaction to Puritan repressiveness or frontier hardship? Did it emerge from the political
satire of the Revolutionary period? Was it unleashed by that tremendous explosion of human energy we have come to term Jacksonian
democracy? Was it the product of oral traditions, or of the gentleman's
study, or of the newspaperman's office? Different students of the subject
might differ in their qualified responses to each of these propositions—
indeed the debate continues in several of the new essays included in the
present collection—but the vast majority of those who have written about
American humor agree on one point: It is at once an outgrowth of and
index to the collective American mind. It is hardly surprising, then,
that periods of particularly intense interest in American humor as a
subject for serious comment have coincided with periods in our cultural
and political history when defining the nature of the American character and the meaning of the American experience has been a matter of
paramount importance.

One such period encompassed the years following the Civil War,
when men and women of letters explored every conceivable way (including the study of "our national humor") to reunite Americans into
a single people, and it extended through the early years of the twentieth
century, as American literature gradually emerged as a formal field of
study worthy of inclusion in the academy. However unsophisticated many
of the earlier discussions of American humor may seem in the light of

subsequent scholarship, taken together they raised important issues later critics would address in detail and helped in no small way to pave the road to respectability for American literary study as a discipline.

As always, popular magazines offer an invaluable glimpse into the preoccupations of an age, and in the last quarter of the nineteenth century and immediately afterward periodicals like *Harper's New Monthly*, *Munsey's*, the *Century*, and the *Atlantic* carried theoretical accounts and evaluative retrospective surveys of American humorous writing that even today repay the investment in time and labor necessary to unearth them, largely because of what they reveal about the values and biases of the time.[8] A veneration, often unspoken, for New England high culture and a distaste for "coarseness," along with a frank admission of its humorous potential, permeate these articles and essays; Mark Twain and the Local Colorists and Literary Comedians are valued highly to be sure, but Oliver Wendell Holmes and James Russell Lowell come in for a measure of praise later readers are likely to find exorbitant. A general agreement about the vital roles exaggeration and the ironies endemic in a pluralistic society play in the shaping of a native humor runs throughout these pieces, as does a recognition of the primacy of the oral humorous anecdote in America, though some commentators are quick to draw a distinction between genuine humor and the lowly joke. Others suggest that American humor is never far from pathos and detect a residual seriousness behind the comic mask. If one wishes to arrange this diverse body of material along the lines of a spectrum, it might be useful to put the rambling, but frequently insightful generalizations of S. S. Cox, onetime member of Congress from Ohio, at one end and an erudite overview of American humor up to the turn of the century by W. P. Trent, Columbia Professor of Literature and early champion of American literary scholarship, at the other.

For Cox, a man of unabashed spread-eagle enthusiasms, the vigor of American humor was an outgrowth of the nation's optimistic expansionist energies, a reflection of the degree of political liberty and relative material prosperity Americans enjoyed above and beyond the lot of other nationalities. This vitality was strengthened by the fact that the United States was a nation made up of widely differing nations; the uniqueness of its humor was in large part a result of converging cosmopolitan influences. However sincere he was in his call for a refinement and domestication of America's seemingly irrepressible comic spirit, Cox nevertheless gloried in its very exuberance, describing it at one point as "a slashing humor, which will sacrifice feeling, interest, sociality, philosophy, romance, art, and morality for its joke; an overriding, towering humor, that will one day make fun of all the rest of the world, not forgetting itself."[9] Professor Trent's no less readable, but much more systematic "Retrospect of American Humor" compared humor to a weapon "in the shape of a stick pointed at one end for prodding, just thick enough in the middle for castigating without severe results, and knobbed at the other end for knocking the adversary completely out." Americans, Trent remarked, tended to employ this weapon in readily-identifiable ways: "As we are a kind-hearted people, we seldom prod; but as we are healthy and full of common sense, we knock out extreme folly and moroseness, and castigate all forms of eccentricity. A reason for our conduct in this respect may be found in the fact that we had a new world to settle and subdue, and hence could tolerate no ineffectiveness and repining."[10] There follows a surprisingly broad discussion of the principal figures and movements in the development of American humor through the nineteenth century that amounts to an implicit attempt to identify and establish a canon. Trent's penchant for cataloguing humorists was bolstered by his sensitivity to the way in which social factors molded literary expression. He observed, for example, that the "incongruities" that emerged at each new stage in the development of the American nation triggered a corresponding series of shifts in the nation's evolving body of humorous writing, and he was especially insightful in his brief discussion of the conditions that gave rise to what we now know as the humor of the Old Southwest. Trent was quick to draw a distinction between those writers like Irving, Paulding, Holmes, and Lowell, who were primarily citizens of the Republic of Letters, and humorists like Twain and Artemus Ward (Charles Farrar Browne) whose writings seemed to spring from the very richness of the national life itself, while he insisted on granting each group its due. He was fully aware of the extent to which American humor was nurtured by the forces of popular culture, the "ubiquitous" newspaper in particular, and while he made no claims for much of our humor as high literature, neither did he stoop to condescension in commenting upon it.

Though Trent's essay was aimed at a general audience, his approach was unmistakably academic, and a number of his fellow scholars shared his willingness to take American humor seriously as an important adjunct to understanding the way in which American life and literature meshed. In his monumental *A History of American Literature, 1607–1765*, Moses Coit Tyler had missed much of the spirit of colonial humor, though he did have praise for Nathaniel Ward's *The Simple Cobbler of Aggawam* (1647) and Ebenezer Cook's *The Sotweed Factor* (1708), despite the latter's "filth and scurrility."[11] Brander Matthews addressed himself to the problem of the humorist's marginal respectability in the realm of letters and meditated upon the essence of American humor in two important essays,[12] and F. L. Pattee included an astute chapter on "The Laughter of the West" in his *History of American Literature Since 1870*,[13] in which he identified Irving's *Knickerbocker History of New York* as the "first really American book" and made connections between the humor of the decades preceding the Civil War and that which followed upon it, citing, like many of his predecessors, Lincoln as an embodiment of the American comic spirit and arguing that not until after the war did American humor become truly "national." Yet another indicator of the extent to which the study of humor had been seriously appropriated by students of American writing was Will D. Howe's essay "Early Humorists" in *The Cambridge History of American Literature*.[14] Howe's work is also a good indication of the degree to which an accepted canon of American humorous writing had evolved by the time of the First World War. Upon the foundation provided by men like Trent, Tyler, Matthews, Pattee, and Howe would be erected the impressive scholarship of the 1920s, 30s, and early 40s—a period that might justly be termed the Golden Age of American humor studies.

Kenneth S. Lynn is quite right when he notes that the "anxiety" of many intellectuals "to establish contact with . . . a usable past" in the wake of the Great War fueled a widespread interest in the study of American humor, especially with regard to its folk elements.[15] Such a concern reflected a broader postwar fascination with unearthing the roots of American experience, both mythic and socio-historical, that nourished a strong nativist bent in American literature and literary scholarship even at a time when many younger writers were leaving the United States to follow Ezra Pound and Gertrude Stein to the Old World. It is useful to regard Van Wyck Brooks' *The Ordeal of Mark Twain* against such a backdrop, for that book, itself the product of nationalist fervor of a sort, flew squarely in the face of most of the commentary on American humor that came before and after. It was Brooks' contention that Twain's satiric gifts, amounting to "genius," were stifled rather than nourished by his western background and sojourns in Nevada and California. Brooks had undisguised contempt for the American tradition of vernacular humor, arguing that Twain in opting to follow that tradition early in his career "was arrested in his moral and aesthetic development."[16] For Brooks, Twain's "failure" as a genuine artist resulted from his inability to rise above the shortcomings of the America into which he was born and his reluctance to fully dissociate himself from the values of the Gilded Age. A dozen years later, Bernard DeVoto, a westerner like Twain, set about to demolish Brooks' thesis in *Mark Twain's America*. DeVoto explicitly denied the notion that the role of humorist was in and of itself demeaning: "Laughter is not ignoble, nor is the small company of those who have been able to make it a living force, a mean fellowship."[17] More specifically, DeVoto depicted frontier humor as a mode of honest realism wedded to mythopoeic forces of remarkable creative potential, a veritable dynamo of folk expression that Twain harnessed to the best possible artistic advantage. Far from being a victim of his time and place, Twain drew upon the rich heritage frontier America provided him, and his greatness lay in the fact that his humor and compassion represented the culmination of· an indigenous tradition.

The present introduction cannot, of course, presume to address itself to the extensive body of critical commentary on Mark Twain, though obviously much of that work is germane to the understanding of American humor,[18] but we cite the Brooks/DeVoto controversy as the most obvious example of a debate about the legitimacy of vernacular humor and the value of its literary treatment that raged throughout the period in question, a debate that had its political as well as scholarly dimensions. For all practical purposes, the champions of the vernacular tradition won the battle of the books, so that even today much if not most of the writing about American humor makes an obligatory bow in the direction of the folk and frontier humorists, more particularly the humorists of the Old Southwest.[19] The sympathetic attention that V. L. Parrington gave in passing to writers like Augustus B. Longstreet and Joseph Glover Baldwin in the second volume of his *Main Currents in American Thought* played a not inconsiderable role in this regard. Far more important, though, was Jennette Tandy's ground-breaking *Crackerbox Philosophers in American Humor and Satire*, which appeared in 1925.

As her title indicates, Tandy's study traced the development of the "unlettered philosopher" as a characteristic comic type, the simple but sensible countryman whose unpretentious mother-wit made him an ideal foil for his pretentious and folly-ridden superiors. For Tandy, "There is a continuity about the persistence of this homely type in our American literature which suggests a national ideal."[20] Noting that this figure had his origins in oral tradition, she proceeded to follow the evolution of the folksy philosopher from his early beginnings as the conventional stage Yankee through his more skillful treatment at the hands of Seba Smith and Thomas Chandler Haliburton, leading up to James Russell Lowell's use of the type for purposes of impassioned satire in his *Biglow Papers*. Tandy was occasionally simplistic, even inaccurate, in her portrayal of the complex political and social realities of antebellum America, which marred an otherwise excellent chapter entitled "The Development of Southern Humor," but her critical insights were unusually reliable and her style often matched the spirit of the matter at hand. She was surprisingly even-handed in her discussions of Bill Arp (Charles Henry Smith) and Artemus Ward, who spoke for opposing sides during the Civil War, while she devalued the vituperative spirit behind David Ross Locke's persona Petroleum V. Nasby. Tandy's appreciation for Josh Billings (Henry Wheeler Shaw) may not be shared by many readers today, but her concern with the origins, contexts, and contributions of American humor, and with the biographies of the humorists themselves,[21] has made her book an early landmark in systematic humor studies.

Tandy's work was, however, soon overshadowed by that of another woman—Constance Rourke, whose 1931 book *American Humor: A Study of the National Character* remains even today something of a touchstone. The opening paragraph of Rourke's Foreword is revealing, not only of her own intentions, but of what she regarded as some of the temptations the study of humor was heir to:

> In pursuing humor over a wide area, as in the nation, certain pit-
> falls lurk for the unwary. An antiquarian interest is likely to develop.
> An old piece of humor is discovered, and one turns it over like a worn
> carving or figurine, with mounting pride if one can name it as pre-
> Jacksonian, early Maine, late Arkansas, or perhaps not American at
> all but of doubtful origin, say neo-French. But other interests may
> [and should, Rourke implies] transcend this beguiling pedantry. . . .[22]

Thus Rourke forsook the "pitfalls" of mere cataloging in favor of a more ambitious enterprise—investigating the workings of the comic spirit in America as one important source of a distinctly American national identity. In the portrait of American humor *and* the American charac- ter that unfolds in the course of her book, it is instructive to note the frequency with which words like "primitive," "pioneer," "folk," and "homely" recur. Rourke emerges as champion of the vernacular, though with qualifications, and her book commences with memorable discus- sions of the two dominant comic types in early nineteenth-century Amer- ican literature—the crafty Yankee and his western counterpart, the Gamecock of the Wilderness. Rourke dealt in some detail with the role the stage played in disseminating indigenous comic materials, and the attention she paid to Black American contributions to the ever-popular minstrel show tradition was one example of her critical pioneering, well-intentioned though rather condescending in the light of contem- porary scholarship.[23] Even so, her willingness to bring minority humor into consideration was an important step in broadening the field of American humor study. More daring still was Rourke's insistence upon the impact American humor had on venerated nineteenth-century masters like Whitman, Poe, Hawthorne, and Melville. In her view, Henry James too was touched by the same spirit, as were the poets Emily Dickinson, E. A. Robinson, Vachel Lindsay, Robert Frost, and Carl Sandburg. From the publication of Rourke's book on, students of American humor did not need to limit their labors to describing and analyzing the work of acknowledged "humorists." The entire sweep of American culture, high and low, was a territory open to exploration.

Rourke's emphatic coupling of a native American comic impulse with the national character did not receive universal acceptance. For one thing, there was the nagging question of how much of American humor was genuinely "American." DeVoto and Rourke had regarded the tall tale as one of the chief glories of American humor, but J. DeLancey Ferguson begged to differ with them in a 1935 essay, assert- ing that the scholar who "limits his study of Americana to America is . . . in some danger of making a fool of himself" and advising that "collectors of American humor would do well to take a sharper look at the British analogs."[24] Ferguson found examples of "American" exaggeration in earlier English jests, ballads, and folktales and suggested that such American comic heroes as Davy Crockett, Mike Fink, and Paul Bunyan shared a common ancestry that could be traced back to the Celtic *Mabinogion.* Rourke responded immediately, and rather testily, to Ferguson's essay, dismissing much of it as a straw-man, and pointing out that while American humor owed much to Britain it differed radically from British humor in kind (as a number of nineteenth-century British commentators had noted).[25] That inveterate radical Max Eastman, who was hardly blind to America's shortcomings, likewise weighed in on the side of the nativists in the debate on American humor's claims to uniqueness, going so far as to suggest that it was "the origin and almost the central stem of America's distinctly own imaginative culture,"[26] and Sculley Bradley took up the comparison of British and American humor at some length in an article in the *North American Review*, admitting their obvious relationship, but adding that there was an overriding difference: "... the corrective laughter of England is satiric; that of America is ironic. The British laugh at a thing for being so ridiculously what it is; the Americans ... because the thing is not what it should be, or what they expected it would be."[27] The question of precisely what constituted an exclusively American comic sensibility was at least as old as the ruminations of S. S. Cox alluded to earlier, and perhaps it will never be definitively answered. But, the demurral of critics like Ferguson to the contrary, by the mid-1930s a consensus had emerged to the effect that there was indeed a "native" strain of humor, whatever its disparate origins, running throughout American culture, and one unquestionable mark of the ascendency of that view was a book published in 1937, a book that Bernard DeVoto, writing for the *Saturday Review of Literature*, said "must hereafter be taken into account in all critical study of American literature at large."[28]

The book in question was Walter Blair's indispensable *Native American Humor*, and Blair's sensitivity to the thorny problem of definitions was clear from the very opening of his Introduction, in which he rejected the broad notion that American humor was simply "all humor produced in America." Instead, Blair argued that American humor "is *American* in that it has an emphatic 'native quality'—a quality imparted by its subject matter and its technique."[29] This brand of humor did not come into its own, he maintained, until the 1830s, though its roots were easily traceable to Colonial times in writings about the American environment and its inhabitants that were sometimes unintentionally funny. Blair's subsequent treatment of the gradual evolution of a native humor was thoroughly annotated, a model of scholarly professionalism that by comparison made most of the previous work in the field (with the exception of Blair's own articles) seem a bit impressionistic.[30] Blair's long and detailed Introduction, which culminated in a discussion of Twain's place in the tradition, provided subsequent scholars with a working vocabulary, and his categories of nineteenth-century humor and humorists (Down East, Old Southwest; Literary Comedians, Local Colorists) still enjoy a wide currency. He followed his Introduction with an extensive bibliography that was itself something of a first in terms of its inclusiveness, but the bulk of his book was given over to a judicious selection of humorous pieces, with an appendix of annotations, that dramatically illustrated the main points of his thesis. With the publication of *Native American Humor*, Walter Blair emerged as the preeminent scholar in his field. In 1942, he further consolidated his claim to preeminence with *Horse Sense in American Humor*,[31] which superseded Tandy's study of crackerbox philosophers and examined the perennially popular comic type in writers from Franklin to Ogden Nash. Blair's chapters on Crockett, Lincoln, and Twain were seminal, and his treatment of the members of what came to be called the *New Yorker* school, humorists like Robert Benchley, S. J. Perelman, and James Thurber, was one sign of a growing interest on the part of scholars in the contemporary humor scene.

Meanwhile, an ominous new world was emerging out of the global turmoil of World War II and its uncertain aftermath, and these conditions had a profound effect on the direction American humor was taking and, concurrently, on the personalities and perspectives of a new generation of commentators on that humor. Blair himself, in an article on wartime humor, had noted that American humorists during the nation's past wars had ultimately affirmed widely-held sets of traditional social values while World War II humorists tended to be more alienated and skeptical.[32] In time, it became clear that there was a great deal more to this shift in temperament and perspective. The jubilation Americans felt after V-J Day was soon displaced by a spreading sense of insecurity and foreboding which many cultural historians attribute in part at least to a belated awareness of the magnitude of death camp atrocities and of the sinister implications of Hiroshima and Nagasaki. The attrition of age-old verities had been going on for well over a century to be sure, but the process was accelerated in post-World War II America as intellectuals and laymen alike increasingly began to react to everyday realities as by turns absurd or hostile. Before the war, students of American humor, while they might take note of the despair that colored Twain's last years and of dark undercurrents in Old Southwest humor and the work of writers like Ambrose Bierce, tended to regard our humor largely as an expression of a relatively new nation's healthy optimism.[33] But the 1950s and 60s saw the rise to dominance of a more disarming kind of laughter in America; this was the age of the "sick" joke and of a grim and sardonic development termed Black Humor. Humor no longer seemed a by-product of common sense and sanity; it might be an auxiliary symptom of neurosis and rage. This was the view articulated by many critics like Bruce Janoff, whose essay "Black Humor:

Beyond Satire" focused upon novelists like Barth, Heller, and Vonnegut and saw the phenomenon as essentially a departure from the past,[34] though an earlier essay by Hamlin Hill which stressed continuities in American humor provided something of a corrective to an overemphasis on the newness of the "new" humor,[35] as did two important books by Jesse Bier and Richard Boyd Hauck.

Indeed, Bier's impressive *The Rise and Fall of American Humor* pursued a darker strain in American humor in popular forms, including cinema, as well as in the work of major writers, that had manifested itself a full century before World War II. His approach to the evolution and "decline" of American laughter bristled with his own version of Hegelian dialectics; notions of tension and antithesis dominate his discussion. In Bier's view, the American humorist was caught up in a corrosive love-hate relationship with his culture that threatened to end in either self-defeating nihilism or a retreat into sentimentality resulting from a "voluntary failure of nerve."[36] In keeping with the dictates of his thesis, Bier undervalued much of the humor prior to the Age of Jackson, while he found depths of significance in the Literary Comedians that many earlier commentators had missed. Despite its innate subversive quality, American humor seemed to Bier to have fared best in periods, however difficult, in which a strong sense of national purpose existed against which the comic artist could establish his stance. Post-World War II America seemed adrift, and this accounted for the failure of contemporary humor from his vantage point. Bier insisted on distinguishing between that Black Humor which sprang from a revulsion against intolerable social hypocrisy and that which represented a perverse surrender of moral responsibility. For all the stimulating originality of his approach to the question of the relationship between humor and American society at large, Bier was at bottom a critical conservative who valued the comic spirit primarily for its corrective function—hence his disparagement of certain trends in contemporary humor.

Richard Hauck, on the other hand, undertook a retrospective analysis of American humor in which Camus' theory of the "absurd" was a given. Where Bier's approach was Hegelian and normative, Hauck's was informed by an existential perspective. It was Hauck's contention that "The logical response to nihilism is despair, but there is a power in the American character to organize, to build, to act, and to laugh in spite of a clear recognition that creation may mean nothing."[37] Hauck presented the frontier humorists as proto-absurdists, and proceeded to discuss the divergent achievements of Melville and Twain in the light of his evolving thesis before turning his attention to Faulkner and to John Barth, who emerged as a kind of exemplar of the absurd comic artist under the terms of Hauck's definition. Hauck's aims in *A Cheerful Nihilism* were less far-reaching than Bier's in *The Rise and Fall of American Humor*—he made it explicitly clear that he was concerned primarily with the absurdist impulse—but in many ways the two books were complementary and representative of a new level of sophisticated critical thinking about American humor that was going on in the 1960s and 70s.

Indeed, by this time American humor studies had fully come of age. The American Humor Studies Association was founded during the early 70s, and at Southwest Texas State University Jack Meathenia launched the publication of a new journal, *Studies in American Humor*. It would be impossible within the confines of the present introduction to do justice to the stream of significant articles that appeared in that and other journals during the decade, but special note should be taken of a number of edited collections of criticism that the student of humor will find of particular interest.

Harry Levin's *Veins of Humor*[38] contains essays on diverse "humors," including pieces by Joel Porte on the American Transcendentalists, Walter Blair on the continuous influence of oral story-telling on American humor, Roger Rosenblatt on Langston Hughes' Simple, and Robert Alter on Jewish humor. In this same connection, Louis D. Rubin, Jr., collected thirty-two essays by various authorities on American writing under the title *The Comic Imagination in American Literature*.[39] These pieces had originally been commissioned under the auspices of the United States Information Agency for Voice of America broadcast—testimony to the value of American humor as a cultural export. In addition to Rubin's fine introduction, his book included suggestive studies by Lewis Simpson (on the early national wits), James M. Cox (on Southwestern humor and on Twain), Brom Weber (on the "Misspellers" and on Black Humor), Blyden Jackson (on minstrel humor and on the Harlem Renaissance), and Arlin Turner (on Local Color humor). Bernard Duffey's essay on the Chicago school in the same volume and Robert D. Jacobs' treatment of Faulkner's humor likewise merit favorable comment, as do Allen Guttman's study of Jewish humor and Richard K. Barksdale's account of the "comic mask" in Black American literature. The perennial interest the humor of the Old Southwest has held for students of American culture was admirably attested to by M. Thomas Inge's useful anthology of criticism *The Frontier Humorists: Critical Views*,[40] and O. M. Brack's *American Humor: Essays Presented to John C. Gerber*[41] featured an insightful article by Hamlin Hill on Black Humor, as well as studies in topics ranging from Poe and Melville to Russell Baker and *Mad* magazine. *Comic Relief: Humor in Contemporary American Literature*,[42] edited by Sarah Blacher Cohen, printed important work by Stanley Trachtenberg ("Berger and Barth: The Comedy of Decomposition"), C. Hugh Holman ("Detached Laughter in the South"), Charles H. Nichols ("Comic Modes in Black America"), Sanford Pinsker ("The Urban Tall Tale"), and a number of other critics.

The Cohen book was made even more valuable by the inclusion of a generous checklist of criticism on contemporary American humor.

In a way, the 1970s wave of intense critical interest in the study of American humor reached something of a culmination with the long-awaited appearance of Walter Blair's and Hamlin Hill's comprehensive study *America's Humor: From Poor Richard to Doonesbury.*[43] The range of inquiry in this eminently readable book actually went beyond the limits suggested by its subtitle to include European sources of early American humor and contemporary comic expression in a variety of "non-literary" forms such as film, television series, comic strips, and the standup comedy of celebrities like Lenny Bruce. *America's Humor* is by far the most encyclopedic account of the progress of the Comic Muse in America that has yet appeared. Still, it manages to arrange all the complexity and seeming contradictions of our national humor into a cogent pattern, however elaborate and complicated. The authors' close analyses of representative masterpieces like Franklin's Revolutionary satires, Irving's "Rip Van Winkle," George Washington Harris' "Parson Bullin's Lizards," Thorpe's "The Big Bear of Arkansas," and Thurber's "Walter Mitty" stand as models for elucidating a humorous text. One dissenter, James M. Cox, in a clever review in which he adopted the crackerbox philosopher persona, faulted the book for a lack of theoretical emphasis,[44] but nevertheless *America's Humor* clearly represents a watershed in the history of writing about American humor. A synthesis and extension of the best work done on the subject in the past, it establishes the direction future explorations are likely to take.

The original pieces commissioned for this volume in the G. K. Hall Critical Essays on American Literature series are an indication of the breadth and vigor of American humor studies at the present time, and Hamlin Hill's Postscript points toward the shape of things to come. In selecting a limited number of items to reprint, out of a seemingly limitless number of worthy possibilities, the editors have tried to establish an implicit chronological outline of the evolution of commentary on the subject.

We owe a special debt of thanks to David H. Stewart, Head of the English Department at Texas A&M University, who provided us with a graduate assistant to facilitate our research. That assistant, Sally Dee Wade, wore out several pairs of jogging shoes while combing the stacks: all future editors should be blessed with like assistants. Special thanks are also due to Norman S. Grabo, friend and former colleague, whose advice was invaluable in the early stages of our project.

WILLIAM BEDFORD CLARK
W. CRAIG TURNER

Texas A&M University

Notes

1. *A Plato Reader,* ed. Ronald B. Levinson (Boston: Houghton Mifflin, 1967), p. 154.

2. *The Heart of Thoreau's Journals,* ed. Odell Shephard (1927; rpt. New York: Dover, 1961), p. 18.

3. *Studies in Classic American Literature* (1923; rpt. New York: Penguin, 1977), p. 68.

4. H. W., "Slick, Downing, Crockett, Etc.," *London and Westminster Review,* Dec. 1838, p. 137.

5. *American Humorists* (New York: Funk & Wagnall's, 1882), pp. 10–11.

6. *Lost Leaders,* 2nd ed. (London: Kegan Paul, 1889), p. 76.

7. For an account of Gallic reactions to American humor, see James C. Austin's *American Humor in France: Two Centuries of French Criticism of the Comic Spirit in American Literature* (Ames: Iowa State University Press, 1978), especially the concluding chapter by Daniel Royot, "American Humor and the French Psyche," pp. 120–38.

8. Typical examples would include S. S. Cox, "American Humor," *Harper's New Monthly,* 50 (1875), 690–702, 847–59; J. L. Ford, "A Century of American Humor," *Munsey's,* 25 (1901), 482–90; Henry Clay Lukens, "American Literary Comedians," *Harper's New Monthly,* 80 (1890), 783–97; and H. W. Boynton's eulogy over the supposed decline of the comic spirit in America, "American Humor," *Atlantic Monthly,* 90 (1902), 414–20.

9. *Why We Laugh* (New York: Harper, 1876), p. 30.

10. "A Retrospect of American Humor," *Century,* 63 (1901), 45–64. The passage quoted appears on p. 45.

11. *A History of American Literature, 1607–1765* (1878; rpt. Ithaca, N. Y.: Cornell University Press, 1949), p. 488. Much remains to be done in the field of Colonial humor. A step in the right direction is *Laughter in the Wilderness: Early American Humor to 1783,* ed. W. Howland Kenney (Kent: Kent State University Press, 1976).

12. "The Penalty of Humor" in *Aspects of Fiction,* 3rd ed. (New York: Scribner's, 1902), pp. 43–56; "American Humor" in *The American of the Future* (New York: Scribner's, 1909), pp. 161–76.

13. (New York: Century, 1915), pp. 25–44.

14. William Peterfield Trent and others, eds. (New York: Putnam's 1918), pp. 148–59.

15. *The Comic Tradition in America: An Anthology* (Garden City, N. Y.: Doubleday Anchor, 1958), pp. xiii–xiv.

16. *The Ordeal of Mark Twain* (New York: Dutton, 1920), p. 242.

17. *Mark Twain's America* (Boston: Little, Brown, 1932), p. 268.

18. Perhaps the most obvious titles to fall under this category are Kenneth S. Lynn's *Mark Twain and Southwestern Humor* (Boston: Little, Brown, 1959) and James M. Cox's *Mark Twain: The Fate of Humor* (Princeton: Princeton University Press, 1966).

19. The book that firmly established the importance of the humor of the Old Southwest was Franklin J. Meine's anthology *Tall Tales of the Southwest* (New York: Knopf, 1930). Meine's Introduction (pp. xv–xxxiii) is still worth reading. The extent to which Old Southwest Humor has been subjected to critical examination

is dramatically revealed in "Humor of the Old Southwest: A Checklist of Criticism," compiled by Charles E. Davis and Martha B. Hudson, *Mississippi Quarterly*, 27 (1974), 179–99.

20. *Crackerbox Philosophers in American Humor and Satire* (Port Washington, N. Y.: Kennikat, 1964), pp. ix–x.

21. Tandy was able to draw upon a massive biography of the creator of Sam Slick by V. L. O. Chittick, *Thomas Chandler Haliburton: A Study in Provincial Toryism* (New York: Columbia University Press, 1924). A book on the creator of Jack Downing by Mary Alice Wyman, *Two American Pioneers: Seba Smith and Elizabeth Oakes Smith*, was likewise published by the Columbia University Press (Tandy's publisher) and appeared in 1927. These three books testify to a strong interest in humor among those engaged in the American studies work that thrived on or around the Columbia campus in the 1920s.

22. *American Humor* (New York: Harcourt, Brace, 1931), p. ix.

23. Many of Rourke's regrettable preconceptions about Black Americans were shared by Carl Wittke in *Tambo and Bones: A History of the American Minstrel Stage* (Durham: Duke University Press, 1930). *Blacking Up: The Minstrel Show in Nineteenth-Century America* (New York: Oxford University Press, 1974), by Robert C. Toll, is more reliable. See also Gary D. Engle's Introduction to his *This Grotesque Essence: Plays from the American Minstrel Stage* (Baton Rouge: Louisiana State University Press, 1978), pp. xiii–xxviii.

24. "The Roots of American Humor," *American Scholar*, 4 (1935), 41–42.

25. "Examining the Roots of American Humor," *American Scholar*, 4 (1935), 249–53.

26. "Humor and America," *Scribner's Magazine*, July 1936, p. 13. Eastman took a serious interest in humor indeed, devoting two volumes to the subject: *The Sense of Humor* (New York: Scribner's, 1921) and *Enjoyment of Laughter* (New York: Simon & Schuster, 1936).

27. "Our Native Humor," *North American Review*, 242, No. 2 (1936), 352.

28. "The Lineage of Eustace Tilley," *Saturday Review of Literature*, 25 Sept. 1937, p. 3.

29. *Native American Humor* (New York: Chandler, 1960), p. 3.

30. Two fine examples of Blair's early writing are "Burlesques in Nineteenth-Century American Humor," *American Literature*, 2 (1930), 236–47; and "The Popularity of Nineteenth-Century American Humorists," *American Literature*, 3 (1931), 175–94.

31. (New York: Russell & Russell).

32. "Laughter in Wartime America," *College English*, 6 (1945), 361–67.

33. A classic, and relatively late, statement of this view appears in Mody Boatright's *Folk Laughter on the American Frontier* (New York: Macmillan, 1949), pp. 159–77.

34. *Ohio Review*, 14, No. 1 (1972), 5–20.

35. "Modern American Humor: The Janus Laugh," *College English*, 25 (December 1963), 170–76. See also Hill's "Black Humor: Its Cause and Cure," *Colorado Quarterly*, 17 (Summer 1968), 57–64.

36. *The Rise and Fall of American Humor* (New York: Holt, 1968), p. 27.

37. *A Cheerful Nihilism: Confidence and the Absurd in American Humorous Fiction* (Bloomington: Indiana University Press, 1971), p. xi.

38. (Cambridge: Harvard University Press, 1972).

39. (New Brunswick: Rutgers University Press, 1972).

40. (Hamden: Archon, 1975).

41. (Scottsdale: Arete, 1977).

42. (Urbana: University of Illinois Press, 1978).

43. (New York: Oxford University Press, 1978).

44. "Correspondence," *Sewanee Review*, 86 (1978), 618–20. Cox's own theory of humor informs his essays "Toward Vernacular Humor," *Virginia Quarterly Review*, 46 (1970), 311–30; and "Humor and America: The Southwestern Bear Hunt, Mrs. Stowe, and Mark Twain," *Sewanee Review*, 83 (1975), 573–601.

DOCUMENTS IN AN
EVOLVING CRITICISM

[From "Slick, Downing, Crockett, Etc." (1838)]

H. W.*

These books [of regional humor] show that American literature has ceased to be exclusively imitative. A few writers have appeared in the United States, who, instead of being European and English in their styles of thought and diction, are American—who, therefore, produce original sounds instead of far-off echoes,—fresh and vigorous pictures instead of comparatively idealess copies. A portion of American literature has become national and original, and, naturally enough, this portion of it is that which in all countries is always most national and original—because made more than any other by the collective mind of the nation—the humorous.

We have many things to say on national humour, very few of which we can say on the present occasion. But two or three words we must pass on the heresies which abound in the present state of critical opinion on the subject of national humour: we say *critical*, and not *public*, opinion, for, thank God, the former has very little to do with the latter.

"Lord Byron,"—says William Hazlitt, in a very agreeable and suggestive volume of 'Sketches and Essays,' now first collected by his son,—"was in the habit of railing at the spirit of our good old comedy, and of abusing Shakespeare's Clowns and Fools, which, he said, the refinement of the French and Italian stage would not endure, and which only our grossness and puerile taste could tolerate. In this I agree with him; and it is *pat* to my purpose. I flatter myself that we are almost the only people who understand and relish *nonsense*." This is the excuse for the humour of Shakespeare, his rich and genuine English humour!

In Lord Byron the taste which the above opinion expresses is easily accounted for; it was the consequences of his having early formed himself according to the Pope and Gifford school, which was the dominant one among the Cambridge students of his time. Scottish highland

*Reprinted from the *London and Westminster Review*, December 1838, pp. 136–45.

scenery, and European travel, aided by the influences of the revival of a more vigorous and natural taste in the public, made his poems much better than the taste of the narrow school to which he belonged could ever have made them; but above the dicta of this school his critical judgment never rose. We thought the matter more inexplicable as regards William Hazlitt, a man superior to Byron in force and acuteness of understanding—until we found the following declaration of his views:—"In fact, I am very much of the opinion of that old Scotch gentleman who owned that 'he preferred the dullest book he had ever read to the most brilliant conversation it had even been his lot to hear.' " A man to whom the study of books was so much and the study of men so little as this, could not possibly understand the humour of Shakespeare's Clowns and Fools, or national humour of any sort. The characters of a *Trinculo*, a *Bardolph*, a *Quickly*, or a *Silence*, are matters beyond him. That man was never born whose genuine talk, let it be as dull as it may, and whose character, if studied aright, is not pregnant with thoughts, deep and immortal thoughts, enough to fill many books. A man is a volume stored all over with thoughts and meanings, as deep and great as God. A book, even when it contains the "life's blood of an immortal spirit," still is not an immortal spirit, nor a God-created form. Wofully fast will be his growth in ignorance who prefers reading books to reading men. But the time-honoured critical journals have critics— "The earth hath bubbles as the waters hath"—and William Hazlitt, with his eloquent vehemence, was one of the best of them.

The public have of late, by the appreciation of the genuine English humour of Mr Dickens, shown that the days when the refinement which revises Shakespeare and ascribes the toleration of his humour to grossness and puerility of taste, or a relish for nonsense, have long gone by. The next good sign is the appreciation of the humour of the Americans, in all its peculiar and unmitigated nationality. Humour is national when it is impregnated with the convictions, customs, and associations of a nation. What these, in the case of America, are, we thus indicated in a former number:—"The Americans are a democratic people; a people without poor; without rich; with a 'far-west' behind them; so situated as to be in no danger of aggression from without; sprung mostly from the Puritans; speaking the language of a foreign country; with no established church; with no endowments for the support of a learned class; with boundless facilities for 'raising themselves in the world'; and where a large family is a fortune." They are Englishmen who are all well off; who never were conquered; who never had feudalism on their soil; and who, instead of having the manners of society determined by a Royal court in all essentials imitative to the present hour of that of Louis the Fourteenth of France, had them formed, more or less, by the stern influences of Puritanism.

National American humour must be all this transformed into shapes which produce laughter. The humour of a people is their institutions, laws, customs, manners, habits, characters, convictions,—their scenery, whether of the sea, the city, or the hills,—expressed in the language of the ludicrous, uttering themselves in the tones of genuine and heartfelt mirth. Democracy and the 'far-west' made Colonel Crockett: he is a product of forests, freedom, universal suffrage, and bear-hunts. The Puritans and the American revolution, joined to the influence of the soil and the social manners of the time, have all contributed to the production of the character of Sam Slick. The institutions and scenery, the convictions and the habits of a people, become enwrought into their thoughts, and of course their merry as well as their serious thoughts. In America, at present, accidents of steam-boats are extremely common, and have therefore a place in the mind of every American. Hence we are told that, when asked whether he was seriously injured by the explosion of the boiler of the St. Leonard steamer, Major N. replied that he was so used to be blown-up by his wife that a mere steamer had no effect upon him. In another instance laughter is produced out of the very cataracts which form so noble a feature in American scenery. The Captain of a Kentucky steam-boat praises his vessel thus:—"She trots off like a horse—all boiler—full pressure—its hard work to hold her in at the wharfs and landings. *I could run her up a cataract.* She draws eight inches of water—goes at three knots a minute—and jumps all the snags and sand-banks." The Falls of Niagara themselves become redolent with humour. "Sam Patch was a great diver, and the last dive he took was off the Falls of Niagara, and he was never heard of agin till t'other day, when Captain Enoch Wentworth, of the Susy Ann whaler, saw him in the South Sea. 'Why,' says Captain Enoch to him 'why, Sam,' says he, how *on airth* did you get here, I thought you was drowned at the Canadian lines.'—'Why,' says Sam, 'I didn't get *on earth* here at all, but I came slap *through* it. In that are Niagara dive I went so everlasting deep, I thought it was just as short to come up t'other side, so out I came on these parts. If I don't take the shine off the sea-serpent, when I get back to Boston, then my name's not Sam Patch.' "

The curiosity of the public regarding the peculiar nature of American humour seems to have been very easily satisfied with the application of the all-sufficing word exaggeration. We have, in a former number,[1] sufficiently disposed of exaggeration, as an explanation of the ludicrous. Extravagance is a characteristic of American humour, though very far from being a peculiarity of it; and, when a New York paper, speaking of hot weather, says:—"We must go somewhere—we are dissolving daily—so are our neighbours.—It was rumoured yesterday that three large ridges of fat, found on the side-walk in Wall street, were caused by Thad. Phelps, Harry Ward, and Tom Van Pine, passing that way a short time before":—the humour does not consist in the exaggeration that the heat is actually dissolving people daily—a common-place at which no one would laugh—but in the representation of these respectable citizens as producing ridges of fat. It is humour, and not wit, on account of the infusion of character and locality into it. The man who put his umbrella into bed and himself stood up in the corner, and the man who was so tall that he required to go up a ladder to shave himself, with all their brethren, are not humorous and ludicrous because their peculiarities are exaggerated, but because the umbrella and the man change places, and because a man by reason of his tallness is supposed too short to reach himself.

The cause of laughter is the ascription to objects of qualities or the representations of objects or persons with qualities the opposite of their own:—Humour is this ascription or representation when impregnated with character, whether individual or national.

It is not at all needful that we should illustrate at length by extracts the general remarks we have made, since the extensive circulation and notice which American humour has of late obtained in England have impressed its general features on almost all minds. But, we may recall them more vividly to the reader, and connect them more evidently with the causes in which they originate, by showing very briefly how institutions infuse themselves into men, how the peculiarities of the nation re-appear in the individual, and how, in short, the elements of the society of the United States are ludicrously combined and modified in the characters, real and fictitious, of Sam Slick, Colonel Crockett, and Major Jack Downing.

Note

1. *London and Westminster Review* (January, 1838), p. 266.

Ed. note: The review concludes with lengthy excerpts from Thomas Chandler Haliburton, Seba Smith, and Crockett.

[From *Why We Laugh* (1875-1876)]

S. S. Cox*

"Those confused seeds which were imposed upon Psyche as an incessant labor to cull out and sort asunder, were not more intermixed."—JOHN MILTON.

What, then, is the quality of American humor? How much of the electric talent do we possess?

As to the last inquiry, there are many reasons which might be urged,

*Reprinted from *Why We Laugh* (New York: Harper, 1876), pp. 34–50.

a priori, why we should be wanting in its finer development. We are too engrossed in practical matters, our eyes too much bent on the golden pavement, to cultivate that hilarious spirit which is the offspring of leisure, laziness, fatness, freedom, carelessness, and unrestraint. We shall see by-and-by how much force there is in this antecedent probability against our humor.

It is urged as a reason against our having the humorous gift that, as humor flows out of peculiarities of character and conduct, we can not have a national humor original and unique because of our cosmopolitanism; that if we have any humor, it will so partake of the quality of every other people as to be wanting in a distinct American quality.

This objection is worth examining. Let me give it the strongest statement. In illustration of it, the objector points to the richness of English humor; and triumphantly asks, "Is it not due as much, if not more, to English isolation than to the unequalness of the climate? Do not England's insular position and crabbed exclusiveness give her a mold of her own, so that an Englishman can never be mistaken for any one else, either in a play, at home, or abroad? Is not this, in connection with the changes of English climate, that which makes the Englishman such an incarnate incongruity? and is not this near a definition of humor? How, then, can America, with her roving disposition, her open ports, and her armies of immigration, ever attain that distinct form of manners which England in her isolation has attained?"

Let us weigh this statement. It is true that no people were ever so composite as ours. On the Atlantic side the nations of all Europe have a theatre for the blending of their divers tempers, while on the Pacific side the Chinaman and Japanese, with their pig-tails and shorn crowns, lean forward to blend their laughterless physiognomy with the motley groups which people the *placers*, do the cooking and washing, and build the railroads of the Occident. It was only the other evening the writer addressed a meeting in New York City. It was composed of Hungarian Hebrews. They drank lager, while the band played "The Mulligan Guards." It was more than *E pluribus bragh, Erin go unum!*

Our institutions have made us the most affiliative people known to history. It may be that, in grafting so many and divers shoots upon our national stock, we are overburdening our productive energy, and neutralizing our native temper and tone. But I trust not. The predominant genius is *American!* Like the genius of the Grecian artist, it is eclectic, for out of many models it will educe the highest type, from divers discordances it will develop a comely concordance. Bancroft has said that our land was not more the recipient of the men of all countries than of their ideas. Annihilate the past of any one leading nation of the world, and our destiny would have been changed. Italy and Spain, in the persons of Isabella and Columbus, joined together for the great discovery that opened it for emigration and commerce; France contributed to its independence; the search for the origin of the language we speak carries us to India; our religions are from Palestine; of the hymns sung in our churches, some were first heard in Italy, some in the deserts of Arabia, some on the banks of the Euphrates; our arts come from Greece, our jurisprudence from Rome, our maritime code from Russia; England taught us the system of common law, and Ireland the heart to love and defend the constitution of our federation; the noble republic of the United Provinces bequeathed to us the prolific principle of federal union. Our country stands, therefore, more than any other, as the realization of the unity of the race. It may be asked, "Where, then, in all this Babel of tongues, jangle of ideas, crosses of race, and confusion of systems, is there any individual Americanism in our temper, tone, or humor?" Where, indeed, I answer, if not in the blending of the many-tinted phases of the varied civilizations which time and sacrifices have furnished for our own exquisite mosaic? It is this absorption of characteristics of every clime and time which makes our society the most incongruous, grotesque, odd, angular, and *outré*, ever yet known in history. Instead of destroying our peculiar humor, this medley has turned us from the old English channel, where we had ever been coypists, into new channels of our own. [The actor Joseph] Jefferson, in his Rip Van Winkle, could never have played his part so well had he not combined the thin, jolly American with the Dutchman. Instead of this unexclusiveness breaking down our humor, it is a resource for it as inexhaustible as it is varied. If the power of man consists in the multitude of his affinities, in the fact that his life is intertwined more with his fellows of every caste, degree, and nation—if he thus becomes a more complete compend of all time, with all its tastes, affections, whims, and humors—then the American man ought to be more potent in his individuality than any other. From *his* mind, as from the Forum of ancient Rome, proceed the great avenues north, south, east, and west, to the heart of every other people, multiplying his relations, and drawing to itself all the resources which human nature can furnish. Out of these derivatives from the Old World we have our originals. The greater the variety of our life, the more golden are the veins of that humor which is so loud, large, uproarious, and rollicking in exaggerations.

Prosperity, Liberty, and Humor.

There are elements in our country from which, *a priori*, we may infer that we shall have abundant harvests of humor, if we have them not already. These elements are our Plenty and Freedom. The same reasons given by an old English writer for the variety of the vein in England may be applied to America with even more fitness. I extract their essence thus: 1. The native plenty of the soil: plenty begets wantonness and pride; wantonness is apt to invent, and pride scorns to imitate. 2. Easy government, and liberty of professing opinions: liberty with plenty begets stomach and heart, and stomach will not be restrained. Thus we come to have more that appear what they are. We have more humor, because every man follows his own bent, and takes both pleasure and pride in showing it.

This philosophy will hold everywhere. Plenty, unless gorged to dyspepsia—and even then it becomes ludicrous—is the very father of fun. Whether plenty has the ribless side or the thin anatomy, laughter lives in its company. Does not a man "well-to-do"' feel good? Is he not more genial? Can he not laugh more heartily, invent merrier thoughts? And will he not, if unconstrained by a tyrannic government, let out more of the native peculiarities of his disposition? His independence precludes imitation, and disdains obedience. He is more of an individual sovereign, and in the wrestling of life he will show more muscle and point. Nast's caricatures furnish plentiful illustrations, and the newspapers, in both picture and type, are not less evidences of our unlicensed printing than of our love of the most grotesque fun. If you would deaden humor, put your government to work with the Procrustean bed, and make men all of a length, and you have machines, not men, and no humor....

Our Humorous Writers.

There is much of Franklin's shrewd, practical humor disguised under the mask of Josh Billings's sayings. With a Puritan face all severe and sour; without a hearty open laugh to welcome the coming or speed the parting joke; with nothing but an odd pucker of the mouth, and an elfish twinkle of the eye; with an inward chuckle which has no outward sign—Billings (aside from the small fun of bad orthography) hits the target of humor in the centre when he says that with some people who brag of ancestry, their great trouble is their great descent; or when he thanks God for allowing fools to live, that wise men may get a living out of them; when he says that wealth won't make a man virtuous, but that there ain't any body who wants to be poor just for the purpose of being good; when he says that if a fellow gets to going down hill, it seems as if every thing were greased for the occasion; or when he gives us his way of keeping a mule in a pasture, by turning it into a meadow adjacent and letting it jump out; or when he has known mules, like men, keep good for six months just to get a good kick at somebody—he makes a species of drollery which even our English reviewers have begun to appreciate, and which does not require the drawl of bad grammar and worse spelling. I once had occasion, in a deliberative body, to use Billings's illustration that one hornet, if he felt well, could break up a camp-meeting. The effect amazed me. The application was made; and Billings himself afterward said, "My name will go down to the fewter coupled with the hornet; we will be twins in posterity." The description of the nature of the insect, especially the use it makes of its "business end," of the way it avoids the thousand attempts to "shoo" it and to fight it, and the consequent consternation of a pious body, has in it exaggeration of the raciest kind.

But this kind of humor, like that of Nasby, does not rise to the dignity of literature. It can not compare, of course, with Washington Irving, who, in his *Knickerbocker* and other works, has given us the very choicest brand, all sparkling and stimulating. But Irving is too refined, sweet, and shy for general appreciation. Besides, Irving is not an American humorist. He is more English than American, more cosmopolitan than either. Paulding, Hawthorne—alas for our humorous literature! Oh for one man for America what Richter is to Germany, or Dickens is to England!

Mrs. Stowe has plenty of the genuine indigenous humor in her "Uncle Tom." But can there be a more gentle and genuine humor than that of Mrs. Sparrowgrass and her "cozzens?"

Our humorous writers, with a few exceptions, are not strictly national. Even Franklin, our first, best humorist, stifled his humor in the Addisonian style. His was too earnest a character to make the humorous trait very prominent; but his sly, shining threads of observation, intertwisted into the strong strand of his practical sense, have had their effect on the older men of this generation.

Sam Slick and Jack Downing—they are the caricature of caricatures. We have had printed at Philadelphia a series of works on American humor, giving graphic pictures of the pioneer times of the South, South-west, and West, which, if purged of their grossness, and artistically inwoven with some genial purpose, would better represent our national idiosyncrasies, with their reckless heroism, quaint extravagances, and novel parlance, than any other portion of our literature.

But, after all, the American humor does not reside altogether in books. It is to be found in our newspapers, with their spicy dialogues, practical jokes, Mrs. Partingtonisms, Artemus Wards, Josh Billingses, Nasbys, Max Adelers, Twains, Bret Hartes, and the infinity of little jets of fun on the outside, and measureless ridicule and cuts on the inside, local items, advertisements, and all.

There is no room in this volume to run the round of our newspaper humorists. One might begin with Doesticks, quote Breitmann's Anglo-German verses, turn over the versatilities of Mr. Newell, chuckle at Max Adeler's demure extravaganzas, Apoth. E. Cary's humorous nostrums, and the dry jocoseness of the *Danbury News*, roar with Donn Piatt till the Capitol itself echoed the "cave of the winds," or shake with the "Fat Contributor" until the lean earth was larded, and just begin to have an appreciation of the illimitably broad hyperbole which marks our ephemeral newspaper fun.

The Athenians frequented the theatre of Bacchus to hear a play of

Aristophanes, wherein the spite and fun of the day were concentrated; the Romans gathered at the Baths of Caracalla to laugh over the gossip and humor of the city. What theatre and bath were to Athens and Rome, the journal is to the American. In our five thousand American journals, sending out a billion of copies per annum, the American finds a mirror of his own nature, reflecting his opinions and feelings, and those distorted and grotesque images and scenes which are the life of American humor. . . .

The general sources of our humor are those from which all people draw, which would make a Laplander laugh as well as an American. These have been frequently catalogued. They are a portion of the categories to which reference has been made. Let us reproduce a few. The balking of our hopes in trifling matters makes us smile. An unlooked-for accident that is absurd, as when a dandy slips up on an icy pavement, makes us laugh. We laugh at that which is against custom, as at a man in a bonnet. We laugh at the weaknesses of others, as at a politician who brags much and polls a small vote. We laugh at amateur farmers who fail. We laugh at incongruities, as when we see a little man walking arm-in-arm with a giant; we laugh more if the little man marches with a big bass drum and the big man with a baby drum. We laugh at a little man on tiptoes, thrumming a base viol. We laugh at insignificant distress, as at a lady who loses her lap-dog. We laugh at extravagant pretension which suddenly collapses, as at an orator who soars to a star-lofty climax and breaks down. We laugh at cool impudence, for the ready and courageous invention pleases. We laugh when it is foiled, as at a lawyer in court who gets a saucy cut from a female witness. We laugh at a sudden or stealthy surprise, as at the large stranger who kicked an ornamental dog on the steps of a brown-stone house, merely to see if it was "holler." He is said to be at his aunt's, ill, but he is not over his surprise. Young ladies laugh at young men—and that is queer: they can not tell why; but oftentimes the more they like them, the more they laugh at and smile on them. We laugh at what is serious for others, as at a man looking out of a jail, but never at what seriously affects us, as, for example, if we were in jail. We laugh at disguises, at the dress of foreigners, fops, and slovens. We laugh when we see some men in a clean collar and new coat. We laugh at the meeting of extremes, as at the two well-bred fellows who, being pretty thoroughly soaked with bad whisky, got into the gutter, and, after floundering for some time, one of them proudly said, "Let's go to another hotel; this hotel leaks." It is hard to keep children from laughing at deformity, at negroes, at madmen, at fat men, at long thin men. We laugh often because we ought not to, as in church, from the spontaneous impulse of resistance to sobriety. We laugh at the utter simplicity of some men, and the more so if the laugh is caused by a sudden illustration of it, or by a sudden jerk of the mind to an absurd extreme, as the other day, when an editor, describing the gifted Dr. Holland, said that he would loan money to a man on the collateral notes of an accordion. We laugh—all men laugh, but Americans especially—at the aggrandizement of special foibles of character. Dickens furnishes illustrations of how humorous some preeminent trait may be made to seem by a sort of Hogarthian satire with the false perspective. But this exaggeration is not always humorous.

Our Specific Humors.

But we have in America specific objects of humor—the scheming Yankee, the big, bragging, brave Kentuckian, and the first-family Virginian. We have lawyers on the circuit, as in the Georgia scenes; loafers on a spree, as in Neal's charcoal sketches; politicians in caucus; legislators in session; travelers on cars and steamers; indeed, the history of every Amercian's life is humorous, moving as he does from place to place, and even when he sits down, as restless as the stick which a traveler saw out West that was so crooked it would not lie still!

There is a sympathy running through the American mind of such intensity and excitement in relation to our physical growth and political prominence, that our manners, movements, and mind must become intensified. Why, an American can not repose unless he does it with might and main. He must take an extravagant position. It expresses an imperturbable confidence in the destiny of his native country, and the wonderful flexibility in the human skeleton. Foreigners laugh at him for it. A foreign tourist says it is utterly impossible to mistake an American for any one else *en route*. He either has his feet upon the car-seat in front, the back of which he turns over for that purpose, or, if it be occupied, he sits with his knees let into the back of it, keeps up a continual spitting, invariably reads a newspaper, and chews his *quid* as he rides. It should have been for an American tobacconist that Curran proposed a motto for the panels of the coach: *Quid rides!* The wondrous exaggerations of Jules Verne, in his "Around the World in Eighty Days," are placed to the account of an American. Even the leaping of streams by the momentum of the locomotive and train is located upon our territory. When at home, the American soon tires of sitting still, and paces the floor with restless nervousness. . . .

With all our vanity, energy, and unrest, we are not a dull, cheerless people. Sour-faced fellows, yellow and dyspeptic, are to be met with in our cars and streets; but they are not the type of the American, for he is as ready for a laugh as for a speculation, as fond of a joke as of an office. Wherever the American goes in his tireless round of observation and traffic—whether he breaks the seal which for ages had closed Japan to the world, or wanders through Africa after Livingstone, or roams for gold at the head-waters of the Amazon, or among the Black Hills reservations, or at the Cape in Africa, or for diamonds, salted or un-

salted, in Arizona, or stands with Kane and Hall on the shores of some
newly found sea of the poles, or whether more nearly at home—he leaves
his trail on every mountain-pass, his axe-stroke in every forest; whether

> He's whistling round St. Mary's Falls
> Upon his loaded train,
> Or leaving on the pictured rocks
> His fresh tobacco stain,

he is leaving the rudiments of an empire, the muscle and mind, and the
invincible good nature and sense of the humorous, by which he is
enabled to mingle with all, and to rule as he mingles.

Wherever he goes he exaggerates his country, his position, his
ability; and his humor takes the same size. If he does not enjoy the fun
made at his own dilation, he is the cause of its enjoyment by others.
What with the great sea-serpents, moon hoaxes, spirit-rappings, Shaker-
ism, Barnum's shows, women's rights, free love, cannon concerts, big
organs, much-married Mormonism, and other quackeries and extravagances, if we are not ourselves amused, we export amusement in large
quantities. An English reviewer says, "America is determined to keep
us amused; we are never left long without a startling novelty from the
almighty republic."

Washington Irving, in his quiet way, alluded to the national peculiarity, which he epitomized and incarnated in a man of superior pomposity, as a "great man, and, in his own estimation, a man of great weight—
so great, that, when he goes west, he thinks the east tips up!"

[From *American Humorists* (1882)]   Rev. H. R. Haweis*

American wit has three main roots.

These roots seem part and parcel of the national character, and
are inseparably connected with the early history of our American cousins.

First, I notice the shock between Business and Piety. That is always
a fruitful source of comedy to outsiders. Those famous Pilgrim Fathers
who went over in the *Mayflower*, to create a new civilization and con-
quer a new world, were singularly wide awake as well as pious. They
were martyrs to a religious idea, but they were keenly alive to the
practical interests of real life.

I have nothing to say against religion and business going hand in
hand. The two occupy parallel but not necessarily antagonistic planes,

*Reprinted from *American Humorists* (New York: Funk and Wagnalls, 1882),
pp. 10–13.

and have, or ought to have, frequent side-channels of communication; but the habits and instincts developed by each are too often practically irreconcilable, and sometimes flagrantly inconsistent.

"John," said the pious grocer, "have you sanded the sugar?" "Yes sir." "Larded the butter?" "Yes, sir." "Floured the ginger?" "Yes, sir." "Then come in to prayers."

The brisk competition between business and piety, together with the various cross lines of thought and feeling which it begets—derived no doubt from the thrift and 'cuteness of the early settlers—underlies a good deal of the modern American wit.

The Pilgrims were far too grim and grave to joke; but their descendants, who are fully alive to their peculiarities and weaknesses, while inheriting a full share of both, are not so particular.

Washington Irving's skit on the Yankee lawyer who became a converted man upon seeing a ghost, and after that never cheated—"except when it was to his own advantage," is a fair thrust at that spirit which has the "form of godliness, denying the power thereof," and which, however morally deplorable, has an irresistibly comic side to it.

Another deep undertone of American humor is the forcible and national contrast forever present to the American mind between the Yankee and the poor Red Man whom he has supplanted.

Washington Irving and Artemus Ward have both made great play with this element. The picture in "Knickerbocker" of the wily Dutch trader sitting down opposite the red man, and smoking gravely with him "the calumet of peace," listening to the poetical savage's interminable tirades of oratory à la Fenimore Cooper, and puffing away gravely without understanding a word of it, but never omitting to put in a "Yah! mein Herr!" at each pause, with a stolid and Batavian gravity—that is a feature quite peculiar to and inseparable from the national life and humor.

Lastly, the contrast between the vastness of American nature and the smallness of man, especially European man, seems to be a never-failing source of amusement to Yankee humorists.

Their general ability to "whip creation" turns largely upon the bigness of their rivers, mountains, and prairies, and the superior enterprise generated by these immensities.

By one wit, Niagara is valued because it could put out "our" Vesuvius in "ten minutes." Our biggest rivers are to the Mississippi and Missouri as babbling streams, our lakes are mere ponds; even the Alps and Pyrenees begin to look puny; and as to fields and woods, they are as paddocks and shrubberies to the virgin forests and boundless prairies of yon mighty Transatlantic continent.

The American visitor who was asked how he liked the Isle of Wight, is said to have replied, "It was well enough, but so dangerous"; and when asked to explain, he said the fact was the island was so small that when he got out of bed in the morning, he found himself in danger of tumbling into the sea!

To sum up the peculiarities of American humor:

First, there is the shock between Business and Piety.

Secondly, the shock of contrast between the Aboriginal and the Yankee.

Lastly, the shock of contrast between the bigness of American nature and the smallness of European nature, or, as for the matter of that, Human Nature itself outside America.

[From "American Humour" (1889)]   Andrew Lang*

Two remarkable features in American humour, as it is shown in the great body of comic writers who are represented by Mark Twain and the "Genial Showman" [Artemus Ward], are its rusticity and its puritanism. The fun is the fun of rough villagers, who use quaint, straight-forward words, and have developed, or carried over in the *Mayflower,* a slang of their own. They do not want anything too re-fined; they are not in the least like the farm-lad to whose shirt a serpent clung as he was dressing after bathing. Many people have read how he fled into the farm-yard, where the maidens were busy; how he did not dare to stop, and sought escape, not from woman's help— he was too modest—but in running so fast that, obedient to the laws of centrifugal motion, the snake waved out behind him like a flag. The village wits are not so shy. The young ladies, like Betsy Ward, say, "If you mean getting hitched, I'm on." The public is not above the most practical jokes, and a good deal of the amusement is derived from the extreme dryness, the countrified slowness of the narrative. The humorists are Puritans at bottom, as well as rustics. They have an amazing familiarity with certain religious ideas and certain Biblical terms. There is a kind of audacity in their use of the Scriptures, which reminds one of the freedom of mediæval mystery-plays. Probably this boldness began not in scepticism or in irreverence, but in honest famil-iar faith. It certainly seems very odd to us in England, and probably expressions often get a laugh which would pass unnoticed in America. An astounding coolness and freedom of manners probably go for some-thing in the effect produced by American humour. There is nothing of the social flunkeyism in it which too often marks our own satirists. Artemus Ward's reports of his own conversations with the mighty of the earth were made highly ludicrous by the homely want of self-

*Reprinted from *Lost Leaders,* 2nd ed. (London: Kegan Paul, French and Co., 1889), pp. 73–77.

consciousness, displayed by the owner of the Kangaroo, that "amoosin' little cuss," and of the "two moral B'ars." But it is vain to attempt to analyze the fun of Artemus Ward. Why did he make some people laugh till they cried, while others were all untouched? His secret probably was almost entirely one of manner, a trick of almost idiotic *naïveté*, like that of Lord Dundreary, covering real shrewdness. He had his rustic chaff, his Puritan profanity; his manner was the essence of his mirth. It was one of the ultimate constituents of the ludicrous, beyond which it is useless to inquire.

With Mark Twain we are on smoother ground. An almost Mephistophilean coolness, an unwearying search after the comic sides of serious subjects, after the mean possibilities of the sublime,—these, with a native sense of incongruities and a glorious vein of exaggeration, make up his stock-in-trade. The colossal exaggeration is, of course, natural to a land of ocean-like rivers and almighty tall pumpkins. No one has made such charming use of the trick as Mark Twain. The dryness of the story of a greenhorn's sufferings who had purchased "a genuine Mexican plug," is one of the funniest things in literature. The intense gravity and self-pity of the sufferer, the enormous and Gargantuan feats of his steed, the extreme distress of body thence resulting, make up a passage more moving than anything in Rabelais. The same contrast, between an innocent style of narrative and the huge palpable nonsense of the story told, marks the tale of the agricultural newspaper which Mr. Twain edited. To a joker of jokes of this sort, a tour through Palestine presented irresistible attractions. It is when we read of the "Innocents Abroad" that we discern the weak point of American humour when carried to its extreme. Here, indeed, is the place where the most peculiarly American fun has always failed. It has lacked reverence and sympathy, and so, when it was most itself, never approached the masterpieces of Thackeray and Dickens. To balance its defect by its merit, American humour has always dared to speak out, and Mark Twain especially has hit hard the errors of public opinion and the dishonest compromises of custom.

A Retrospect of American Humor [1901]   W. P. Trent*

It is obviously not easy, and it almost seems impertinent, to subject humor to criticism. Yet butterflies are pinned and catalogued, and flowers are dissected. How, then, shall even the lightest forms of literature escape classification and evaluation, unless, indeed, through their very airiness, they elude the clumsy critic?

*Reprinted from the *Century Magazine*, 63 (November 1901), 45–64.

To some extent wit and humor have eluded the critic, and will continue to do so until the psychologist is able thoroughly to analyze the complex emotions that induce laughter and smiles. Yet perhaps this is a consummation not devoutly to be wished. Should the physical basis of these emotions be laid bare, it might at once appear that our sense of humor depended upon our food and our digestion. The consequent explanation of hitherto inexplicable differences between national standards of humor would not be altogether grateful to us if it were to become clear that American humor should be regarded as merely a by-product of American dyspepsia. Perhaps, after all, the student of literature may not find in the psycho-physicist the ally he craves.

But when he turns to his old ally, the rhetorician, the help he gets is more apparent than real. The numerous attempts to distinguish wit from humor, and to define them both, are seemingly little more satisfactory and authoritative than the distinction between the imagination and the fancy, of which so much used to be made. For example, a famous rhetorician tells us that jesting at one's own expense is humorous, and that in wit we have a combination of unexpected ideas. When Franklin remarked to one of his fellow-Signers, "We must all hang together or we shall all hang separately," was he humorous, or witty, or both?

The late Mr. Haweis thought that humor might properly be likened to the atmosphere, wit to the electric flash. Wit sometimes seems to its victims like forked lightning, humor like harmless sheet-lightning. Probably one is safe enough in using the terms without reference to attempted definitions or substituted metaphors, although perhaps the underlying unity and common aims of wit, humor, and ridicule may be expressed by saying that together they make up a weapon used by wisdom and good nature against folly and moroseness—a weapon in the shape of a stick pointed at one end for prodding, just thick enough in the middle for castigating without severe results, and knobbed at the other end for knocking the adversary completely out. It goes without saying that all save very dull and very sensitive men delight to see this weapon used effectively, except upon themselves.

It is generally agreed that there is a special employment of this weapon peculiar to Americans. As we are a kind-hearted people, we seldom prod; but as we are healthy and full of common sense, we knock out extreme folly and moroseness, and we castigate all forms of eccentricity. A reason for our conduct in this respect may be found in the fact that we had a new world to settle and subdue, and hence could tolerate no ineffectiveness and repining. The weapon metaphor may be dropped, however, and reliance may be placed on the old rhetorical claim that incongruity is a basal element of humor. There has been no lack of the incongruous in American life from the beginning. Even the early Puritans of New England, although their religion repressed their animal spirits, probably contrasted their aspirations, spiritual and material, with their actual surroundings, and did not refrain from innocent forms of grim humor. Their literature, in the main, is serious enough; but the fantastic Samuel [sic] Ward evidently thought that his "Simple Cobbler of Agawam" might be taken humorously, for he protested that he wrote in all earnestness. There are also passages in the writings of the topographers and travelers that seem to indicate that the modern process known as "stuffing" is of considerable antiquity. Some one must have "stuffed" John Josselyn with the notion that the Indians conducted their extempore discussions in perfect hexameter verse.

But, to leave our seventeenth-century pioneers for a moment, it seems clear that a new phase of incongruity in our life is observed to be contemporaneous with each new phase of our humorous literature. For example, much of Franklin's early humor was probably dependent upon the contrast between rural and slowly evolving urban life, while his later humor often depended upon the contrast between the actual American life he knew and the absurd views of it held by Europeans—a department of our humor by no means yet exhausted. War always furnishes incongruities and ample reasons and opportunities for indulging in ridicule; hence humor and satire play important parts in the literature of the Revolution and of the Civil War. Later, the contrast between pretensions of the new government and the tendency to anarchy represented by "Shays' Rebellion," as well as between the aspirations and the unsophisticated character of the people at large, gave rise to satiric and humorous effusions, mainly in verse and now completely forgotten, but doubtless beneficent in their day. Then came the rise of the democracy to power under Jackson, and the incongruities involved in the assumption of leadership by those who had previously been led inspired a literature of political humor which culminated in the "Biglow Papers," but has surely suffered no grievous decline in the hands of "Mr. Dooley" (P. F. Dunne). Almost immediately afterward our eyes were opened wide to the incongruities between the life led in our centers of culture and that led in our primitive outlying districts. Perhaps the satire heaped upon us by foreigners like Mrs. Trollope and later by Dickens, while stinging us into petulance, taught us to laugh at our own oddities. At least, it is clear that the Down-Easter, the Georgia Cracker, the Flush-timer of Alabama and Mississippi, soon made their bows to laughing audiences. The discovery of California brought other reckless specimens of humanity to the front, and as the country has filled up, the contrast between the life of the settled East and of the various Wests has given birth to fresh phases of a humorous literature constant in its main features. The Mormon, the Pike County man, the Mississippi boatman, have all contributed to the gaiety of the nation, largely, it is needless to say, through the agency of the ubiquitous newspaper. Side by side with this extensive growth of our humor, there has been an intensive growth, classes of characters forced into prominence by a developing civilization, such as the freed negro, the vulgar millionaire, the commercial traveler, the immigrant of whatever nationality, and the suburbanite, having furnished themselves as objects of good-natured banter. Writers of local fiction have also left few odd nooks unexplored, until it may be truly said that the American who is in want of something to smile at cannot have long been naturalized. And most of this wide-spread humor has been practically based upon incongruities, themselves based upon a rapidly extending and evolving democratic society.

Naturally the earliest settlers had no such broad field for the display of whatever sense of humor they possessed. Yet the anonymous poem, "New England's Annoyances" (1630), shows a disposition on the part of the Puritans to bear smilingly the discomforts of their bleak abode; and it is quite certain that from the beginning the Southerner loved his jest. With the eighteenth century humor takes a permanent place in our literature. Madam Sarah Knight, traveling on horseback from Boston to New York, and Colonel William Byrd, watching the drawing of the line between Virginia and North Carolina, smiled at all the odd things they saw, and wrote diaries that afford fresh and amusing reading to-day. By the middle of the century, Mather Byles and Joseph Green were making puns and writing skits in that sedate Boston where shortly before Cotton Mather had ejaculated a prayer every time he washed his hands. With urban growth, material development, and political progress, humor was bound to emerge- a humor shrewd enough to represent a shrewd people, full of an exaggeration in keeping with the physical vastness of the country, essentially good-natured, as befitted a primitive democracy in which every man must help his neighbor. These characteristics, which have remained fairly constant in American humor, are seen almost in full development in Franklin. "The very tails of the sheep are so laden with wool, that each has a little car or wagon on four little wheels, to support and keep it from trailing on the ground." Here we have that combination of imagination, matter of fact, good nature, and exaggeration in which we Americans so delight, and at which foreigners so often gasp.

The sixty years that cover the old age of Franklin, the maturity of Washington Irving, and the youth of Oliver Wendell Holmes need not detain us long. During the period quite a quantity of fair, but only fair, humorous and satiric verse was produced by writers of whom Hopkinson and Freneau and Trumbull, together with Drake and Halleck, are probably the only ones honored by being even half remembered. Irving, of course, especially through the inimitable "History of New York, by Diedrich Knickerbocker" and the genial "Sketch-Book" and "Bracebridge Hall," gave American humor, along with American literature, a standing in the world of letters; but, like the poets, his predecessors and contemporaries, as well as the Knickerbocker coterie he dominated, Paulding, Sands, Verplanck, and the rest, Irving was continually showing in his writings the influence of literary models. This fact suggests that American humorists may be conveniently classified under three heads—the writers of humorous verse, the academic humorists, and the socio-political humorists, the last-named class containing most of those amateur depicters of local oddities and those professional purveyors of fun who represent the raciest and most characteristic phases of our national humor.

Not one of these classes—to which we might add a fourth, including those writers of fiction who, from the days of Hugh Henry Brackenridge, author of "Modern Chivalry" (1796–1806), to those of Mr. Stockton, Mr. Cable, and Mr. Joel Chandler Harris, have either made their humor an excuse for writing stories or have infused it into everything they have written—should be overlooked in a careful survey of American humorous literature. But a sketch cannot be thorough, and when the question arises on which class special emphasis should be laid, it would seem that there is only one answer. However truly American Irving, Dr. Holmes, George William Curtis, Mr. Mitchell ("Ik Marvel"), and the late Charles Dudley Warner really are, it can scarcely be denied that they are primarily citizens of the world of letters, that they have their literary analogues, that they are not professed humorists of the type of "Artemus Ward"—a type as distinctively and originally American as the most chauvinistic patriot could desire. So with the writers of humorous verse, with Albert Gorton Greene, author of "Old Grimes," with John Godfrey Saxe, whose popularity was once great and not undeserved, with Charles G. Halpine ("Private Miles O'Reilly"), with Charles Follen Adams ("Leedle Yawcoob Strauss"), and even with the versatile author of "Hans Breitmann's Ballads," Charles Godfrey Leland,—with all their genuinely national humor, these writers are to be classed with Hood and Thackeray—a fact which is not in the least discreditable to them, but which has obvious bearings upon the scope of the present paper. Yet it is truly an ungrateful procedure to pass over a class of writings represented by such an exuberantly burlesque stanza as

> Hans Breitmann gife a Barty—
>   Wo ist dot Barty now?
> Wo ist de lofely golden cloud
>   Dot float on de moundain's prow?
> Wo ist de Himmelstrahlende Stern—
>   De shtar of de shpirit's Light?
> All goned afay mit de Lager Bier,
>   Afay— in de Ewigkeit!

It is fully as ungrateful to pass over the humorous verses of Bret Harte and Eugene Field, the more than humorous poems of Mr. John Hay, the early dialect rhymes of the ill-fated Irwin Russell (1853–79), and the many charming contributions made by Mr. Stedman and other poets to our national stock of *vers de société*. Courage may be found for this, but it is impossible to treat so cavalierly a writer whom many competent readers regard as the greatest humorist America has ever produced—James Russell Lowell. Against this ranking of the author of the "Fable for Critics" and the "Biglow Papers" no protest shall be entered here, although it is conceivable that the less ebullient humor of the genial "Autocrat" should seem more delightful to certain minds. But even Lowell, original and great humorist though he be, has his literary analogues. His prolegomena may well seem to throw all previous similar apparatus in the shade, but the similar apparatus existed previously. So, too, one has but to read Coleridge's "Talleyrand to Lord Grenville" and to remember that Seba Smith and his imitator Charles Augustus Davis had already made a Down-East rustic deal, in his own vernacular, with current politics, in order to perceive that while no more truly original production than the "Biglow Papers" exists in any literature, its author never ceased to be more than what we know technically as a "humorist"—never ceased to be a great man of letters, whose humor deserves an essay or a volume, not a mere paragraph in an article.

Turning now to our third class of humorists, whose special designation, socio-political, seems portentously serious, it is easy to discover from their biographies one reason at least why they are separated by quite a gap from the other two classes. Nearly every one of them has had a variety of typically American experiences, if, indeed, he has not been a "rolling stone." Set over against Dr. Holmes, physician, professor, and man of letters in cultured Boston, Henry Wheeler Shaw ("Josh Billings," 1818–85), who left the East to work on Ohio steamboats, then became a farmer, and finally an auctioneer, before he ever published an article or an almanac, or delivered, with affected awkwardness, a lecture full of pithy humor. In the contrast between these two men's lives we have a key to the contrast between their writings. If, when Dr. Holmes, after the lapse of years, resumed his "Autocrat" papers, he had found himself addressing an obdurate public, is it likely that he would have accommodated himself as Josh Billings did to similar circumstances, changed his spelling, and won popularity? That was the trick of a typical American determined to make his wares sell, just as his phenomenally successful "Farmers' Allminax" was a joint product of his humor and his "hoss-sense." Yet none the less was the critic right who declared that Josh Billings's bad spelling hid but did not obliterate his kinship with La Rochefoucauld. "Cunning, at best, only does the dirty work ov wisdom; tharfore I dispize it," is a saying worthy of any moralist. On the other hand, the following advertisement is worthy only of the "enterprising" American that wrote it: "Kan the leopard change his spots? i answer it kan, bi using Job Sargent's only klensing sope. Job Sargent never told a lie—so did George Washington."

So does biography, one is almost tempted to add when one considers the lives led by Josh Billings's compeers. Where they have not tried several trades or professions, they have generally stuck to one profession that is almost as wide in its scope as American life itself—the profession of journalism. One of the first of our group to attain great popularity, Seba Smith (1792–1868), the creator of "Major Jack Downing," won his fame as a Portland journalist before he served on the metropolitan press. Joseph Clay Neal (1807–47), whose long-forgotten "Charcoal Sketches" described various ridiculous urban types, was a Philadelphia journalist who won the favor of Dickens. Judge Augustus B. Longstreet (1790–1870) would surely not have described Georgia life with such hearty humor if he had not been lawyer, judge, editor, Methodist minister, planter, lecturer, politician, and president of at least four colleges. His co-editor and fellow-depicter of Georgia oddities, William Tappan Thompson (1812–82), creator of that famous lover and traveler "Major Jones," seems to have been the first white child born in the Western Reserve, but to have served later as a volunteer against the Seminoles and as an editor in most of the important towns in Georgia, when he was not making an experiment in journalism in Baltimore. Add to this career a little politics and service in the Confederate ranks, and we have a far from monotonous life. Other examples are scarcely needed, but it is hard to resist citing Benjamin Penhallow Shillaber (1814–90), exploiter of the famous and delightful "Mrs. Partington," who was a printer before he began a varied newspaper career; George Washington Harris (1814–69), who was a jeweler's apprentice, captain of a Tennessee River steamboat, inventor, and political writer, as well as the creator of that egregious East Tennesseean, "Sut Lovengood" [sic]; and George Horatio Derby (1823–61), better known as "John Phœnix," who, after graduating at West Point, saw life in Minnesota, on the Pacific coast, in Texas, and in Florida. Such has been the training these benefactors of their country have received; nor are the two representative humorists, who have been best welcomed abroad, "Artemus Ward" and "Mark Twain," exceptions to the rule. What an experience the latter has had, and to what a good use he has put it! Printer's apprentice, Mississippi pilot, Nevada pioneer, journalist, traveler—what wonder that Mr. Clemens, with his native genius, has evolved from a humorist into a great writer of picaresque fiction and something of an international *censor morum!*

But we are chiefly concerned with the humor of these men, not with their lives; and although the task of describing it is difficult, it must not be shirked. It is, on the whole, a broad humor that frequently does not disdain the aid of bad spelling and bad puns. It deals in incongruities of expression; it accentuates oddities; it sets the commonplace in ridiculous relief; it burlesques pretensions; it laughs at domestic, social, and political mishaps, when they are not too serious; it makes games of foibles and minor vices; it delights to shock the prim, but sedulously avoids all real grossness; it sometimes approximates sheer though innocuous mendacity—but why attempt to describe this Protean something which does not get beyond our national borders often enough to make an elaborate passport description necessary? In its lowest forms it can be found in almost any newspaper, in the shape of what is called "comic copy," receipts for writing which are said to be easily obtained and followed. In intermediate forms it can be found in collections of squibs and sketches like those illustrative of the broader phases of New York life written nearly half a century ago by Mortimer Thomson (1832–75), actor, drummer, lecturer, journalist, who adopted the whimsical penname of "Q. K. Philander Doesticks, P.B.," the initials standing for "Queer Kritter," "Perfect Brick." It is needless to say that such things, which were perhaps as amusing to contemporaries as most of our own humorous effusions are to us, cannot now be read *in extenso* without considerable exertion. Finally, in its higher forms this humor can be found in such political satire as that directed against the "copperhead" Democracy by David Ross Locke (1833–88), better known, in the words of Lowell, as "that genuine and delightful humorist, the Rev. Petroleum V. Nasby," and in such sketches of primitive manners as those contained in Judge Joseph G. Baldwin's (died 1864) "The Flush Times of Alabama and Mississippi." Probably, if only on the ground of their wide-spread popularity, we should include among these higher forms of American humor the diverting lucubrations of "A. Ward, Showman," and the less distinctively national naïvetés of Mrs. Partington.

Further classification is probably unnecessary; but it may be remarked that Mr. Watterson's division of American humor into "that which relates to fighting and that which relates to money," while suggestive, is far too narrow. Political humor, provincial humor, social type and class humor, and the humor of whimsicality—even these broad divisions hardly suffice to include all the important productions of Americans in this very flexible genre. Under these heads may be placed, however, such of our humorists as we shall be able to consider in any detail.

Lowell being put to one side, there are at least five political humorists of importance belonging to the eventful forty years 1830–70. These are Seba Smith, Charles Augustus Davis (1795–1867), Robert Henry Newell (1836–1901), the "Orpheus C. Kerr" whose letters gave Lincoln needed relaxation, and whose sad life was recently unveiled in the daily press, Charles Henry Smith ("Bill Arp," born 1826), and David R. Locke. To these one is almost tempted to add Richard Grant White, whose "New Gospel of Peace," describing "the war in the land of Unculpsalm," somewhat belied its title by being a clever and very popular parody of the style of the historical books of the Old Testament.

Seba Smith's excellent creation, Major Jack Downing of Downingville, who is well worthy of the modern reader's attention, had his origin in political disputes in Maine, where his letters began to appear in a local newspaper in January, 1830. They won instant popularity, and the Major soon began to contribute to the New York "Daily Advertiser," and took it upon himself to act as confidant of General Jackson, and to inform the eager public of all the doings of its hero. Later he took part in the Mexican War, and had some interesting things to say about politics in the days of Polk. The humor and wisdom lavished by him on the public throughout his long career may be found in his far from Bentonian "Thirty Years Out of the Senate" (1859).

So successful was Smith's experiment in humorous political satire that a second Jack Downing soon began to contribute letters to the New York "Daily Advertiser." This Major Downing, the creation of C. A. Davis, who represented the somewhat unusual combination of humor and the iron trade, may be followed in "Letters of J. Downing, Major, Downingville Militia, Second Brigade" (New York, 1834). Like his prototype, this pseudo and less-known Major Downing makes a triumphal tour with Old Hickory, during which Mr. Van Buren shows his political agility and his consideration of the dear public by landing on his feet after a tremendous toss from his horse, and making a graceful bow to the awe-struck by-standers. The Major also enlightens his readers as to the standing of the United States Bank, against which Jackson has fulminated, for did he not visit that institution, slate in hand, and perform some wonderful computations? But let us hear him describe in his own words how Mr. Van Buren tried on the coat of the sleeping President, a scene which looks backward to Shakspere and forward to an Executive supposed to be too small to wear his grandfather's hat:

> Mr. Van Buren's turn came next: as soon as he put on the coat, he riz on his toes; but it would not do; it kivered him to his heels, and the hat fell on his shoulders, and you could n't see nothin' on earth of him. "How does that look, Zekil?" says he. "Why," says Zekil, "it looks plaguy curious." "Is the coat too long, or am I too short?" says Mr. Van Buren. "Well, I don't know exactly which," says Zekil. "I 'll think on 't to rights." "That's right, Zekil," says I, "don't commit yourself." And then they all kinder snickered; and the laugh went ag'in' Mr. Van Buren.

The humor of the "Orpheus C. Kerr Papers" is not so homely as that of the "Downing Letters," whether of Smith or Davis, and although the events they treat of are nearer to us and more important, it is conceivable that the older books might draw more smiles from the reader fairly well versed in American history. Journalistic exaggeration and facetiousness, together with rapid use of the unexpected in matter and phrase, constitute, perhaps, the chief notes of the rather formidable array of pages. There are some clever parodies, and the criticism of men and events is often bright and apt; but not infrequently the humor seems forced. At its best, although droll, it is seldom crisp enough to afford good short quotations. This is not the case with the more direct and racy letters of Bill Arp, Newell's Southern counterpart, who lacks some of the latter's literary merits, but is nearer, as it were, to the soil, and has his affiliations also with whimsical makers of mirth like Artemus Ward, Josh Billings, and his own Southern contemporary, George W. Bagby ("Mozis Addums," 1828–83), whose work should be more widely known. Arp's letters to "Mr. Linkhorn" must be read in the light of the fierce struggle of forty years ago to prove palatable to many readers to-day; but surely the great President himself must have smiled if his eye ever fell upon the following account of how Confederate regiments were recruited in the neighborhood of Rome, Georgia: "Most of 'em ["the boys round here"] are so hot that they fairly sizz when you pour water on 'em, and that's the way they make up their military companies here now—when a man applies to jine the volunteers, they sprinkle him, and if he sizzes they take him, and if he don't, they don't." Lincoln would have relished, also, the following apt use of a good story—a phase of American humor which ought not to be overlooked: "We can't run ag'in, for the reesin urged by the Texin, who, when he got into trubble, took advise of a lawyer as to what he orter do. His kase was so bad that the faithful attorney advised him to run away. 'The devil!' says he; 'where shall I run to? I'm in Texas now.'"

But doubtless the most important member of our political group is David R. Locke, journeyman printer, reporter, and editor of Union papers in Ohio. His "Nasby" letters began to appear in 1861, and were useful to the administration. They were continued to cover the tumultuous years following the war, the various volumes being collected in 1872 into "The Struggles—Social, Financial, and Political—of Petroleum V. Nasby." The late pastor of the Church of the New Dispensation, whose name illustrates some of the absurd features of his autobiography, is made to give unblushing utterance to the worst sentiments that supra-loyal Union men assumed to characterize the embarrassed Democrats of the North, particularly of the State of New Jersey. His situation is naturally not a comfortable one, and he finds no rest for the soles of his feet until he reaches Confederate X Roads, Kentucky, where he gets his indispensable whisky on credit, preaches to such orthodox Demo-crats as Deekin Pogram and his compeers, and deluges Andrew Johnson with applications for the local post-office. His zeal is finally rewarded, and he becomes the confidant of the President, much as Major Jack Downing had done before him. His experiences must be sought in "Swingin' Round the Cirkle," which, with the illustrations of Thomas Nast, is one of the most readable of all the productions of our older humorists. For pungent satire, for good-humored though often unjust exaggeration of party and sectional weaknesses, for clever scriptural parodies and visions, for diverting whimsicalities, the book is almost unique, nor should it be forgotten that few of our humorists have been gifted with an imagination so sustained as that of Locke. No short quotation can do justice to his merits, but the reader may be referred to such typical pages as those that describe the procession in honor of the new postmaster, whose salary was hypothecated for his numerous debts, and the following characteristic utterance may be culled for the light it throws upon Mr. Nasby's notions of finance: "I give him the note becoz he furnished the paper, and it made him easy in his mind—I put down the memorandum becoz it looked businesslike. Benevolence is a prominent trait in my karacter. When givin' my note for borrered money will do a man good, I never begrudge the trouble uv writin' it."

Passing now to the provincial group, the humorists whose specialty it is to depict local oddities, we find considerable embarrassment of riches so far as authors and books are concerned, but not with regard to available specimens of their work. The only way to appreciate "Georgia Scenes," for example, is to read at least four or five of the sketches. One humorist of this class, Judge Thomas Chandler Haliburton (1796–1865) of Nova Scotia, whose well-deserved fame is being kept green by his compatriots, does not strictly belong to us except on the principle that, as the United States was the native land of the immortal "Sam Slick," we have as much right to appropriate Judge Haliburton as he had to appropriate the shrewd clock-maker. The rest of these humorists are for our period mainly Southern, because the South, or rather the Southwest, was then filling up rapidly and presenting the mixture of eccentric types which the Far West was to show later. The Middle West was more orderly in its development, although it also furnished some local humor, and it is needless to add that virtually no corner of the country has since escaped the local humorist or his brother, the provincial novelist. It is worth while to add that the humor of the Southwest was much affected by the extensive use of the Mississippi as a highway of travel, and that over this and other highways jocose stories and quaint extravagances of speech spread to the still more or less unsettled half of the continent. The humor of Bret Harte and Mark Twain may not claim kin with that of Longstreet and Johnson J. Hooper, but this is mainly due to the fact that the family tree has not been drawn.

It is hard to assign the palm among these Southwestern humorists. "Sut Lovengood," "Captain Simon Suggs," "Major Jones," and "Ned Brace" are all worthies whom it is well to have known at one time or another, provided one is not squeamish or puritanical. Captain Suggs, the creation of Johnson J. Hooper (1815(?)–63), a lawyer of Alabama, was a blackleg such as only the new Cotton States of those turbulent times could have furnished, and is fairly worthy of comparison with Jonathan Wild himself, although he would certainly have worsted Fielding's hero at seven-up or in a "horse swap." Major Jones is not so artistic a creation, but he is amusing, as most readers of his courting experiences given in the extract in the "Stedman-Hutchinson Library" will probably admit. As for Ned Brace, the practical joker of Longstreet's "Georgia Scenes," he is, in some respects, nearer to life than any of his compeers; but the scenes in which he figures are hardly those that make the deepest impression upon readers of a book that deserves to be reprinted, if only for its historic importance as the fountain-head of that racy Southern, and especially Georgian, fiction given us since the war by such writers as the late Richard Malcolm Johnston and Mr. Joel Chandler Harris. The scenes that are most characteristic of versatile Judge Longstreet, and of the rough but sterling people he sketched, are those that describe the horse trade, the fight, the dancing-party, and, to name no others, the "gouging" rehearsal. Unless he was mystifying his readers, one of the best scenes in his book was not from Judge Longstreet's hand —that admirable description of the militia company drill which Mr. Thomas Hardy seems to have made free with in the twenty-third chapter of "The Trumpet Major." Almost as amusing as the apparently plundered sketch is the fact that when the "lifting" was exposed by the "Critic" in parallel columns, a writer in the "Daily News"—was it Mr. Andrew Lang?—came to the rescue of the British novelist by pointing out how far the latter had improved upon the crude sketch of the American provincial. But alas! no sooner had this convincing proof of British superiority been given than the "Critic" was forced to explain that by an unlucky (sic) mistake the authors' names at the tops of the columns had been transposed!

If Mr. Thomas Hardy, or any other novelist, will turn to Judge Baldwin's "Flush Times," he will doubtless find things well worth working over. In some respects the book has more literary merit than any of its companion volumes. The experiences of a legal neophyte in that paradise of litigation are told with leisurely humor; the artistic lying of Ovid Bolus, Esq., is described with due elaboration; the pathetic fate of the Virginian emigrants who had no weather eye open for sharpers is set forth with artistic skill; and finally, the fabulous exploits of Cave Burton, Esq., of Kentucky yield place to the astounding triumphs of the eloquence of Sargent S. Prentiss. If the fighting, swearing, drinking, gambling, hail-fellow-well-met Southwest had produced no other literary monument than this, it would not have broken the Ten Commandments in vain. One wonders whether Judge Baldwin, who died Chief Justice of the Supreme Court of California, ever saw on the Pacific coast any life more picturesque than that he left behind him. Surely he never examined a more amusingly ignorant candidate for admission to the bar than Mr. Thomas Jefferson Knowly.

Of social type and class humorists the number is so large as to be fairly disconcerting, especially at the close of an article. Fortunately, such humorists constitute the rank and file of their profession at all times, and the reader, by allowing for changes in fashions and manners, can infer from the similar humor of to-day the kind of jests and skits his father laughed at. A few of the more prominent representatives of the class deserve, however, to be mentioned. Among the earliest are George D. Prentice (1802–1870), the witty Louisville editor, and Frances Miriam Whitcher (1811–52), the only woman on our list,—if the writers of fiction were included this would not be the case,—author of the amusing "Widow Bedott Papers." As Miss Berry she won notoriety by contributions to newspapers and magazines, without dreaming that, when she married, the clamors of the supposed models for her characters would drive her clerical husband from his charge. No such effects seem to have been caused by the mild humor of the "Sparrowgrass Papers" of Frederick Swartwout Cozzens (1818–69), whose work is now but faintly remembered. After the Civil War the humorists of this type, profiting perhaps by the example set them by Artemus Ward and Petroleum V. Nasby, become more aggressive and certainly more attractive to the modern reader. Prominent among them are Melville D. Landon ("Eli Perkins," born 1839), C. H. Clark ("Max Adeler"), Charles B. Lewis ("M. Quad," born 1842), well known for the "Lime-Kiln Club" papers in the Detroit "Free Press," and James M. Bailey (1841–94), the popular "Danbury News Man." The mention of the last-named shows us at once that we have reached the golden age of humorous journalism (*circa* 1875). Hitherto humorous articles had been copied widely by the various newspapers. Now the paper that secured an original humorist on its staff would obtain a large circulation throughout the country. Mr. Bailey, for example, soon carried his "Danbury News" up to a circulation of thirty thousand. Later it was found profitable to establish journals like "Peck's Sun" in Milwaukee and the "Texas Siftings" of Alexander E. Sweet, recently deceased, which existed for and by their humor alone. This type of "funny paper" has passed; but "Puck," founded in 1877, the first really successful comic periodical in the country, still holds its own, although deprived of the guidance of its genial editor, the late H. C. Bunner, himself a humorist of a refined and most attractive type.

The humor of whimsicality alone remains to be treated briefly, its main representatives being John Phoenix, Josh Billings,—who is too large for any one class, and has been dealt with already,—and Charles Farrar Browne (1834–67), better known as "Artemus Ward." Derby's books, "Phœnixiana" and the "Squibob Papers," have been lately republished, which is perhaps a sign that his fame is emerging from its comparative eclipse. Whether he will hold latter-day readers is a moot point. When at his best, as when he lectures on astronomy, plays the editor, proposes a new system of English grammar, and writes a musical review extraordinary, he is a very delightful John Phœnix to some of us—in his own San Diego French, "il frappe toute chose parfaitement froid." But often his fantastic humor seems forced and becomes tiresome. Still it cannot be denied that he introduced the humor of the Pacific coast to the American public, and that he taught his fellow-humorists new tricks of extravagance in expression and thought. As a fair but not thoroughly satisfactory specimen of his quips and cranks, the following descriptions of the moon must suffice: "This resplendent luminary, like a youth on the Fourth of July, has its first quarter; like a ruined spendthrift, its last quarter; and, like an omnibus, is occasionally full and new. The evenings on which it appears between these last stages are beautifully illumined by its clear, mellow light."

The fame of Artemus Ward, showman, lecturer, practical joker, and whimsical writer, is perhaps more persistent than that of most of the other humorists we have dealt with, but it is to be feared that few persons are tempted even to glance through his "Works," and some who have done this confess to having been not a little disappointed. Indeed, it is not certain that Artemus Ward, typical American though he was, has not, on the whole, fared better in England, where he died at what seemed but the opening of a brilliant career, than he has in his native country. Be this as it may, it is impossible to read even a meager sketch of him without yielding him one's heart, yet at the same time realizing that, as in the case of a great orator, no one who did not see and hear the man is at all competent to judge him. His literary remains, although it would be easy to underrate their true wit and extravagant humor, do not of themselves explain his once tremendous vogue; but when to them we add the testimony of men who knew and loved him, it is not difficult to conclude that as a whimsically witty genius, although not as a broad, hearty humorist, he has had no equal in America. It is impossible to prove this conclusion, and it would be useless to attempt to support it by quotations even from his account of his famous visit to Brigham Young, or from his lecture on the Mormons. Perhaps a better test of the man's real greatness is supplied by the fact that his contemporaries at home and abroad, and our later selves, let and still let him say anything he will with impunity. He writes from Stratford to "Punch": "I've been lingerin' by the Tomb of the lamentid Shakspere. It is a success." "It 's Artemus Ward," is our involuntary comment, if we have learned to understand him.

Artemus Ward and Shakspere are good names to close with, for they help to show us that humor makes the whole world akin. And poor Artemus's fate reminds us that American humor, as, for example, in Eugene Field's "The Old Man," is constantly tending to run into pathos. But the bare mention of Field recalls George Ade, Oliver Herford, Charles Battell Loomis, and the many true humorists whom we have omitted,[1]—not forgotten,—some of whom will contribute to these pages, but more of whom, like Edgar W. Nye ("Bill Nye," 1850–96), have passed to a place where their smiles find no counterparts in tears. Living or dead, they have been the benefactors of their people. It may suggest a coarse taste, it may even be uncritical, as superfine criticism now goes, to maintain that their work is an integral and not the least valuable part of American literature; but, however this may be, it seems safe to prophesy that whenever America ceases to produce good humorists, and men and women ready to smile and laugh with them, the country will cease to be the great nation that now engages our love and pride. Yet it is equally safe to prophesy that a people that has a jest for every-thing—even for political corruption—will sooner or later have more need of writers who, like Milton and Dante, rarely smile.

Note

   1. From a working list of eighty—itself a product of selection.

[From "Humor in America" (1909)]
Joel Chandler Harris*

   Much that is best and most characteristic in American humor has never had the advantage of type and binding. Much has been lost, but much has been preserved in the oral literature of the common people, having been handed down from generation to generation; and such of it as still persists is perhaps the cream of the best. The pungent and racy anecdote, smelling of the soil, that is told to illustrate a moral, or to give point to an argument, the happy allusion to some memory or tradition, the dramatic manner giving an added perfection, are all a part and parcel of American humor and give piquancy to its peculiarities.
   It may be said of us, with some degree of truth, that we have a way of living humorously, and are conscious of the fact; that our view of life and its responsibilities is, to say the least, droll and comfortable; and there seems never to have been a day in our history when the American view of things generally was not charged or trimmed with humor. This fact, unimportant and insignificant as it seems to be, has tided our statesmen, as well as the common people, over many rough experiences, and has seasoned many disasters that would other-wise have wrought ruin and despair. At least one humorist of world-wide renown has sat in the President's chair, and it would not be going too far to say that American diplomacy has achieved its greatest vic-tories since the chair of state has been occupied by a gentleman who was noted for his humor long before his statesmanship had been put to the test.
   First and last, humor has played a very large part in our political

*Reprinted from *American Wit and Humor* (New York: Review of Reviews, 1909), I, xx–xxi.

campaigns; in fact, it may be said that it has played almost as large a part as principles—which is the name that politicians give to their theories. It is a fact that is common to the experience of those who embark in politics that the happy allusion, the humorous anecdote, dramatically told—especially if it have the added perfection of timeliness—will change the whole prospects of a political struggle, even on the most extensive field.

The forms of humor that are preserved in the oral literature of the people are very dear to them, and for the best of reasons. It is based on their unique experiences; it is a part of their personality; it belongs to their history; and it seems, in some ways, to be an assurance of independence and strength, of vanity and wisdom, of honesty and simplicity. It need not be said that the hold which the name of Abraham Lincoln has upon the people of the whole country is based largely on the exquisite tact with which he handled the homely humor that runs riot among the common people. Other nations have wonder-tales and the various forms of folk-lore as it is known to our friends the scientists; but the folk-lore of the Republic consists almost wholly of humor, and, as it happens, it is the one quality, apart from religion—and it fits in capitally with that—necessary to keep all things sound and sweet and wholesome. Moreover, the humor that is characteristic of the American mind—that seems, indeed, to be its most natural and inevitable product—can be found in no other nation under the sun, for it is possible only where many mixtures of many peoples have been worked into one homogeneous whole on the broad basis of Anglo-Saxon and Celtic thought. . . .

We speak the English language, or—to be perfectly fair to the genial beef-eaters to whom we are related by blood and finance—a form of English dialect called American, and, whether we will or no, we are all the time trying to conform to the standards of written English in form and expression, and to the general trend of English methods that are to be found in what are termed the British classics. This is inevitable, and no fault is to be found with it; but, at the same time, the fact must be recognized that these forms and methods give rise to a certain degree of artificiality when an effort is made to fit American humor to their measure. In this sense, it could be said that all forms of literary expression are artificial in their nature, but it is not necessary to go so far or to lay undue stress on a poignant truth. The fact remains that the vernacular, as distinct from literary form and finish, is the natural vehicle of the most persistent and most popular variety of American humor: hence the frequent employment of what is called dialect. This necessity has had its influence abroad, and the typical American—the man who represents the common people—is supposed to be a person indifferent to the ordinary refinements of life—a careless galoot, indifferent to the course of events and utterly reckless.

Mr. Kipling's ballad of an American takes the measure of this typical person as he is thought of abroad, and presents him at full length. It must be admitted that the figure Mr. Kipling draws is neither a heroic nor a pretty one; but this is because the poet is inclined to take American humor too seriously. It is far from meaning all it says, and the various antics which it reports as taking place before high heaven are merely pleasing inventions. The poet preserves the unities by placing the American spirit on the witness-stand, and this spirit, after venturing to make a list of incredible faults and virtues, announces that it will save the reckless American at last. American humor is a temperamental quality, and belongs to the many instead of a few chosen ones; and yet, when it is taken as seriously as our foreign friends are inclined to take it, its whole effect is destroyed, and we have a view, not of the genuine American, but of a grinning loafer at the corner grocery, who is willing to match with destiny for beers.

Nevertheless, the insight of the poet is superior to the impression made on him by American humor as a whole, and, in spite of his scorn for the outward aspect of the American, there is something fine and large and free in the figure he draws, for it is not to be denied that there is a certain grimness about the home-made portraits of ourselves painted by our humorists—something suggestive of the soil, in spite of prosperity and in the face of a material and commercial progress without a parallel. There is nothing attractive about them save to those who know something of the motives and the interior workings of the American mind, which, in spite of its humorous idiosyncrasies, stands for business, for the aggressive commercialism that has alarmed the world—and also for the tolerance, the sympathy, and broad views and the generous conceptions that are the basis and groundwork of humor the world over.

To take a concrete example: there seems to be a good deal of truth in the statement that Abraham Lincoln was a typical American; and a number of biographies have been written to prove it. These volumes deal with the events, the troubles, the doubts, the difficulties, the confusion of conflicting interests, the perplexities of the hour, the passions and the prejudices that swarmed about him, and they are exceedingly interesting in and of themselves; but not one of them presents the man as he was, and as the people conceived him to be. They knew perfectly well that the melancholy of which he was said to be the victim was merely the exaggeration of spectators, and that, at its worst, it was but the shadow of a deep-seated purpose—the gentle abstraction that shed a beautiful light on his desires, and that served as an exquisite foil for his humor. They knew that the sorrows from which he suffered merely sweetened his nature and strengthened his soul. It was his humor that was typical. In its exuberance, and in its apparent untimeliness—if we are to believe the reports of stupefied and astonished dignity—it was essentially the humor of the common people, the people who have made the Republic what it is, and who will continue to mold its destiny.

It is well to believe in the social and commercial scheme of salvation which the American spirit has mapped out for itself; for, always and everywhere, it remains true to the ideals represented by the promoters and organizers of the Republic. The American whom it represents has had little time for the enjoyment of luxury, or for the cultivation of the extra trimmings and embroideries of refinement. He has always had much to do; business pursues him as he pursues business; and yet, after all is said, his salute and his "so-long" go as far as those of any man in the world. He has been compelled to reorganize his own social organization to meet the demands made possible and pressing by the results of a great civil war; he has been called on to refashion and, in some sort, extend the operation of his political affairs, in order that he may keep pace with a sort of world development that he has inaugurated. Not only has he been compelled to remold the hordes of refugees from old-world tyranny that have come to these shores, but it has been in the line of his trade and traffic to seize the crowns nearest at hand and deposit them in the trash-pile; and to-day he feels that he is but bending to the will of destiny in carrying liberty and ultimate self-government to new peoples in the far islands of the south seas.

There are those, of course, who enter bitter protest against the American's commercialism, his devotion to the projects of trade and material development; but, so long as he carries his humor into his business, all will be well. There are those, too, who are inclined to criticize his recent adventures in alien and unfriendly seas, declaring that these later exploits come dangerously near to committing the country to imperialism—the imperialism of which Mr. Kipling is the laureate. But, if crowns can have their imperialism, with poets to back them, why may not freedom and independence, freedom and self-government, have their nobler imperialism? And why may not this imperialism of liberty reach out for new lands and new peoples on which to impose the blessings that we are fondly supposed to enjoy? Why may not the imperialism of self-government spread until it becomes not only epidemic and contagious but confluent? To venture the suggestion is not to get very far away from the Spirit that spoke so loudly in the poet's unbelieving ear. . . .

First and foremost, men who can see their own weak points, and laugh at them more heartily than disinterested spectators, can be depended on not to wander far from their own ideals. In the light of his own humor, the American stands forth as the conqueror of circumstance, who has created for himself the most appalling responsibilities, which he undertakes and carries out with a wink and a nod, whistling a hymn or a rag-time tune, to show that he is neither weary nor down-hearted.

An American Comic Character [From
Crackerbox Philosophers (1925)]   Jennette Tandy*

Our literary history contains a remarkable series of satirical portraits of the common American. Every age, every country has its imaginary representations of the boor, the clown, the peasant, and the small bourgeois. Such groups of portraits often grow into recognized character types, or are taken over by men of letters after a long existence in popular anecdote. In drama they afford comic relief, in the novel they furnish atmosphere, local color background for realistic movement or picaresque adventure. There are plenty of persons resembling Launcelot Gobbo or Sancho Panza. Rarely does there arise a Reinecke Fuchs, a Til Eulenspiegel, whose tricks and misfortunes, homely wisdom, and shrewd observations on the life about him are given a certain moral or social or political significance; who becomes a symbol of a class-conscious people, a personification of the folk.

Behind a certain group of American character types, through the veil of American humorous caricatures, I seem to glimpse such a folk-hero, the homely American. This fellow, whether he be Yankee, or Southerner, or Jewish clothing merchant, represents the viewpoint of the man of the people. With wise saws and rustic anecdotes and deliberately cruel innuendo he interprets the provincial eccentricities of American life and the petty corruptions of American political intrigue. Hosea Biglow, Josh Billings, Bill Arp, Mr. Dooley, Abe Martin, are successive incarnations of Uncle Sam, the unlettered philosopher.

There is a continuity about the persistence of his homely type in our American literature which suggests a national ideal. Each one of these creations is fathered by oral tradition. A long succession of Yankee yarns precedes the appearance of Jack Downing of Downingville. Countless sporting tales of the Southwesterner lie back of Bill Arp and Petroleum V. Nasby and Pudd'nhead Wilson. Many generations of comic Irishmen ornamented the vaudeville and the legitimate stage before Mr. Dooley. A century of reliance upon the advice of Poor Richard and the Old Farmer prepared the way by which Josh Billings and Artemus Ward reached the heart of the American public.

We have had, too, many such popular wiseacres in real life. They have always been an integral part of our social scheme. Today every Main Street has its crackerbox philosopher, every daily newspaper its "colyumist" or its platitudinous poet. Some of our best beloved demi-gods have been invested with this tradition. Franklin of the coonskin cap and the wise maxims, Davy Crockett, Lincoln the rail-splitter, with

*Reprinted with permission from Introduction, *Crackerbox Philosophers in American Humor and Satire* (New York: Columbia Univ. Press, 1925), pp. ix–xi. Copyright 1925 by the Columbia University Press.

his "little stories," have been living examples of the sages whom Democracy delights to honor. Popular myth makes these men rustic critics, backwoods philosophers, instead of politicians and men of the world. One might point to present-day demagogues who have adopted the mask of crudity and wit to their own advantage.

There is, then, in America a long succession of these personages. They began to emerge from oral and subliterary written tradition in 1830. From 1830 to 1865–1867 this company made up a body of historically significant political caricatures of some literary merit. During the sixties and the seventies Josh Billings and Artemus Ward excelled in social caricature. In the eighties and nineties the unlettered philosopher existed only in minor capacities and a multiplicity of subtypes. In more recent times there is the same variety in characterization and the same relative unimportance, except for the political and social satire of Mr. Dooley, Mawruss Perlmutter, and Abe Martin. The rural sage peoples the background of the local color novel, the back pages of the magazine, and the far corners of the editorial page of the newspaper. The old rustic types are still with us, the Uncle Henrys and Abe Martins, but many more of the minor critics are today city-dwellers. Frequently they are not native born.

So we live, as always, surrounded, in our books, our newspapers, our films, as in our actual social environment, by advisers and observers from the lower ranks of life. An important phase of our national as well as our literary activity is our reliance on, our apprehensiveness of, the opinions of the Perlmutters and the Lippincutts. Consciously or unconsciously, our lives are shaped by those real or imaginary homely critics, the unlettered philosophers.

The Roots of American Humor
[1934-1935]   J. DeLancey Ferguson*

Nowadays students of our literature have taken up humor in a serious way, and the collecting of its earlier manifestations has become a specialty among enthusiasts for Americana. Mr. Bernard DeVoto draws upon Mr. Franklin J. Meine's unrivaled collection of early books and periodicals for his examination of the matrix of Mark Twain's humor; Miss Constance Rourke has traced from similar sources the development of the stock characters of American drama and American fiction alike. Names of long-forgotten authors such as Augustus Baldwin Longstreet

*Reprinted with permission from the *American Scholar*, 4 (Winter 1934–1935), 41–49. Copyright 1934 by the United Chapters of Phi Beta Kappa.

and Johnson J. Hooper have been disinterred; the gathering and sifting
of tall stories about Paul Bunyan and Mike Fink has become a small
but depression-proof industry. Through all this collecting and collating
runs a naïve idea which threatens to become a creed—the investigators' conviction that they have at last discovered something truly native
to our soil. Mr. DeVoto indeed states the conviction in terms which
leave him no loophole for escape: The tall story, he says, "was an
infinitely versatile art form; and, what is more important, an art sharply
and autochthonously American—unique."

Was it?

Nothing is riskier, in surveying any human institution, than to point
to one specific spot and say, "Here it begins." For if anything is certain
about them it is that institutions have a life history of their own. They
do not spring up suddenly but grow by mutation and adaptation.
Getting to their origins is as long and dubious a task as getting to the
root of our biological family tree. Especially is this true of American
institutions. The transplanting of the English-speaking peoples to
America did not produce a new civilization. We carried with us not
only innumerable vestigial organs of an older society but also the seeds
of all our new developments. Whoever limits his study of Americana to
America is bound to obtain incomplete results and is also in some danger
of making a fool of himself.

What applies to American institutions in general applies *a fortiori*
to American speech and literature. Most people nowadays, except the
testy gentlemen who write letters to the British papers, are aware that
the average "Americanism" is merely an archaic or dialectic English
term which has flourished here after being forgotten or ignored in its
native land. When Francis Grose—he who explained "gouging" as "a
cruel practice used by the Bostonians in America"—published his *Classical Dictionary of the Vulgar Tongue* in 1785 he included dozens of
"Americanisms" such as "cracker" for "biscuit," "frisk" for "search,"
"hick" for a rural simpleton, "kid" as a verb meaning to hoax or deceive,
"leery" as an adjective meaning on one's guard, and "moonshine" for
illicit liquor. It may well be questioned, indeed, whether any of our
older expressions except those of Indian origin is really native to the
soil. Even our spelling of "honor" simply perpetuates the usage of
such sturdy Yankees as John Milton and Robert Burns. Perhaps the
collectors of American humor would do well to take a sharper look
at the British analogs.

The study of literature still suffers from the aristocratic bias which
formerly limited the materials of history to the doings of kings and
their courts. That which engrosses textbook and classroom is mostly
highbrow literature, the carefully wrought product which was written,
and read, only by an educated minority of the population. The undergraduate, and too often his teacher as well, is left with the impression

that Wordsworth and Coleridge were the best sellers of 1798 and Shelley and Keats of 1821, whereas in those years few Britons had even heard the poets' names. Further back in literary history the spread between the tastes of the upper classes and those of their humbler contemporaries becomes still wider. The gentry find their standards in foreign languages and literatures, preferably extinct ones; the plain folk have interests nearer home. We judge the eighteenth century by Pope and Swift and Johnson, by Fielding and Addison and Sterne, but it is doubtful whether a tithe of the population had ever read a word of any of these. The works which circulated by the tens of thousands in print and by hundreds of thousands through oral transmission were very different. The scholarship of nearly two centuries has made us familiar with the popular ballads and folksongs of England and Scotland, but no such work has been done for the popular prose. Johnson's *Rambler*, which as a periodical achieved a maximum circulation of five hundred copies, is in all the textbooks, but no textbook mentions Johnson's contemporary, Dougal Graham, bellman of Glasgow, whose pamphlets sold by the tens of thousands and were in the pack of every peddler in Scotland.

Investigators of our humor, if they have sought its origins in Great Britain, have read the literature which gets into the histories. Finding no humor of exaggeration there they have concluded that it did not exist. Nevertheless the roots of our folk tales are in Britain, though we must look for them in men like Dougal Graham and not in Pope and Johnson. America was not settled by highbrows, though they have written its history, thereby misleading their own descendants as well as the rest of the world. If the colonial history of New England had not been recorded by ministers and elders of the church so many misconceptions of New England life would not be current today. Behind the clergy, and making up the real life of the colonies, were plain farmers, artisans, fishermen and sailors, working hard for small reward, much interested in their families and their bread and butter and not at all interested in theology, bawdy in their cups and grimly stoical or acidly humorous under hardship—in short, men of a piece with mankind the world over. And this stock had not cast aside its traditions when it crossed the Atlantic. As it perpetuated and adapted to American use the local speech of all the parts of the British Isles whence it came, so it perpetuated and adapted folk literature.

The only part of this transplanted folk literature which has received adequate attention is the ballads which even today are found in remote spots among the decendants of Scottish, Scotch-Irish, and North of England stock—ballads which prove by their multitude of variants and alterations that they are something more than mere fossilized remains. But the ballad after all is a specialized form. Effective composition of a new ballad—this remark is made with a defiant glance at the adherents of the "communal" theory of ballad-making—requires not only a specific talent but also an education in the traditions of the form. Popular prose is under no such handicap. It is infinitely versatile, as Mr. DeVoto says, and the man who has had or imagined a single vivid experience or who strikes out a single metaphor has as good a chance of adding to the common stock as has the born raconteur.

When we turn back, not to the seventeenth and eighteenth century authors who bulk largest in the textbooks but to the proverb collections and chapbooks of the period, we are in no strange world. As Mark Twain discovered about well-drawn characters in fiction and biography, we have known it before—met it on the river. The plain people of Great Britain, two centuries ago, were no strangers to exaggeration and far-fetched metaphor and tall stories—these things were part of their daily speech. The following examples of the simplest form of the humor of exaggeration—the grotesque or startling simile, the "tall tale in miniature," as Miss Rourke calls it—are drawn from a variety of sources. To avoid confusion from dialectic details, and to remove clues, the spelling has been normalized and one or two localisms have been replaced by their standard English synonyms. How many can classify them according to country of origin?

As lazy as Ludlam's dog, that leaned his head against a wall to bark.

I am perfectly honest! When I was only a child, my mother would have trusted me with a house full of millstones.

Mean enough to steal acorns from a blind hog.

He'd drive a louse to London for the hide and tallow.

As wise as Waltham's calf, that ran nine miles to suck a bull.

They drive their own car, though you wouldn't think they had money enough to keep a mousetrap baited.

No more chance than a cat in hell without claws.

It is well that the alleys are not wider, because they hold as much smell now as a person can stand.

I nearly slept myself to death with hunger.

As brisk as a bee in a tarpot.

Tongue enough for two sets of teeth.

"Salt!" said the cobbler, after he had eaten the whole cow except the tail.

One of the above is quoted from Mark Twain, one from James Russell Lowell, and one from an elderly Manchester merchant who used the expression in casual conversation with the writer some years ago. The others are to be found in John Ray's *English Proverbs* (first published in 1670), Grose's *Classical Dictionary of the Vulgar Tongue* (first published in 1785), and Dougal Graham's *The Comical Sayings of Paddy from Cork* (*circa* 1760). Since Ludlam's dog appears in both Ray and

Grose, as do a number of other similar sayings, we may reasonably infer that he was well-known in British talk for more than a century. And he was not too lazy to cross the ocean. Turning to the apocryphal or ghost-written *Account of Colonel Crockett's Tour to the North and Down East* (1835) we find this speech by a Yankee peddler recently returned from the South: "They're great for huntin' of foxes; and if you were to see their hounds! lean, lank, labber-sided pups, that are so poor they have to prop up agin a post-and-raid fence 'fore they can raise a bark at my tin-cart." According to the *English Dialect Dictionary* "labber" is North of England and means wet or muddy or sloppy; and therefore out of this particular "pristine little story" only the post-and-rail fence and the tin-cart are really entitled to wear the "lustrous air of new birth" which Miss Rourke finds surrounnding the earlier tall tales. In other words, the only details by which this tall tale in miniature differs from its British parents are those which relate to the physical elements in the American scene. The humor is the same in both.

It may be objected that these metaphors and similes are too simple to base an argument on. The full development of American humor gives us not merely this brief dry wit but the full-blown flower of extravaganza—the saga of Paul Bunyan or John Henry or Mike Fink. The chapbooks and the proverbs offer nothing to compare with the Big Bear of Arkansas or with the exploits of Paul Bunyan and his blue ox Babe. Perhaps not, though if one were not warned in advance would one be wholly certain that Paddy from Cork's rooster had not strayed in from one of Paul's camps? "I remember one long-necked cock that my mother had of an overseas brood, that stood on the midden and picked all the stars out of the north west, so they were never so thick there since."

But let us go back a little further. It may not be irrelevant and immaterial to recall that any first settler of Pennsylvania or the Carolinas would have had plenty of time, if he chose, to read Urquhart's translation of Rabelais before starting for the New World; that any settler in Virginia—like any Pilgrim Father who wasn't too pious—might have seen Falstaff and Bardolph on a Bankside stage. Passing by these reminders, however, that exaggerated humor was not unknown even to the cultivated classes in the seventeenth century, we turn from the chapbooks to folk tales and from folk tales to the medieval sagas and epics and romances whence they sprang. And wherever we look we find the same thing.

Consider, for instance, some of the heroes of the *Mabinogion*. There was Drem the son of Dremidyd who "when the gnat arose in the morning with the sun, he could see it from Gelli Wic in Cornwall, as far off as Pen Blathaon in North Britain." Gilla Coes Hydd "would clear three hundred acres at one bound: the chief leaper of Ireland was he." Clust the son of Clustveinad, "though he were buried seven cubits beneath the earth, he would hear the ant fifty miles off rise from her nest in the morning." Medyr the son of Methredydd could from Gelli Wic "shoot the wren through the two legs upon Esgeir Oervel in Ireland"; Gwiawn Llygad Cath could cut a haw from the eye of a gnat without hurting him, and Kai was of so warm a nature "that, when it rained hardest, whatever he carried remained dry for a handbreadth above and a hand-breadth below his hand; and when his companions were coldest, it was to them as fuel with which to light their fire." And like these heroes was Cailleach Bheurr, "a colossal old deer-goddess, the best known in the Gaeldom, a being who could wade across the deepest straits—whose washtub was the mighty whirlpool of Corryvreckan—who could carry islands with her in a basket."

The further an American reads in the Celtic legends, in fact, the more familiar they seem. What essential difference is there between Davy Crockett who could grin a coon to death at thirty yards and Kilhwch who could shout with so deadly an effect that every pregnant woman within a hundred-mile radius would miscarry and all the rest would be so blighted as to become barren from that day forth? What difference between Paul Bunyan who dug Lake Superior as a drinking trough for his ox and Finn MacCool (or, to go Celtic all over, Fionn Mac Cumhaill) who built the Giant's Causeway to call the bluff of a Scotch giant who had challenged him to fight? The folk heroes of American mythology are descended in royal lineage from the gods and demigods and heroes of Scotland and Wales and Ireland, and from Sigurd and Beowulf and Thor himself.

It is not mere fancy to make such a claim. Though the legends from which our epics stem had sunk below the attention of the highbrow world while America was being colonized, the stories, like the language, went on growing in the mouths of the common people, regardless of what the court and the universities talked about. But the tales of Finn or of Guy of Warwick were intertwined with Old World geography; the very bricks and stones were alive to corroborate their truth. Retold in America the legends lacked roots. It was inevitable that the best adventures of heroes who had never heard of America should gradually be transferred by narrators who had never seen Europe to real or imaginary native sons. It is needless to seek as far as Scandinavia for the main elements of the Paul Bunyan cycle, for example. Lumbermen from the British Isles could have furnished them all, long before the Norse immigration began.

Even the twist of surprise or anticlimax at the end, often supposed to be characteristic of the American story, has its roots elsewhere. Everyone who has seen *Lightnin'* recalls the hero's classic tale of driving a swarm of bees across the plains in the dead of winter and never losing a bee. "Got stung twice" he adds as an apparent afterthought. In the *Mabinogion* Kilhwch, as one of the seemingly impossible tasks he must perform to win Olwen, is required in a single day to gather up nine bushels of flax-seed which had been sown broadcast long before. Like Psyche in the Greek story he accomplishes the task with the help of the ants: "They fetched the nine bushels of flax-seed which Yspaddaden Penkawr had required of Kilhwch, and they brought the full measure without lacking any, except one flax-seed, and that the lame pismire brought in before night."

In short, to anyone who has dipped into British folk literature the whole world of American humorous characters as outlined by Miss Rourke, from Jonathan the peddler onward, is a familiar world with only a few labels changed. We meet that Yankee peddler in Miss Rourke's first chapter—shrewd, sly, and taciturn, disliked in many places because he always gets the better of a bargain, oppressed and made the victim of tricks by his enemies but usually coming out on top by reason of superior cleverness. His Southern customers insult him by telling him that "Down east a cow and a calf and a calico frock is said to be a girl's portion"—and the insult is merely a bowdlerized version of "Tipperary fortune" as defined by Francis Grose. No English or Scots or Irish farm lad of the eighteenth century would have been misled for an instant on meeting this Yankee. He is no stranger; he is John Cheap the chapman, or Leper the itinerant tailor, dressed in different clothes and speaking with a different intonation. His adventures are familiar and recognizable—even as Leper the Tailor relates among his other encounters the tale which John Millington Synge took by divine right as the framework of *In the Shadow of the Glen*. Miss Rourke claims Jonathan as a parthenogenetic birth of the American soil, but his father was John Cheap and his grandfather was Autolycus.

Probably the chief reason why these obvious facts have not been more generally recognized is that American folk tales have rarely reached the modern reader in their original form. The earliest printed versions are already corrupted and revamped far more devastatingly than were the "improved" versions of old ballads which some of the first editors perpetrated. The rare genius like Mark Twain or Joel Chandler Harris who could *think* in folk language was the exception. Most of the sketches of such early humorists as Augustus Baldwin Longstreet and Johnson J. Hooper—adequately represented in Mr. Meine's *Tall Tales of the Southwest*—are the work of highbrows self-consciously patronizing the people they write about. The style, modeled on the *Spectator* and the *Sketch-Book*, embodies all the worst features of both. The author talks about his subjects instead of letting them talk, and every word or phrase which to his quivering ear is not pure Addisonian English is enclosed in quotation marks. This is not folk literature. One must painfully disinter and piece together the real folk stuff as the archeologist strives to reunite the sculptured fragments of a classical temple which he finds built into a modern Greek pigsty. The simple speech of the people was too low, too vulgar; it must be condescended to and apologized for. Joseph G. Baldwin can write a twelve-page essay on Ovid Bolus, champion liar of his district, without ever giving Ovid a chance to tell a single story in his own words, and even T. B. Thorpe's *The Big Bear of Arkansas*, generally regarded as one of the gems of these early collections, seldom rings true for two consecutive sentences.

Some day, perhaps, before it is too late, lovers of American folklore may realize the importance of setting down prose as well as verse exactly as it is told to them. If that day comes we shall have more books like Mr. Dobie's *Coronado's Children* and fewer like Mr. Stevens' *Paul Bunyan*. And then it should be plain to everyone that American humor is not a new creation, the fruit of some "unrecorded overthrow of all the world has ever known or even been," but something far more important and significant—the free growth on American soil of a literary heritage as old as our race.

Examining the Roots of American Humor [1935]

Constance Rourke*

"The study of literature still suffers from the aristocratic bias which formerly limited the materials of history to the doings of kings and courts. That which engrosses textbook and classroom is mostly highbrow literature, the carefully wrought product which was written, and read, only by an educated minority of the population."

This statement appears in Mr. J. DeLancey Ferguson's article on "The Roots of American Humor." I should be obliged to go far to find an observation with which I am more heartily in accord. The complementary position as to the importance of popular evidences governs my approach in *American Humor*, and Mr. Ferguson has also been concerned with popular expression. It is therefore with surprise that I find him concluding that some of us who have considered American humor have disregarded well known popular British materials. It may be assumed, I think, that we have read the *Mabinogion*. The sources of British popular humor to which he briefly alludes, Ray, Grose, and Dougal Graham, are not the exclusive possession of any student. And surely such a generalization as the following is unwarranted: "Investigators of our humor, if they have sought its origins in Great Britain, have read the literature which gets into the histories. Finding no humor of exaggeration there, they have concluded that it did not exist." Let me say that I for one have never searched for the origins of American humor

*Reprinted with permission from the *American Scholar*, 4 (Spring 1935), 249–53. Copyright 1935 by the United Chapters of Phi Beta Kappa.

in the formal literature of Great Britain, nor have I drawn such conclusions as to the humor of exaggeration.

There is one body of British popular expression with which Mr. Ferguson seems unfamiliar, though it is germane to his present argument, i.e., the popular reactions to American humor when this first appeared in force on the British stage, in the early eighteen thirties. If American and British humor are essentially the same we might expect a hearty acceptance of that fact from British audiences. The time for a test was auspicious, for Americans were then still close to the period when they were nominally Britons—close to the "roots." But the British were sombrely puzzled by our comedians. "The humors of our own Anglo-Saxon flesh and blood transported to America, and often located in wildernesses, are like nothing among the family which has remained at home," said a newspaper critic of the time whom I have quoted further in *American Humor*. Such summaries of the popular reaction may be found in William Jerdan's *Yankee Humor and Uncle Sam's Fun* (London, 1853), in *The Spirit of the Times* (New York, *seriatim*), in the considerable literature having to do with the adventures of our early comedians abroad, and in other literature of a popular character which I have cited. American humor was regarded as a novelty in Great Britain.

This is far from saying that English and American humor have had nothing in common. It must be clear that our forefathers brought an imaginative inheritance with them when they migrated to these shores, humor included. I develop nothing like the theory of parthenogenesis which Mr. Ferguson ascribes to me, or even the particular thesis that the Yankee Jonathan of the early American stage was "a parthenogenetic birth of American soil." I have, rather, stressed the mixed ancestry of the Yankee, indicated the natural comparisons with the Yorkshireman, accepted the frequently made suggestion that the early Jonathan was derived in part from the Yorkshireman of the British stage, and used a considerable number of references to Irish influences. Mr. Ferguson advances a theory of Gaelic origins controversially as if this were his own discovery, but I had already indicated the possible use of "Gaelic fragments" in the making of American legend and in another connection suggested that "fragments of Gaelic lore brought by the earlier pioneers may have strengthened a sense of natural magic." In my more recent *Davy Crockett* possible alliances between Gaelic myths and the large cycle of Crockett myths are referred to, as are obvious identities between certain of these stories and common general patterns in European folklore.

Some of Mr. Ferguson's difficulties become plain as his collection of "roots" is examined. In drawing upon the *Mabinogion* he is under a handicap since this body of literature has never been regarded as comical. "The further an American reads in the Celtic legends," he says, "the more familiar they seem." The implications of this statement are rather wide. He has drawn his illustrations from the *Mabinogion* from the single story of "Kilwch and Olwen." This is of course one of the great Celtic romances, and the labors of Kilwch are no more comical than the labors of Hercules. Mr. Ferguson might have mentioned Ychdryt Varydraws in this tale, who could thrust his stiff red beard across the forty-eight rafters of Arthur's hall; this perhaps was something of a trick whereas the feats of the heroes or giants he does mention represent only an excess of muscular, visual, vocal, or auditory power, or of natural heat. Exaggeration is not humor, and to the contemporary mind of the mabinogs such excesses were not even exaggeration. They were believed. These stories of heroes and demi-gods and ugly giants sprang from an earlier primitive body of myth and magic; and the continuance of belief even in a later period when the tales were set down for bardic use is attested by many internal evidences, among them the inclusion of genealogies. Mr. Ferguson asks, "What essential difference is there between Davy Crockett who could grin a coon to death at thirty yards and Kilwch who could shout with so deadly an effect that every pregnant woman within a hundred-mile radius would miscarry and all the rest would be so blighted as to become barren from that day forth?" There is the difference in the contemporary mind between belief and comic fantasy. Kilwch is not a comic hero, and the contrast illustrates a peculiar American bent. Many mythologies have been created in which men believed; the inflated fancy belongs to all myth. But where, except on our frontiers, have been invented mythologies which men disbelieved in and still riotously enjoyed, heaping invention upon invention? And this special form of mythology has sprung up not once or transiently among us but many times and in many places, having to do with Mike Fink, Crockett, Paul Bunyan, John Henry, and a host of minor figures.

In further argument Mr. Ferguson sets down twelve examples of comic similes, defies us to say which are English and which are American, and then discloses that only two of them belong to us. He obviously expects us to say that they are all American and it is very easy to give him this point. To my certain knowledge at least six of the similes are or have been common in this country, and the whole lot may have been known here. The English may have invented them all. The practise of culling from the English joke books was common among us in the early part of the last century and even later. The English *Joe Miller* was a prime source. But borrowing was gradually superseded among us by invention, a transition admirably illustrated by the passage from *Colonel Crockett's Tour to the North and Down East*, cited to the contrary in "The Roots of American Humor."

Mr. Ferguson discovers that "labber" is a North of England word. He has also found the English simile "As lazy as Ludlam's dog, that leaned his head against a wall to bark"—which may be called the bones of the joke. But out of these and even throwing in the rails and the tin-cart, I do not believe that Mr. Ferguson could have concocted the Crockett passage: "They're great for huntin' of foxes; and if you were to see their hounds! lean, lank, labber-sided pups, that are so poor they have to prop up agin a post-and-rail fence 'fore they can raise a bark at my tin-cart."

The passage is too brief to hang a whole interpretation on, but it illustrates that combination of highly concrete description with magnified overflow which has been characteristic of our humor. Mark Twain combined these gifts in superlative measure. No one could be more exact in matters of observation, as to scenes, individuals, dialect. No one could at one and the same time cut the strings of reality and soar into the comic empyrean. I think the same things may be said of the whole passage from which Mr. Ferguson has drawn the phrase about "a cow and a calf and a calico frock" which is, he believes, only a Bowdlerized version of the "Tipperary fortune." And I wish to add that none of this is to be construed as an assertion that American humor is superior to English humor. I consider the phrase about Ludlam's dog rather poor as humor, but I do not consider it as characteristically English.

Every point which Mr. Ferguson makes as to identities between American and British humor may be granted. The same patterns, as of exaggeration, may appear in each. An analogue for one of the Paul Bunyan stories appears in the *Spectator*. The same tale is told in Russia. But this is not to say that we had the story from Russia or England or from Sweden, or that the effect of humor in each is the same. Apart from the theory of independent origins, known to students of folklore, the main consideration appears elsewhere. When the individual uses common or traditional materials and does something indubitably his own with them, we call this genius. When the achievement is that of a people we are justified, I think, in using the same word with the implication of fresh creative energy which it carries.

Whatever the common base, something incontestibly our own has been expressed in that highly mixed aggregation which we call American humor. Twists have been given, strong colors added, and the whole patterned into contours often bearing small resemblance to the original base and not to be summed up by the simple word "exaggeration." The original base, when this can be discovered, has importance for careful study, but not a final importance. All literature, all folklore, uses common stuffs. Mr. Ferguson believes that the difference between American and English humor is a mere matter of changing labels. It is nothing so dull. The differences have to do with the creative fancy. Nowhere is this plainer than in relation to the physical scene, which he regards as a minor matter. He makes this point in connection with the English line about Ludlam's dog, but he has failed to notice that in this line there is no scene. Our comic similes, our humor, have abounded in scenes. The wild scene with its white oaks, raccoons, possums, bears, sprawling rivers, and lush growth made a subject of which our early humorists never seemed to tire. Comically, poetically, yet exactly, they drew these subjects again and again, and this turn of absorption makes one of the fresh imaginative contours which our humor has followed.

There will not be space to consider Mr. Ferguson's argument as to certain lively English archaisms still used by Americans. The subject is large, and I believe that Mr. Ferguson's points have been ably met by others elsewhere. But the general query raises a final question. It would seem that one of Mr. Ferguson's difficulties has to do with language. He quotes a phrase of mine which includes the words "new birth," which I believe may rightly be used in relation to American humor. From this he makes a broad leap to a theory of "parthenogenesis," which he says is mine, and finally reaches the amazing statement that American humor is not "the fruit of some 'unrecorded overthrow of all the world has ever known or ever been.'" No one has said anything so absurd. I must assume that Mr. Ferguson knows the meaning of the word "parthenogenesis." I must assume that he has read *American Humor*. Perhaps in an interval it has been remade in his mind, with a touch added here and there, and a considerable amount subtracted. The process is well known. It belongs to folklore, but one does not expect to find it in serious criticism.

Our Native Humor [1936-1937]   Sculley Bradley*

A painstaking scholar recently classified 30,000 jokes in pigeonholes, finding that there were only thirty original jokes (which was more than one would suspect). Afterwards, he discovered another, and he had to rearrange the entire lot in thirty-one categories. This was probably a useful enterprise, but simple folk, who prefer their laughter undiluted, are inclined to seek another pigeonhole for the critic.

Yet humor, of all human qualities, lies closest to the heart. Other animals share with man the ability to think, but not that highest perception of the intellect which flowers into laughter. The true nature of an individual is revealed by what makes him laugh. If Lucrezia Borgia ever smiled, no one has remembered it, but the laughter of the wise and good, of the Buddhas and the Shakespeares, is immortalized in bronze or in their own words.

As with individuals, so with nations—the collective laughter of a race will reveal its most secret qualities. It is not simply accident that

*Reprinted with permission from the *North American Review*, 242, No. 2 (Winter 1936–1937), 351–62. Copyright 1936 by the *North American Review* Corporation.

has given each nation a distinctive humor. Above the bed-rock of universal humor, the common heritage of mankind and understood everywhere, lies the top-soil formed by the erosion of national life. Humor is deeper and more fertile in the United States than in some less fortunate places. Critics are just beginning to see it as an important key to our national character. To understand its spiritual sources is to comprehend more fully the American attitudes revealed in the sober pursuit of our daily lives, and in our language, literature, and art.

The common origins of the English and the earlier American cultures have produced certain similarities in humorous points of view. Since the Anglo-Saxon is always a moralist, the laughter both of England and America is prevailingly corrective. Yet there is an important difference; the corrective laughter of England is satiric; that of America is ironic. The British laugh at a thing for being so ridiculously what it is; Americans are more prone to be laughing because the thing is not what it should be, or what they expected it would be. This American attitude was demonstrated, years ago, by the wide currency of stories about the Ford car. And after that remarkable machine had achieved a perfection beyond humor, our typical jokes fastened themselves upon certain blond or platinum personalities in Hollywood, and then, more recently, found a perfect subject in the depression. British life offers little parallel for this sort of humor, a blend of admiration or awe with irony.

English humor rejoices in the simple humor of a situation. For instance, when Sheridan learned that the theater which afforded him his livelihood was burning, he repaired with a friend to an alehouse across the street where he watched the destruction over a comforting glass. As their spirits revived, a formal little gentleman at an adjoining table, not recognizing the writer, admonished them sternly for their gaiety "while poor Mr. Sheridan's theatre was burning down."

"Well," said Sheridan, "things are at a pretty pass when a man dare not be merry at his own fireside."

This, of course, is a variation of a universal comic situation, the "downfall of dignity." In its simple form it generally suffices for British humor. When Americans employ it, however, they are tempted to treat it with embellishment or exaggeration which would seem in bad taste to our English cousins. An old American story, for example, deals with the corpulent and dignified Senator who sprawled on the icy steps of the Capitol and slid to the bottom. Part way down he encountered a stout lady, who crumpled up helplessly on his chest and rode to the sidewalk below. There the Senator lay panting, "Madam, you will have to get off now; this is the end of my route." Thus a simple and universal comic situation is made American.

Characteristic English humor is defensive, while American humor prefers to strike first. The English enjoy the sudden, defensive brilliance of wit under fire. They do not understand why Americans like to play jokes on the unwary. It does not occur to an Englishman to give his friend a cigar that will explode. The British tell another story of Sheridan which is one of the best examples of defensive wit. As dramatic critic for a periodical, he had praised a play which some spectators had thought to be immoral. An irate lady of sturdy principles wrote a letter to the editor, remarking that for the opinions of such a man she "would not give three skips of a louse." Sheridan published the letter with the comment that, although the language was violent, a woman must always be forgiven for mentioning whatever was going through her head at the moment.

Americans employ such defensiveness, of course, but even more they seem to enjoy the unexpected and unprovoked attack. They tell of the explorer in the jungle who was informed by his wife that a tiger was pursuing his mother-in-law; and "What do I care what happens to a tiger!" replied the explorer. Judged by British standards, this story is in bad taste; in America, it is simply funny. Far reaching differences in social history are responsible for these divergent attitudes.

The national characteristics of American humor are plainly rooted in the conditions of American life. A people chiefly occupied with the conquest of a wild and unfriendly continent will develop unique attitudes which their humor must represent. The frontier spirit has been the strongest element in our national consciousness for three hundred years. In 1607 the frontier, for Captain John Smith, was Pocahontas in Virginia; in 1900 it was the great Northwest. But as the margin of conquest moved westward it left behind an increasing area of frontier consciousness which survives today even in eastern cities. Frontiersmen must live their lives with the mother of invention. They must be quick and cunning and strong. They must not be taken in by the appearance of things. They will come to value simple integrity of character and homely philosophy. As these attitudes grew in American thought they were reflected in American humor, and they still persist.

A principal trait of American humor is its anti-romanticism. We love to puncture an illusion, to burst an iridescent bubble of hot air. Pretensions of grandeur, false family pride, snobbishness, or conceit annoy us, and we enjoy destroying them with the sharp weapon of irreverence. As a necessary corollary to our anti-romanticism, we have chosen as our most comic figue the "sucker." He is the "goat," the victim of our practical jokes, the romancer who is fooled by the mere surface of things. At different periods he was the tenderfoot who walked blithely into an Indian ambush, the fool who thought he could go up in a balloon, the loon who believed a carriage would run without a horse, the apprentice who runs to fetch a left-handed monkey wrench or a bucket of steam, the sucker who "bites" on the leading question, or the simple soul who is taken in by those odd novelties, decent and otherwise, in which American merchants do a thriving business just before the first of April. The more easily the American "sucker" may be "taken," the funnier he is.

Reflect upon the origins of all this in pioneer life. From the time of Columbus onward, European publicity men and real-estate brokers painted alluring pictures of America in the effort to induce colonization and stimulate trade. The land flowed with milk and honey, gold lay in lumps on the ground, and wild game obligingly came into the settlements to be shot. As late as 1880, according to the story, an Irish immigrant, leaving the immigrant station in New York, saw a blind beggar standing outside, with a ten dollar gold-piece glittering at his feet. Stooping down, Pat tossed the coin into the beggar's cup with the remark that "the poor divil couldn't see thim fer himself."

Whether in New York in 1880 or in Virginia in 1607, the expectations of the immigrant were to receive a rude shock. The Indians were not noticeably friendly, the game was unaccountably shy, the trees were tough and the gold turned out to be chiefly iron pyrites. A family of settlers would pole a raft laboriously up the mammoth tides of the Mississippi or Missouri, past the forlorn settlements, looking for a place less muddy and unfriendly. At last, finding it all to be the same, they would choose a spot and build a log house. In three weeks of perspiring toil they would achieve a romantic dream of abode. Then one night, just as the new mansion was nearly completed, the floods would descend, the river would capriciously change its course, and the house would become an island, if indeed it did not float off toward the gulf.

Experiences of this nature were the common lot of our forefathers. If you could not laugh at this or at yourself in the role of the sucker, you were doomed. And the laughter grew. It became a national trait. Such anti-romanticism is a fundamental quality of our typical humorists, writers like Mark Twain, for instance, whose *Petrified Man* is as characteristic a story as we have. It deals with a party of silver miners in Nevada. They have labored across the continent and up the steep hills. They have sweated fruitlessly through many veins of pure quartz, with no trace of silver. At last they strike something different. They do not understand it, but hope springs high. For days they labor to uncover the curious object. At last it is revealed, a gigantic petrified man. There he had been sitting hundreds of years, facing eastward toward the oncoming pioneers, his nose and thumb cooperating "in the immemorial gesture of derision."

This story is almost a perfect pattern for the anti-romantic American story. It was a fertile field for Davy Crockett, Petroleum Nasby, Artemus Ward, John Phoenix and almost every other early American humorist. It is a principal characteristic in our humorous fiction. It is a fundamental American stamp on the work of such contemporary writers as Dorothy Parker, Ogden Nash, Robert Benchley, or Clarence Day. In John Phoenix, for example, the anti-romantic climax emerges exuberantly in the case of the ingenious surveyor who invented a pedometer for measuring distances in road building. The instrument had a neat dial which was hung on the "seat of the pants," and a long rod attached to the knee. Unfortunately the surveyor stopped at a tavern for some frontier whiskey, and in the next ten miles achieved a speedometer reading which suggested a transcontinental journey. When a bottle of Phoenix' hair tonic was accidentally broken on a marble step, a doormat grew up at once. In our modern humorists there is only a change of setting; the principle of anti-climax is retained. A typical heroine of Dorothy Parker has looked forward to a certain dance as a big moment of her life. She is carefully dressed for the advent of Prince Charming. Suddenly her garter snaps and her stocking begins to slither down. To her horror she finds that she is on the side of the room remote from the haven of feminine repair. She spends the evening as a gloomy wallflower, holding her knee, waiting for the guests to leave, with thoughts of such brilliant ineptitude as only Mrs. Parker can master. Clarence Day's *Father* was a master of the anti-romantic conclusion. Stephen Leacock thrives upon it, as for instance in *My Financial Career*, in which a "simple soul" goes crazy opening his first bank account. Anti-romantic expectation is so deeply rooted in our national consciousness that even today, in any part of the country, the current slang of "So what?" or "Oh, yeah?" are conclusive if impolite remedies for inflated illusions.

Contemporary writers still employ frontier irreverence. Ogden Nash's *Quartet for Prosperous Love-Children* ("the banker, the broker, the Washington joker," and the Forgotten Man) coming pat upon the inevitable moment in national politics, was convincing proof that the appeal of irreverence is as strong now as it was when Major Jack Downing poked fun at President Jackson, or when Abe Lincoln kept thirty important political leaders waiting while he read to Sumner the satiric remarks on politicians from the pen of Petroleum V. Nasby, or when Will Rogers, in *Letters of a Self-Made Diplomat*, addressed President Coolidge by cable as Calcool, or called the United States senate "just a cheap club that ninety-six men belong to, and pay no dues." This sort of thing will naturally give pain to British critics, one of whom recently reviewed Ogden Nash as a poet who might produce important work if he could learn the use of rhyme.

Another element noted in our humor by the critical is its endless capacity for exaggeration. To this the English have impolitely referred as the habit "of telling a lie and laughing at the person who believes it." This disparagement may indicate a natural resentment on the part of the British. Again and again, stories from American newspapers and magazines, which no American was intended to believe and which passed as good hoaxes at home, have been reprinted in England as the solemn truth. There was the story, out of a frontier newspaper in Nevada, of the invention of "solar armor," a refrigerating device intended for use in crossing the great southern deserts; and how its inventor, neglecting to turn off the refrigerator at the proper time, had been found frozen to death. English papers reprinted this, with grave comments on the usefulness of such an invention for the British army in the tropics. This sort of episode has continually embarrassed our foreign diplomacy.

Actually, the exaggeration in our humor has the same cultural sources as our anti-romanticism. Probably the first settlers who ever wrote letters home began the practice. Many of them had come over against the earnest advice of family and friends and they all were anxious, above all else, to make good. Children who have left home against their parents' wishes are notoriously unreliable in reporting their adventures; and young wives who have made questionable marriages are given to the public praise of their husbands. Just so, we may imagine, the new settlers tried to enhance the attractiveness of their new situation. The letters home passed into literature as books about the new country. Captain John Smith, as early as 1608, began his remarkable series of publications about Virginia, and today their charm as literature rests chiefly on the quaint exaggerations which render them wholly unreliable as history. As late as 1778 the same attitude was still prevalent among writers on the new country. In that year one Samuel Peters, a clergyman, published a *History of Connecticut* which reads as though some portions of it had been written by Sir John Mandeville's ghost. The rapids of the Connecticut river, for instance, were said to be so swift that an iron crowbar would float there.

Another powerful impulse to exaggeration was the worship of strength and size which were principal requisites for survival in forest and frontier life. The traditional exploits of the frontiersman are unblushingly exaggerated for humorous effect. He could run down a deer. He had killed a bear so big that he could not carry the pelt. Davy Crockett told of shooting an eye through the head of a weathercock across the Ohio river. At the same distance he punctured a pail of milk which a girl was carrying on her head. Bill Merriweather lost his brother in an extraordinary manner. During a drenching rain his new deerskin breeches shrank so rapidly that he was shot high into the air and never was seen again. Paul Bunyan, at the age of two, built Niagara Falls for a cold shower.

Fishermen and huntsmen even today preserve the frontier tradition, and an allusion to "the one that got away" will always provoke a knowing wink. Sporting magazines unblushingly conduct a Liar's Club while the amalgamated reformers are undisturbed by this menace to the public virtue.

Indeed, the "tall story" was highly regarded in early American life. Such yarns were repeated until they constituted a native folk-lore; they were reprinted in the newspapers as a regular branch of journalism from the Jacksonian era until long after the Civil war. They inspired a school of fiction which flourished for a half-century. The adventures of Simon Suggs, Major Jones or Sut Lovingood are unfamiliar now, and such authors as Longstreet, Baldwin, Thorpe, and W. T. Thompson have passed from memory, but they were the popular literature of the generation of Mark Twain. It is natural, therefore, that exaggeration should leaven every anecdote in *Roughing It* or *Tom Sawyer*; or that *A Connecticut Yankee* should be a tall tale of Arthurian times.

The tall story survives exuberantly today in our daily conversation, in our jokes, in the anecdotes which we so shamelessly tell about our friends. Our speech is full of absurd "gags" which we continuously employ. The one about the man so tall that he had to climb a ladder to shave himself is very old, but one recently heard of the professor so absent-minded that he put his trousers to bed and hung himself over a chair-back where he froze to death. Any reader can add a score of such current oddities. And recently one of the most popular features on the American radio was Baron Munchausen who fascinated millions of auditors every week by the monstrous audacity of his lies. It seems unlikely that this could have occurred in any other country.

Two principal elements of American humor have been indicated. It is interesting to see exaggeration and anti-romantic irreverence joining forces to give the typical American quality to Mark Twain's work. A certain heroine, he said, was "virtuous to the verge of eccentricity." "In this chapel," wrote the Innocent, "were the ashes of St. John. We had seen St. John's ashes before, in another church. We could not bring ourselves to think St. John had two sets of ashes." Romantic Italy proved to be a place where you couldn't get a bath. "Each of us had an Italian farm on his back. We could have felt affluent if we had been officially surveyed and fenced in." The coyote of the Western plains proved to be not a noble wolf, but "a living, breathing allegory of want, . . . and even the fleas would desert him for a velocipede." Mark Twain's enduring popularity rests in large measure upon his ability to make immortal use of the qualities which differentiate our native character.

Today these are still the principal traits of our humorists. I have before me one of those omnibus volumes of contemporary mischief containing nearly a hundred widely varied pieces from pens of such writers as Lardner, Benchley, Leacock, Sullivan, Nash, Thurber, Stewart, and Mrs. Parker. Almost every one of these sketches achieves its quality and strength through the same combination. "I was a poor little girl born in a tenement and my mother and father used to be drunk all the time and beat me so I grew up to be sweet and pure and beautiful." . . . "Only an expert can tell a live Penguin from a stuffed one. It is probable that most Penguins are stuffed." . . . "Children are embarrassed to have their parents along when they are attending certain movies or plays. A child never knows at what point in a play his uninformed old father will start to giggle." . . . "I knew if I came to this dinner, I'd draw something like this baby on my left. I should have stayed at home. I could have had something on a tray. The head of John the Baptist, or something." These quotations fall at random from various parts of the volume, and they all bear the same stamp. It is not so much the tradition of Mark Twain as it is the democracy of frontier laughter amid the sophistication of New York city today.

Finally, our humor is distinguished by homeliness. This, again, is the result of our homespun past. It has a blunt directness, learned along gunsights. It preserves the laconic reflectiveness of wide and lonely vistas. It is the philosophy of the countless crossroads stores that dotted the countryside a few years ago. The bustling towns sprung up around the old Corners have not forgotten the circle of chairs about the wood-stove at night, the box of sawdust with its brown stains, and the slow wisdom. It is as though the shrewd commonsense of *Poor Richard* had been sharpened to laughter by adversity. Our most typical humor still preserves the vernacular and seldom employs the balanced brilliance of wit. Across the pages of our social history moves an array of characters with linsey-woolsey names—Jack Downing, Hosea Biglow, Petroleum Nasby, Bill 'Arp, Artemus Ward, Josh Billings, Mr. Dooley, and many others. They have made our humor as characteristically American as the California redwoods or a baseball game.

Courage and necessity were the original sources of our especial variety of humor. It lined the faces of men and women who were crossing prairies, and conquering forests, and building cities. It may be that with all its strength it is a bit boisterous. Perhaps it lacks refinement or finish according to British standards. But if we were free to choose, we should probably prefer the American variety. As Mr. Dooley said, "a man can be r-right an' be the President, but he can't be both at the same time."

The Lineage of Eustace Tilley
[Review of *Native American Humor*, by Walter Blair (1937)]   Bernard DeVoto*

"An Amerikan luvs tew laff," Josh Billings says in a passage reprinted in Mr. Walter Blair's new anthology,[1] "but he don't luv tew make a bizzness ov it; he works, eats, and haw-haws on a canter." Josh was making a pretty profitable business of it in the *Century* and other mag-

*Reprinted with permission from the *Saturday Review of Literature*, 25 September 1937, pp. 3–4, 20. Copyright 1937 by the *Saturday Review of Literature*.

azines and especially on the lecture platform when he wrote the aphorism, but his observation was sound. American humor developed under the amateur spirit and began to decline—as a literary form, that is—when it was professionalized. In the same essay, Josh (whom Mr. Max Eastman recently described as the father of Imagism, which is pretty hard on King Solomon) made another observation that will bear repeating: "Americans love caustick things; they would prefer turpentine tew cologne-water, if they had tew drink either. So with their relish of humor, they must have it on the half-shell with cayenne."

Let us place on file some American state papers, and then return to our business in an orderly manner. Under date of October 24, 1862, the President writes to Gen. George B. McClellan commanding the Army of the Potomac:

> I have just read your dispatch about sore-tongued and fatigued horses. Will you pardon me for asking what the horses of your army have done since the battle of Antietam that fatigues anything?
>   A. Lincoln.

A year later, the President sends a note to his Secretary of War:

> I personally wish Jacob Freese, of New Jersey, to be appointed Colonel of a colored regiment, and this regardless of whether he can tell the exact shade of Julius Caesar's hair.

The Americans' fondness for haw-hawing on a canter may be observed in the fines assessed against it at Plymouth Plantation, and as soon as there are Englishmen on tour in the provinces it is made clear that the provincials were a people incurably addicted to telling stories. Before the end of the seventeenth century they must have forged an idiom, accent, and turn of thought as recognizably American as the last clause quoted from Lincoln, but for another century you will find little of it in what they wrote. The humor of Benjamin Franklin's formal writing is eighteenth-century London humor; that of his letters is more native, but it is only in his quoted remarks that you get the pure thing. If he truly said that we must all hang together or we should hang separately, he was speaking classical American, though the classics were not yet written. Even more unmistakably, so was the first Yankee who remarked of Franklin's birth that though Ben's keel was laid on Nantucket, his mother went to Boston to launch him. The provincials had been talking that way for a long time, but it took them a good many years to learn to write that way.

This oral humor was the compost in which our native literary humor sprouted—an indefinable but sharply individual humor with more poetry and more fantasy in it than most, with its own imagery, its own accent and intonation, its own patterns of thought. The sound of the human voice, in fact, was a direct conditioner of all American literature throughout its early stages: down to the middle of the nineteenth century the historian can read the printed page aright only if he keeps in mind the lectern, the lyceum, and the innumerable forms of American oratory.

Mr. Blair repeatedly stresses the oral foundations in his long introduction, which is the best and most comprehensive critical history of American humor yet written. He appears to have read all the humor there is, everything that has ever been written about it, and the full range of American literature on which it impinges. He is occasionally, in fact, too scholarly for my taste: in his enthusiasm for his subject he almost persuades himself that metaphor is a purely humorous invention, and not all his exploration of sources impresses me. In any department of literature the source-hunt is usually dubious the moment it gets beyond fashions and conventions, and the basic situations and mechanisms of humor are so implicit in experience that you might as well turn to Aristophanes at once and do your further groping backward into the old stone age. But Mr. Blair is too intelligent and too learned to take his occasional ventures into scholarly technique very seriously. His study is historical, analytical, and critical. It brings its variegated and essentially chaotic subject into as much order as can be imposed on it. It contains fundamental judgments on American humor; and, unifying and extending much pioneering work that has been done in the last few years, it phrases principles that must hereafter be taken into account in all critical study of American literature at large.

Humor became a literary form in America, Mr. Blair finds, when writers began to utilize in print the delight in native character, native types, and native eccentricity that had so long fertilized our oral literature. Two types long matured in anecdote and folklore, the Yankee and the Frontiersman, suddenly found memorable celebration in print at about the same time, and the significant thing is that Major Jack Downing and Colonel David Crockett were figures of both fiction and political satire. Let us pass quickly over the latter, since I shall be writing about it at some length later on this year. It is one of our most important and has been one of our most continuous traditions, though Mr. Lewis Mumford once announced that there were only three American satires before "The Theory of the Leisure Class" and that these three (one of them being "A Connecticut Yankee in King Arthur's Court") were pretty weak and footless. Our literature would be immeasurably poorer without the distinguished line that begins with Jack Downing and moves through Simon Suggs and Hosea Biglow to Mr. Dooley and Alexander Throttlebottom. Realistic, disenchanted, completely devoid of reverence, that tradition has been an active force in our democracy, and that it has been watered down in recent years is one of the graver phenomena of the times. Mr. Blair admits Will Rogers to the company of crackerbox commentators, but though the highest-paid of them all he fell miles behind Bill Arp and Petroleum V. Nasby, and light-years behind Mr. Dooley and Mark Twain.

It was in the realistic perception of native character that humor first invaded and then processed the American novel. Here also it was a democratizing force. The earliest realism in our fiction is the intrusion of some low and usually rustic fellow as comedy relief to the gothic goings-on of the romantic leads. He is condescended to but he is drawn with a sharp eye to truth. The heroes tend to come from Mrs. Radcliffe and the heroines, as like as not, are from Bernardin de St. Pierre, but Nimrod Wildfire is from the life. Nimrod was born in the newspaper humor of the thirties and forties, and this rested squarely on the anecdotal humor, the insatiable yarning of the natives. It took him less than twenty years to capture fiction, he has never relinquished his domination, he has not been condescended to, and the main current of American fiction has been realistic primarily because our humorists made it so.

The job was done by a group most of whom lived on and wrote about the southwestern frontier. Augustus Baldwin Longstreet, George W. Harris, Johnson J. Hooper, William Tappan Thompson, and Joseph G. Baldwin were the best of the group, which numbers several dozen principal names. Their importance in our literary history had been singularly neglected until recent years. They were humorists, they were even amateur humorists, but they created American realism. Mr. Blair argues persuasively that they, with their Yankee colleagues, created our regionalism as well, and it is certainly true that the path leads straight from them to the "local color" school of a later generation, and past that to the more self-conscious theorists of today. They gave our fiction, if not its first localities, then certainly its first living communities. But, what is most important, they were the first American writers to make fiction out of the life immediately about them. They enormously enjoyed it and they were shrewd men, men with a gift not only for dramatic story-telling but for style as well. Much of what they wrote is dull now, of course, but it is astonishing how much more is far from dull. Much of Longstreet, much of Hooper and Thompson, and rather more of Harris will last indefinitely. One of Longstreet's stories (which, to be sure, he picked up from an elder friend) was good enough to serve Thomas Hardy's uses, and at least once Hooper beat Mark Twain at Mark's best game.

Mark Twain is, of course, the culmination of one part of this humor. "Huckleberry Finn" is a masterpiece of American fiction percisely as it brings the moods and materials and methods of this humor to expression on the level of genius. Other strains went on to create the local color writing of the eighties and nineties and still others to beget Br'er Rabbit. Like Mark Twain, Joel Chandler Harris is a phenomenon of southwestern humor. That area of fantasy, which includes not only such mythology as Harris practised but the tall talk and the tall tales as well, is native to our humor but has lain fallow for a long time. There are hints of it in Faulkner, Andrew Lytle touched it briefly but memorably in "The Long Night," Roark Bradford and occasionally other Southern novelists glance at it, but mostly it has reverted to its original condition. Give an accomplished Southerner a hooker of corn and the center of the stage and you soon learn that the stories are still there, waiting for literature to overtake them again and be enriched.

This area of our humor has been too little studied and will repay further investigation. It is most important, however, to study the images and intonations of our native humor. Everything that can be said about its mechanisms and devices has been said, and our gain has not been inordinate. But if it is really desirable to isolate the essential American qualities, the most promising approach is to examine the way the thing is said. Mr. Blair quotes a phrase of Mark Twain's, "The calm confidence of a Christian with four aces." No English reader would get the full beauty of the phrase and no Englishman who ever lived would, or could, have written it. It lifts the American pulse-beat because it is a perfect marriage of meaning, rhythm, and expression flowering in a poetic image. In exactly the same way an American esthetics is gratified when Mr. Lincoln forestalls argument about his appointee's ignorance of military minutiae by dragging in Caesar's hair. When A. Ward writes an editor, "My perlitical sentiments agree with yourn exactly. I know they do, becawz I never saw a man whoos didn't," the comment is international but the phraseology, which has nothing to do with the spelling but is intimately bound to the rhythm, is absolute American. The criticism of humor ought to devote itself to style, to the ring of the words in the ear, to the thought finding a native idiom.

I have remarked that the important Southwestern humorists were amateurs. They were lawyers, doctors, country editors, army officers, planters, even parsons, anything but literary men. They were superseded by professionals, and in a way the rise of professionalism signalized the decline of American humor. On the one hand, it was absorbed in the novel. Having given fiction instruments, types, a manner, and a new occupation, having permanently shaped the American novel, humor forfeited the field in which it has most justified itself. One main stream of our humor, probably the principal one, has since then flowed through the novel.

But the amateur humorist yielded not only to the novelist but also to the professional funny man, whom Mr. Blair calls the literary comedian. Humorous magazines flourished during the forties and fifties, and the last few years before the Civil War saw the birth of the columnist and the comic Lyceum lecturer. They were usually different phases of one career. Artemus Ward was the first nationally famous one, Mark Twain was the greatest (he was foremost in most aspects of our humor), and to the genus belonged most of the men whom criticism speaks of as humorists. Petroleum V. Nasby, Orpheus C. Kerr, Bill Arp, Josh Billings, Eli Perkins, the Danbury News Man, and Bill Nye are merely the most celebrated of dozens.

To generalize too sweepingly, most of these humorists turned from the absorption in native character that had marked their predecessors to explore the resources of purely verbal humor, the wise crack, the parody, the set piece, the scrambled association, the unexpected turn, the mere joke. They were joke-makers, only incidentally satirists, and never writers of fiction. With them humor forsakes literature and becomes a department of journalism—topical, lively, ad hoc, well paid, and popular, but ephemeral. Little of what they wrote can be read with amusement today. Hooper and Thompson of the older school are still fresh, but Bill Nye is as unreadable as the sermons of any minor Puritan divine, only a historian can endure Orpheus C. Kerr, and even Artemus Ward is in great part obsolete. Again the process shows clearly in Mark Twain. "Huckleberry Finn" is immortal, but "Sketches New and Old" is dead and mummified.

An Amerikan luvs tew laff and these comedians flourished through the remainder of the century. In a different phase they flourish today. Our humorists stand squarely on their shoulders, though there are only a handful of humorous magazines where there used to be dozens, though mass production has standardized most of the newspaper product, and though humor, revisiting its oral sources by way of the radio, is debasing them.

When, in delicate tribute to the intuitions of this magazine, the last Writers' Congress elected a literary comedian President, he vindicated us by remarking in his inaugural address that the cruelty and injustice of modern American life had produced what he described as the insane humor of today. A funny man must work at his trade, but if Mr. Stewart is to be a spearhead of revolt, he should study his ancestry. Our various Golden Days must have been hideous with cruelty too, for Mr. Stewart and his contemporaries have only played variations on themes and in forms which their more robust great-uncles had by heart. The "Parody Outline of History" was written by Bret Harte in the sixties and was rewritten by a good many of his contemporaries in the next few years. "Aunt Polly's Story of Mankind" and Mr. Stewart's other books glimmer through Mark Twain, Sol Smith, John Phoenix, and a dozen more. If you turn to page 448 of Mr. Blair's collection you will encounter "The Treasurer's Report," and Charles Clark was only making respectful acknowledgment of a situation and a mechanism grown elderly in our humor. Mark Twain was doing Corey Ford's stuff before he wrote "The Jumping Frog," and was but following after the ways of his fathers. By insane humor Mr. Stewart means only humor which derives its laughs from erratic association. And so long as there has been verbal humor in this country, which is much longer than there has been literary humor, there has been that deliberate exploitation of psychological dissociation. The literary comedians who specialized in it after the Civil War presented themselves as Perfect Fools, whereas our comedians present themselves as Perfect Neurotics. There is no other difference; themes, styles, situations, all were there in great-grandfather's time.

We still luv tew laff but humor as a literary form exists but precariously in America today. On the one hand, nearly every novelist has to be a journeyman humorist; on the other, what amuses us today has little in it that can carry over to tomorrow. Since Dunne our political satire has been toothless. Since George Ade only Don Marquis has attained the stature of his forefathers. The verbal humor of the daily press is stereotype, stencil, and formula. Fantasy, once a powerful yeast of the national humor, has all but departed from literature and has sought regeneration in the animated cartoon. Let us, for decency's sake, say nothing of the radio skit—after all, there has always been feloniously bad humor.

It is significant that the best of our current humor has evolved a new kind of fiction. The true and most flourishing successors of the southwestern school are to be found in *The New Yorker*. Mr. and Mrs. North, Hyman Kaplan, President Galbraith, Ruth McKenney's Sister Aileen, and their like are blood relatives of Major Jones, Simon Suggs, and Sut Lovingood's Pa. Like their ancestors, they issue from the life immediately at hand, they speak the living language, and their vitality springs from a rich and delighted perception of the human animal as it really is. In Clarence Day, in James Thurber, and occasionally in those who consciously follow their ideas, the new form rises higher. Mr. Thurber is like Mark Twain at least in this: whether he is playing it straight or writing wild extravaganza his humor derives from a sharply individual and deeply philosophical intelligence that is oriented by a comic sense of life. If fiction has contributed a good deal to this humor it is but returning a loan made a hundred years ago which was invaluable to the American novel.

Buoyancy and exuberance, the earliest qualities of our humor, are hard to come by these days. Most of the poetry is gone too. The language of immigrant groups, of such metropolitan entities as the Bronx, and of the rural places which our humorists visit on vacation effectively maintains the philological tradition. But the snapping turtle will never bark from the canebrakes again, tall talk is done forever and cannot be counterfeited as Caleb Catlum abundantly makes plain, and the successors of the Sazerac Lying Club are small bore, though bores indeed. American humor came of age in the ecstasy of first testing the qualities of the American tongue in print, but the dew and breeze and colors of that sunrise can never be revisited.

All these are missed but there are greater losses. We could use Mr. Dooley, these troubled days—Mr. Dooley and the noble line of his peers, who spoke so much more savagely and so much more courageously than any speaks to or about our statesmen and masters today. The republic would be both a happier and a securer place if a post-depression Nasby or Ward appeared to speak its mind about, well, say, the Supreme Court and the Ku Klux Klan. "Alone in Cuba" has not been followed by "Alone in Utopia"—a frightening weakness in our literature, and plain proof that something ominous has happened to America.

There is a still greater tragedy. We could not spare the elegant Mr. Eustace Tilley nor any of the distorted figures at whom he sometimes briefly glances through his eye-glass. But neither he nor they are full compensation for the passing of Colonel Crockett, the Big Bear of Arkansaw, Brother Jonathan, and other figures once large against the sky. What American literature needs most today is a blood transfusion from those myths. There are vast sun-spots this year but they do not mean, as they once did, that Colonel Sellers is blowing us a kiss across the universe. It will remain a lesser literature till they mean that again. But do not despair. Like Tyl Eulenspiegel, of whom he may well have been the late nineteenth century avatar, Sellers is immortal. He and Jim Smiley and their whole company are certain to return, changed but recognizable, when American literature again strikes a major chord.

Note

1. Walter Blair, ed., *Native American Humor (1800–1900)* (New York: American Book Company, 1937).

Gentlemanly Humorists of the Old South [1953]

Louis J. Budd*

Frederick Jackson Turner's theories about the American frontier have been challenged seriously by some historians, especially during the last twenty years. Yet many students of American literature and folklore, and the compilers of anthologies in these fields, continue uncritically to accept Turner's epic construct of the democracy-loving pioneer who created a new culture on the new land. These analysts go on to claim that our native American humor was inspired by the frontier folk-mind

*Reprinted with permission of the author from *Southern Folklore Quarterly*, 17 (December 1953), 232–40. Copyright 1953 by *Southern Folklore Quarterly*.

and by frontier ideas of individualism, equality, and self-reliance. Such a view is too facile and too sweeping. It slurs over deep differences among Southern, Yankee, and Far West humor. Where the South's best-known antebellum humorists are concerned, it has obscured their literary aims and their provincial prejudices and loyalties. For these writers were from Dixie, not from the frontier. By returning to this obvious but neglected emphasis we can read all our humorists more sensitively and can better enjoy the Southern writers as bearers of a sectional heritage.

Native humor flowed into print in such quantities that sampling is a primary problem, for countless and contradictory tendencies appeared. However, most scholars have agreed that Southern antebellum humor was dominated by five names: Augustus Baldwin Longstreet, Joseph Glover Baldwin, William Tappan Thompson, Johnson J. Hooper and George Washington Harris.[1] Because of their past popularity and their intrinsic merit these men have been stressed more than "Madison Tensas," Joseph B. Cobb, or a host of others. Flourishing after 1830, when the South had emerged as a distinct economic and cultural area, they shaped their region's most enduring wit before the Civil War. To cite these men as appreciative recorders of democratic-minded frontier comedy is to ignore their less folksy and their belletristic qualities and, indeed, is to ignore the true structure of the Old South.[2]

The case of Davy Crockett further shows how the study of native humor has been confused by superficial groupings. Crockett is often linked with Longstreet or Hooper. But he belonged patently to the rawer generation which preceded the Deep South's maturity, and his cultural kin drifted west like Davy himself. He was after all an oral artist and a barely literate hunter who retreated with the canebrake. Of course, rough-and-tumble humor roared on in the Old South. However, this oral tradition was increasingly adapted for newspaper columns by gentlemen or would-be-gentlemen who did not need Crockett's ghost-writers and who satirized much of what he had stood for. While Crockett trudged toward immortality, Southerners applauded into renown a group of volumes quite different in style and tone from his autobiography. Despite its varied prolixity and its plebeian borrowings, printed Southern humor after 1830 produced a group of writers who stood well apart from backwoods yarning.

Perhaps because anthologies reprint only his earthy pieces like "The Fight" or "The Horse-Swap," Longstreet is credited with depicting the Southwestern frontier. However, his Georgia Scenes (1835) described a complex social web, for seven of the eighteen sketches dealt with a citified upper group or with country gentry. In Swallow Barn (1832) John Pendleton Kennedy had lovingly recorded the Old Dominion's plantation life with only brief glances at the peripheral squatters. Longstreet chose to show both polite culture and piney-woods crudity in his unevenly settled state. Possibly echoing Kennedy, he claimed that his main purpose was documentary rather than comic. But, inescapably, his transcribing of real life was controlled by his basic outlook. Edward Eggleston and Hamlin Garland were to give quite grimmer pictures of ragged farmers and squatters.

Far from being corrupted by frontier leveling, Yale-educated Longstreet was careful to dissociate himself from illiterate crackers. He did not try to create an oral narrator or to pose as the willing scribe of such a folk-artist. Quite typically he wrote in a sketch, " 'Now blaze away!' (the command for an onset of every kind with people of this order)." His commoners stumbled through a militia-drill, cheered a gory fight, and gossiped or ranted with dull incoherence. But when Longstreet satirized the elite he showed himself lounging within the select circle. Despite his sandpapering of overpolished spots in upperclass Augusta and his nostalgia for bucolic simplicity, Longstreet's most unrelieved satire scored against whites who fell short of gentility. Secure in his feeling for older social standards, he genially disapproved of sweaty rascality or insolence.

That many Americans, especially Southerners, long admired the coffee-house wits is a scholarly truism. As John D. Wade suggests, Longstreet adopted the eighteenth-century British ideal of the essay which fused durable literary texture with lightly snobbish moralizing. This ideal had been reinforced on our side of the Atlantic by Washington Irving's successes. In turn, Longstreet's combining of fastidious commentary and localized detail further lured writers toward the essay-sketch framework. Throughout the 1840's Joseph B. Cobb, who dedicated his *Mississippi Scenes* (1851) to the Georgian, signed urbane sketches as "The Rambler." Mixed with fresher diction persisted the transparent names for characters and the fanciful pseudonyms used by the Queen Anne essayists. As late as 1853, "Peter Pickle" (Joseph Addison Turner) tried to start the *Tomahawk* in Macon, Georgia, in order to "dissect the various follies and absurdities of the day."[3] Our Southern humorists pushed their celebrated trail-blazing slowly and with backward glances, for Crockett had sky-rocketed too erratically to be a reliable guide.

Baldwin's *The Flush Times of Alabama and Mississippi* (1853) showed how long the foreign models kept guiding Southern humorists. Continuing the practice of mixing British literary fashions with native subjects, Baldwin produced pieces shiftingly reminiscent of Addison, Goldsmith, and Lamb. He larded these essays with verbal and intellectual wit, sophisticated diction, and classical and historical gleanings. Friendly toward Blackstone's country like so many American lawyers, he alluded freely to British events and to British authors, especially Shakespeare, Scott, Byron, and Dickens. It is true that his volume, which was the usual reprinting of random bits in newspapers or magazines, contained anecdotes and tales borrowed from oral currency. But, like the author of *Georgia Scenes*, he tended to elevate himself above vulgar idiom while he exploited it, as in gracefully referring to the "doggery, grocery, or juicery, as, in the elegant nomenclature of the natives, it was variously called."

In the tradition of Kennedy and Longstreet, Baldwin was not willing to write mere comedy. He aspired to "illustrate the periods, the characters, and the phases of the society" during the boom days of the trans-Appalachian cottonbelt. However, of the twenty-six items in *The Flush Times* only one kept legal affairs from the foreground. Several soberly eulogized the Alabama attorneys and judges who had toiled to impose order on the nascent state. In effect, *The Flush Times* amusingly argued that law had to come to the brawling Old Southwest and reform its "hell-carnival," its era of "credit without capital, and enterprise without honesty." Admiring the bustling ambition of the boom days, Baldwin wished for a "gentleman of the Old School with the energy of the New." Yet that ebullient era had teemed with boors who were laughable only in retrospect and who had kept "as unsophisticated ignorance of conventionalities as could be desired by J. J. Rousseau or any other eulogist of the savage state." They had abounded most in the lower reaches and there won popular support as petty elective officials "among the rustics—who usually mistake the silent blank of stupidity for the gravity of wisdom." Looking back after order had tamed anarchy, Baldwin, a wellborn Virginian who quickly won honors in his new home, could praise the flush times for offering wide opportunities. But in the Old Southwest's speculators or pioneering yeoman, he saw little serious merit.

Like Baldwin, Thompson was often compared to Longstreet. But his Major Joseph Jones never lounged in high society or brawled with poor-white loafers. At first he seemed like a Jack Downing who had blundered into a domestic novel. But he rose from a prosperous yeoman to a middleclass planter who could paraphrase Shakespeare and write up his experience (in unsure spelling).[4] Except for obvious satires, *Major Jones's Courtship* (1843) was unique among important Southern works until George William Bagby let his "Mozis Addums" write letters which mixed sense and naiveté. Unfortunately, in *Major Jones's Sketches of Travel* (1847) Thompson later used Jones to expound racism, thus acidifying the cotton-grower who had confessed his own missteps while satirizing the grosser faults of piney-woodsmen.

In the meantime, Thompson had followed the courtship cycle with stories about a "few more interesting specimens of the genus 'Cracker'." In *Major Jones's Chronicles of Pineville* (1845), the placid domesticity of Jones's village was jarred by denizens of the Ticklegizzard settlement like Boss Ankles and other clay-eaters with "bilious-looking eyes, and tanney, shrivelled faces." In the *Chronicles*—reissued under the imitative title of *Major Jones's Georgia Scenes*—the essayist reappeared.[5] Literary allusions and polite diction were woven into a box which set off the riches of oral anecdote. Thompson's tone here often echoed Longstreet's, particularly in "The Fire Hunt." Though Thompson professed to use the term of cracker with "all due respect," his treatment of indigent whites lacked the friendly warmth surrounding Major Jones. In *Major Jones's Courtship* antebellum New England and Dixie humor came closest to touching in method and spirit. In the *Chronicles of Pineville* they were again divergent, despite the fact that William T. Porter's *Spirit of the Times* encouraged the mixing of regional stereotypes.

Hooper's *Adventures of Captain Simon Suggs* (1845) tried to use the more autocthonous device of a mock campaign biography. Yet, unlike Baldwin, Hooper did not worry too much about the electioneering heirs of Crockett. He gave most of his attention to the subsistence farmers and seedy rascals who eked out a livelihood on the fringes of Alabama's cotton domain. While following the legal circuit into the backwoods, Hooper had met vestiges of the older rawness and lawlessness. Through Simon Suggs's posturing and carousing ran the boisterous humor which we like to think of as native, and his vigorous success guided later treatments of Alabama. In *Fisher's River* (1859) Harden Taliaferro ("Skitt") wrote somewhat respectfully of his impoverished childhood friends in North Carolina; however, his "Ham Rachel of Alabama" presented a copperas-trousered grotesque from the "cow counties."

It is evident that neither heady love of "folk" character nor rigorous belief in human equality dominated Hooper's attitude toward Suggs's intimates or the rustics whom he met while visiting old Kit Kuncker and while taking the census. His introductory essay set a mocking tone. And although Hooper let his characters hold the spotlight, he studded the artfully brief expository passages with French and Latin and with cultured asides. He further avoided fraternizing with Suggs by writing, for instance: "In his own energetic language, 'he had tuck his persition, and d——d if he didn't keep it so long as he had yeath to stand upon'." The very capstone of the comedy was cemented when Suggs, in all his ragged military might, was defied by a dirt-eater. Hooper avoided Longstreet's gentility, Baldwin's reverence for the legal caste, Thompson's sentimentality, and Harris's narrow range. His burlesque biography profited enough from native techniques to mold the masterwork of a school which clearly edged Down East rivals in enduring robustness. It also well typified his section's habit of finding in society's least prosperous levels its most risible type, like the slow-witted yokel or like the shifty sharper who preyed on the Deep South's unstable beginnings.

Although Harris started writing in the Addison-Irving vein,[6] in his Sut Lovingood yarns the belletristic facade had been sapped finally by rough comedy. But current Southern political and social principles still guided his literary strategy. His raw, isolated mountaineers of the Great Smokies were hilarious but brutal clowns who, while viable in the single sketch, soon stiffened into dehumanized agents of those duckings and skinnings which other Dixie writers like "Madison Tensas" had chortled over too frequently. While seemingly untamable at first glance, Sut never escaped from the limits set by Harris, who appeared as the scribe to whom Sut was always respectful despite the ridge-runner's antipathy toward well-educated men. Just as Hooper made Suggs oppose nullification, Harris later appointed Sut as Lincoln's friend and adviser merely to belittle the President.[7] The Yankee rustic had ripened into a cracker-box sage who was fit company for any man. In his most frequent role, Jonathan's Dixie cousin was a scorned, linsey-woolsey Cinderella until Charles Henry Smith ("Bill Arp") slowly discovered his admirable qualities during the stresses of the Civil War.

Few Southern humorists before 1860 had thought of themselves as entertainers, and seldom was their output purely comic. It often included antiquarianism, autobiography, or sporting chronicles in varying proportions. Thomas Bangs Thorpe, despite his epic account of the big bear, was a historian of local curiosities while Thompson was a purveyor of reading matter for the respectable family circle. Most Southern wits honored the current habit of literary didacticism. Many sought to correct ethical and social mores; a second volume of Longstreet's pieces, posthumously collected, was well christened as *Stories with a Moral*. Others professed the useful aim of recording faded or fading customs and, like Hooper and Baldwin, steadily scouted rearward. Both Longstreet and Hooper were particularly unanxious to be recalled as humorists, and William T. Porter felt obliged to hide the identity of most of the authors represented in his collection, *The Big Bear of Arkansas and Other Tales* (1845).

Indeed, Porter's book was highly selective, favoring broad tales about hunts in the canebrake and swamp which had appealed to the sporting clientele of his *Spirit of the Times*. His choices did not represent fully the contents of his journal. Companion collections, perhaps slanted toward Northern audiences, also favored pieces which played up uncouthness or muscular rascality. Later anthologists have continued to mine the veins which glitter most invitingly, and books like Meine's *Tall Tales of the Southwest* (1930) or V. L. O. Chittick's *Ring-Tailed Roarers* (1941) have tried to satisfy the growing passion for colorful Americana, preferably in blood-red or copperas shades. Such samplings have been enjoyable but they have tempted us to force antebellum humorists into a mold instead of accepting them on their own terms.

Most mechanical of all, perhaps, have been the attempts to label these writers flatly as frontier humorists. More in truth than in apology, it seems, Porter claimed that the pieces in his first volume were "mainly

by country gentlemen, planters, lawyers, &c. 'who live at home at ease'."
Of the men emphasized in my essay, only Hooper had, briefly and
gingerly, probed into virgin terrain.[8] Hunting and fishing had acquired
amusement value in place of survival value. Viewed from the rising
edifice of a cotton economy, one-mule farmers and poor-whites were
woefully backward. They furnished relatively new stereotypes but they
were seen through the veil of more settled values, for the transplanting
of Tidewater attitudes to the Gulf states had been determined and rapid.
Indeed, the cultural pattern of any frontier is guided by local geography
and by the ideas which the settlers bring along.

Of course, from the amorphous mass of Dixie writers, some minor
ones treated the westering man rather gently and even let him upset the
lawyer, dandy, or gentleman. The major representatives likewise felt
the pioneer's presence. We must recognize their borrowings but we
must not confuse casual stretching with a fool's gold of tallness. Thompson had wanted to "portray Southern rustic life and character, with no
more of exaggeration than was necessary to give distinctiveness to the
picture."[9] We can distinguish between humor written in the cotton
states and that retailed near an advancing frontier by or about roarers
like Crockett or Mike Fink who spurned polite life. To be sure, Dixie
humor seldom treated the Old Dominion or the Carolinas, for it was the
friction between plantation amenities and Southwestern crudities which
agitated the feeling of comic incongruity. Baldwin, ensconced in a reasonably stable community, deplored the splurging times before cotton
economics had jelled the Deep South. In *Mississippi Scenes* Cobb contrasted suaver Columbus with its lagging environs, and others lampooned
scrimping folk in the pockets of "inner" frontier. In brief, Southern
wits often depicted individualistic pioneers and primitives but they did
not often glorify these shaggy variants from older social norms.

By the 1830's the main frontier line had been pushed across the
great river valley by hustling Alabama and Mississippi planters; the Old
Southwestern frontier had come swiftly under the rule of the cotton
kingdom.[10] If they wished to be applauded at home, humorists could
not resist this authority and its doctrine of natural inequality. Despite any
wish to study an age or to emulate the accurate detail of Scott's romances, their realism was like that of other eras in being distorted by
current attitudes.[11] The planter escaped almost unpricked. Hard-working
independent farmers, the largest white class in the pre-Civil War South,
were either ignored or else caricatured beyond easy recognition. Poor-
whites, the mudsill of the yeomanry, received overdrawn features and
an undue emphasis. They reflected rollicking discredit on all but the
professional and planter echelons. Muted but ever-recurring in Dixie
humor, especially in Longstreet's "Darby, the Politician," Baldwin's
sketches, and Kennedy's *Quodlibet* (1840), was the fear that men from
the clearings might dare to dominate the hustlings as Crockett had done.

Essentially, the master values of Longstreet and his breed were shaped by Calhoun's ideology for the settled South which, as Henry Nash Smith shows in his *Virgin Land* (1950), rejected after 1830 the myth of the stalwart yeoman drawing physical and political independence from free American soil.

In other words, the leading humorous gentlemen of the Old South did not merely transcribe popular anecdotage, which is itself multifarious and multivalent. While responding to their region's demand for an original literature, they did not forget their gentlemanly standing. From social as well as stylistic compulsions, the barrier between the author and unlettered folk was kept up. Lowell had even let Hosea Biglow write passable poetry, yet although Major Jones, the cotton-bale emulator of the cracker-barrel thinker, wrote sensible letters, his inferiors needed Thompson's supervision. Nor does a need to contrast the expository box with the tale itself fully account for such estrangement between the humorists and their uncouth subjects. Finding their models in Addison, Goldsmith, and Irving, Southerners clung to the method of urbane essayist and interpreter for the purpose of keeping their distance. This literary overlay decomposed slowly. When it was gone the regional humorist was ready to bow to the sentimentalizing local color artist, who also preceded the folklorist in the South.

Native humor varied importantly from region to region in the loose federal union. Despite counter-currents, Down East myth-making centered around the sturdy freeholder whose mother-wit enabled him to comment intelligently on private and public affairs. This led Yankee humor toward aphoristic monologue while its Southern counterpart aimed at literary grace and an urbane provincialism. Such contrasts illumine Southern antebellum humor's unique qualities and its distinctive reaction to oral tradition and the frontier experience.

Notes

1. Allowing for slight variations, see Constance M. Rourke, *American Humor* (New York: Harcourt, Brace, and Company, 1931), pp. 69–70; Bernard DeVoto, *Mark Twain's America* (Boston: Little Brown, 1932), p. 257; F. J. Meine, Foreword, *Alias Simon Suggs* by W. S. Hoole (University, Ala.: University of Alabama Press, 1932). Although Walter Blair's discussion in *Native American Humor (1800–1900)* (New York: American Book Company, 1937), pp. 62–101, concentrates on the five named here, he lists others. Of these, however, "Madison Tensas" is not widely recalled; Joseph M. Field and John S. Robb, in St. Louis, mixed the various strains of humor, native and British; T. B. Thorpe earned wide reprinting in only one of his sketches.

2. In the Introduction, p. xvi, to his very influential collection, *Tall Tales of the Southwest* (New York: Knopf, 1930), F. J. Meine says of the work of these humorists and others: ". . . these sketches, humble enough in intent, were the earliest literary expression of the frontier, and, remain its most revealing expression." Bernard DeVoto has staunchly insisted upon the frontier spirit behind native

humor. Constance Rourke discusses Longstreet and his school under the chapter heading of "The Gamecock of the Wilderness." While very perceptive, Walter Blair in his *Native American Humor* places emphasis on the debt to the frontier and oral tradition. More recently, Gregory Paine, Introd., *Southern Prose Writers* (New York: American Book Company, 1947), p. lxxvi, says these humorists belong under "folk literature"; Meine, Foreword, in Hoole's *Alias Simon Suggs*, p. xv, discerns in these men the "beginnings of a true American folk literature." Daniel G. Hoffman, *Paul Bunyan* (Philadelphia: University of Pennsylvania Press for Temple University Publications, 1952), pp. 66–73, sees Longstreet, Baldwin, Hooper, and Harris primarily as "frontier authors who retained folk humor intact."

3. B. H. Flanders, "Humor in Ante-Bellum Georgia," *Emory University Quarterly*, 1 (1945), 150. See also Joseph Addison Turner, *Autobiography of "The Countryman": 1866* (Atlanta, Ga.: The Library, Emory University, 1943), pp. 12, 18–19. Also relevant here are Guy A. Cardwell, "The Influence of Addison on Charleston Periodicals, 1795–1860," *SP*, 35 (1938), 456–70; and J. D. Wade, *A. B. Longstreet* (New York: Macmillan, 1924), pp. 157–60.

4. Henry P. Miller, "The Background and Significance of Major Jones's Courtship," *Georgia Historical Quarterly*, 30 (1946), 274, speaks of Jones's "middle class plebeian attitudes," and Clement Eaton, "The Humor of the Southern Yeoman," *SR*, 49 (1941), 173–83, classes Jones as a yeoman. But Walter Blair, *Horse Sense in American Humor* (Chicago: University of Chicago Press, 1942), pp. 107–08, correctly points out that Jones became a planter who owned house servants and field hands.

5. Far from being a voice of the Southwestern frontier, Thompson reflected the British "village" school. He dramatized *The Vicar of Wakefield*. His *Augusta Mirror* was self-professedly a journal "devoted to polite literature, music, and useful intelligence," and Thompson served for a while as co-editor of *The Family Companion* and *Ladies Mirror*; see Gertrude Gilmer, "A Critique of Certain Georgia Ante-Bellum Literary Magazines . . . ," *Georgia Historical Quarterly*, 18 (1934), 299, 304.

6. Donald Day, "The Humorous Works of George W. Harris," *AL*, 14 (1943), 393–94.

7. Hooper, always a states-righter, in 1861 became Secretary of the Provisional Congress of the Confederacy. For Harris's violently pro-Southern opinions, see Donald Day, "The Political Satires of George W. Harris," *Tennessee Historical Quarterly*, 4 (1945), 320–38.

8. Hoole, *Alias Simon Suggs*, pp. 33–34. Hoole remarks that Hooper, the "young aristocratic North Carolinian," from the very first "had access to the homes of the affluent slave holding and not infrequently aristocratic planters" in Alabama. However, Hoole argues that the frontier was "completely democratic: and that Southern antebellum humor was the "frontier in action"; see pp. 24, 30.

9. William Tappan Thompson, Preface, *Major Jones's Courtship* (New York: D. Appleton, 1872).

10. See Ray A. Billington, "Settling the Gulf Plains, 1815–1850," in his *Westward Expansion: A History of the American Frontier* (New York: Macmillan, 1949), pp. 310–28. Clement Eaton, *Freedom of Thought in the Old South* (Durham, N. C.: Duke University Press, 1940), traces in detail the hardening of intellectual conformity before the Civil War.

11. Of course, realism is a slippery term. However, it is almost always used to characterize these humorists. Hoole, *Alias Simon Suggs*, pp. 178–79, summarizes relevant comments by others.

Realism and Fantasy in
Southern Humor [1958]

Arlin Turner*

Joel Chandler Harris wrote once, in introducing a collection of wit and humor he was publishing: "There seems never to have been a day in our history when the American view of things generally was not charged or trimmed with humor." He went on to say that "the American stands forth as the conqueror of circumstance, who has created for himself the most appalling responsibilities, which he undertakes and carries out with a wink and a nod, whistling a hymn or a ragtime tune, to show that he is neither weary nor downhearted."

Harris was probably looking as far back as the Revolutionary soldiers, who combined fun and plain effrontery in suitable proportions to take over a song which the Redcoats sang to lampoon them, and to make it their own "Yankee Doodle." He may have been thinking of the bumpkin characters who had peopled newspaper narratives and sketches through most of the nineteenth century and had enjoyed actual existence from Down-East Maine to the Southwestern frontier, varying but little from one region to another except in such superficials as dialect and dress and ways of making a living. It is not likely that Harris had in mind primarily the formal literature of either North or South, and it seems especially unlikely that he would have cited the recognized authors of the Old South to support his statement; for in the editorial columns of the *Constitution* he had declared more than once that the Old South had produced no literature worthy of the name.

It is not easy to say whether the South has had a more or a less active sense of humor than other regions; or whether the people, as a whole, have taken themselves more seriously than others, and as a consequence have indulged less often in a hearty laugh. The written record, however, the literary record, seems to furnish answers for the period of the Old South. Those who left that record, mainly the educated and the wealthy, that is, lacked something in robust humor. One student of the polite literature of the Old South has said that the Southern authors either lacked humor or were remarkably successful in concealing it.

That is not to say that there were no smiles or laughs and no lightness in the literature which was honored in the early South. At least from the time when William Byrd of Westover described the Lubberlanders living beyond the Dismal Swamp in North Carolina, there had been an Addisonian wit and light satire. As issues of class and caste and section became in time more acute, the satire was on occasions

*Reprinted with permission of the *Georgia Review* and Mrs. Arlin Turner from the *Georgia Review*, 12 (Winter 1958), 451–57. © 1958 by the University of Georgia Press.

more acid and the political lampooning was more ruthless. But this wit and satire, however sparkling or piercing it may have been, was derivative, if not consciously imitative. Its roots were in the eighteenth-century English authors, Joseph Addison and Alexander Pope chief among them; and it belonged with those manners and fashions and habits of the times such as the Greek-columned mansions and the code of the duel, which had models abroad. It had little chance of outliving the support it drew from an imported culture.

Yet it was in the South, or more specifically the Old Southwest, and at the very time we are talking about that the most significant American humor had its beginnings. This was a humor without readily identifiable ancestors. It grew from the soil. It was satisfied to employ homely scenes and characters and incidents and to speak in the native idiom. Extravagant, unlettered, raucous, this humor exploited contrasts and incongruity; it knew little reverence and it strained at the bonds of accepted taste. The boundlessness and the variety of the land, the people, and their experiences supplied its tempo and its tone. The length and breadth or swiftness of the rivers, the fertility of the soil, the abundance of game, the phenomena of weather—such were in actuality hardly believable to the uninitiated. Similarly the skill of the backwoodsman with his squirrel-rifle, or the prowess of the Kentucky keelboatman in rough-and-tumble, eye-gouging fights, preceded as a rule by boasting and threatening which would honor his ancestor, the epic character Beowulf. What could be better or more natural fun than to embroider tales of such phenomena and such doings beyond all recognition and to pass them off with a wink to the knowing and a solemn face to the incredulous? Hence the tall-tales, tales of speed or strength or endurance that would beggar the exploits of the Homeric gods, or accounts to the same scale of ignorance or miserliness or downright meanness. Tall tales came naturally to such men as Ovid Bolus, one of the humorous characters who became an accomplished liar, it was said, simply because the truth was not big enough for him.

Henry Watterson, writing as Joel Chandler Harris did from the South at the end of the nineteenth century, remarked that Southern literature was "full of imitation"; but he added, "our anecdotes are our own, the outgivings of a nature, habit of thought, and mode of existence whimsically real." Likewise, this humor did not wince before criticism coming from overseas, nor before local criticism either, for that matter.

The native humor did not move in good society, however—did not move in good society openly, that is. It was not displayed on the parlor table of the Grangerford family in *Huckleberry Finn*, for example, alongside *Friendship's Offering* and other such ornamented collections of sentimental poems and sketches, and it rarely found a place in the plantation libraries beside the morocco-bound volumes of English and

Classical authors. The *North American Review*, published in Boston and taking as a rule only condescending notice of anything written with less dignity and less seriousness than was usual in its own pages, remarked that "the humor of today is written for the multitude," and added, "The mass of the community has a coarse digestion. . . . It likes horse-laughs." That neither the writers nor the readers of this homely humor considered it literature can be easily demonstrated. And the fact that it originated and existed on a sub-literary level is of very great importance, I believe, in the larger view. Thus liberated in considerable degree from the restraints of polite literature, from sentimentality and imitativeness and false elegance, this humor was free to incorporate a realism of materials and language unthinkable in the accepted literary mode of the time. One consequence of this greater freedom, accentuated at times by a deliberate rebelliousness, as I think was undeniably the case, was an audacity of conception and with it a richness of imagery which has given us our nearest approach to indigenous fable and a native mythology.

We have known for some time how much Mark Twain owed to the early humorists and to the folk background which produced them, and from time to time we discover that others of our authors have learned something or other from the humorous tradition.

Beginning with Augustus Baldwin Longstreet's *Georgia Scenes*, which had first appeared as newspaper sketches and had been gathered into a volume in 1835, several authors in the Old Southwest undertook to record the characters, incidents, and manners peculiar to the region. In doing so, they found occasion to describe the fabulous men and beasts of local tradition and to recount the speech and actions appropriate to them. It was usual for the writers to say that their first purpose was to record a peculiar way of life before it disappeared, but they did not conceal the pleasure they had in the hunting-camp yarns and the earthy language; and one often suspects that the main interest was the anecdotes and the tall tales.

Thomas Bangs Thorpe, an Easterner who came to Louisiana and moved about in New Orleans and the towns and parishes, wrote sketches of hunting and other characteristic activities of the region in which he echoed the note of romantic awe common to Washington Irving, Francis Parkman, and others who visited the Western frontier. Thorpe heard the tales current in the Baton Rouge area of a bee hunter named Tom Owen. He wrote about Tom Owen as a part of the scene, but in letting Tom say, among other things, that he could see a bee for a mile, easy, he was moving, though only a mincing step, from the actual toward the fabulous. In the best of Thorpe's pieces, "The Big Bear of Arkansas" (1841), he moved farther in the same direction.

In this story we are first introduced to a group of real passengers in a real cabin on a Mississippi River steamboat. The conversation, in convincingly real speech, touches on such commonplace subjects as mosquitoes and crops and hunting dogs. Then, before we realize the change in tone which is taking place, the Arkansas bear hunter has declared that he is from the *creation* state, where the soil runs straight down to the center of the earth and is so rich that when you plant a seed you must jump back or else suffer dire consequences. The leisurely tale turns finally, in its last quarter, into an account of hunting what is perhaps an unhuntable bear. Here we are dealing, unobtrusively, to be sure, with the elemental in man, animal, and land. The narrator of the tale hints at a mystery in what he is recounting, seems to recognize the deep forces of nature around him; but he is not so intimidated as to be ill at ease in his homely language and the earthy anecdotes he has to recount. In him, in fact, appears the altogether comfortable juxtaposition of the commonplace and the mythical, the real and the fabulous, which is characteristic of this humor.

The characters drawn by the humorists did not always display the household virtues or the most wholesome living. Ovid Bolus, in Joseph Glover Baldwin's *The Flush Times of Alabama and Mississippi* (1853), was a man to whom lying was an art and a calling. To Simon Suggs, the character created by Johnson Jones Hooper (1845), his exploits as a frontier sharper are a source of no little satisfaction. Though himself a scoundrel, Suggs is nevertheless the vehicle for conveying a pointed indictment of the human race. Like Mark Twain's King and Duke in *Huckleberry Finn*, Suggs thrives in his sharp practices because his victims are themselves bent on cheating others or else are gullible or superstitious or simple-minded in such extremes as to make one ashamed of the human race. This is the view of man reflected over and over in Mark Twain. And it is to be noted that among Simon Suggs's escapades Mark Twain found one, the taking up of a collection at the revival meeting, which he adapted for his own use in *Huckleberry Finn*.

Sut Lovingood, as created by George Washington Harris (1867), is a "natural-born durned fool," in his own words, who means no evil, actually, but falls into escapades producing an astonishing amount of crude action and physical suffering. Yet there is a poetic quality in Sut's speech, and there is an elemental, a universal quality in the imagination with which he enters into his outlandish actions and later tells about them. This is the earthiest of the books I have mentioned, but Sut Lovingood's adventures are fantastic in spite of the earthiness and the commonplace surroundings. Just as his long legs take him over the Tennessee hills at super-human speeds, so it is that the "skeers" he throws into Yankee peddlers and circuit riders and the commotion he sets going at Sicily Burns's wedding and at Mrs. Yardley's quilting party reach such gargantuan proportions as to give the realistic details heroic overtones. In Sut's adventures the real and the fabulous have been used in a way to suggest the myth-making habit of the folk imagination.

The combination of realism and fantasy, of the fabulous and the commonplace, in the Southwestern humor is nowhere better illustrated, perhaps, than in the figurative language which abounds in the tales. In this language is clear evidence, I believe, that the authors had such a respect for the speech of the folk as was uncommon at any time in nineteenth-century America. It is clear also that the writers knew they were sinning against current taste by using this language, and it is equally clear that they found delight in what they were doing. They required an audacity or a crudeness or a rhapsodic quality of imagery to match the characters and incidents of their yarns. Moreover, the metaphorical language dramatizes the development which I believe can be detected in the humor, from realistic reporting in the early pieces to imaginative representation of human nature and human character later.

Among the early authors like Augustus Baldwin Longstreet and William Tappan Thompson who were less concerned with writing humorous narratives than with recording what was peculiar to their time and their locality, the figures of speech seem realistically appropriate enough to the backwoods characters who speak them. They have the tone of everyday speech and the tang of the soil, and they reinforce the sense of actuality. We learn, for example, that someone's eyes "glared like two dogwood blossoms," or that an old maid was "as ugly as a tar bucket." One man looked at another "as spunky as a Dominicker rooster"; the night was "about as dark as the face of Cain," and there was a "wind that would tear off a shirt collar."

But as the authors thought less of their role as social historians and looked more imaginatively at the materials they were handling, their metaphors changed accordingly. At their best the figures kept the flavor of the life and the characters represented but gained a fillip from added hyperbole or from a further touch of earthiness. A stingy man might be described as "closer than the bark on a hickory tree" and might have it said of him further that "he was cotch one day stealin' acorns from a blind hog." One character especially handy with unkind language had been known to "cuss the bark off'n a dogwood saplin." This man may have been a blood relation of David Crockett's, whose grin could be used to knock a squirrel out of an oak tree or the bark off a knot on the tree. There were times when the men, we are told, were "so poor and thin that they had to lean up agin er saplin to cuss!" One of the sharpers in the new country to the southwest found that cheating one of his victims was "like catching a cow with a lariat, or setting a steel trap for a pet pig." A jug of especially efficacious whisky was recommended with the testimonial that it would "make a fellar talk as iley as goose-grease—as sharp as lightnin', and as persuadin' as a young gal at a quiltin'."

At times the figures multiplied and supported each other in sequence. For example, one man reports his encounter with another: "Oh, I giv him thunder and lightnin' stewed down to a strong poison, I tell you, I cussed him up one side and down tother, twell thar warn't the bigness of your thumb nail that warn't *properly* cussed." A description, in another instance, grows by segments: "His face were pucker'd like a wet sheepskin afore a hot fire, an' he looked sorter like he'd been studyin' a deep plan to cheat somebody, and he'd miss'd."

In the earlier humorous pieces, the figures were likely to stay close to real speech. Someone "howled like a full pack of wolves"; someone else stuck where he was, "like a tick under a cow's belly"; others were "as pleased as a young couple at their furst christenin'." The earthiness and the crudeness remained to later authors, and in fact such similes as these appear in all the humorous pieces. Alongside them in the later works, however, appear less natural, more deliberately fabricated figures. A person sat "as quiet as a sick cow in a snow-storm"; something was "as thin as a step-chile's bread an' butter"; a woman was "es big es a skin'd hoss, an' ni onter es ugly"; another, not so fat, "outrun her shadder thirty yards in comin half a mile." Such similes were commonplace: "quicker than hell could scorch a feather," "tight as a friz oyster," "restless as a cockroach in a hot skillet." At times the effect grew from understatement rather than exaggeration, as when a narrator told of a quarrel he had been in: "We didn't make quite as much noise as a panter and a pack of hounds, but we made *some*."

More than one of the humorists before Mark Twain had used their metaphorical language as a way of stunting with words and ideas, of producing outlandish effects. And all of them taken together had explored the possibilities of this instrument, as they had done also with other instruments available to the humorist. As a consequence, Mark Twain could learn from the practices of others and, by relying on his infallible ear for oral speech and his genius for effective turning of thought and expression, could make figurative language one of his most useful tools for gaining humorous effects.

Mark Twain and others of his time and later, such as Vachel Lindsay, Carl Sandburg, John Steinbeck, Jesse Stuart, Erskine Caldwell, and William Faulkner, have followed the early humorists in different ways and to different degrees, as they have mixed realism and fantasy in their handling of characters, action, speech, and figurative language. Thus they have found precedent of long, if not altogether honorable, standing for the fusion of sturdy realism with unbridled fantasy which has produced some of the best effects in their works.

Modern American Humor:
The Janus Laugh [1963]   **Hamlin Hill***

Critics of American humor have been commenting for several generations on the decay of that full-blooded, masculine, vigorous streak that
ran through nineteenth-century literature and reached its apotheosis in
many ways in the character of Sut Lovingood. Generally, they have
found the creation of the *New Yorker* in the 1920's a convenient mile-
stone to mark off the separation of "native" humor from what has been
dubbed "dementia praecox" humor, urbane, sophisticated, witty, reflecting
the tinge of insanity and despair of contemporary society. Actually,
though, the native element in American humor, far from having disappeared except when it has been sublimated into the proper fiction of
such authors as Faulkner, Robert Lewis Taylor, and to a lesser extent,
J. D. Salinger, is flourishing today as much as it ever did in the nineteenth century; and the causes for the rise in a not-so-new school of
humor antedate the glitter and uncertainty of the roaring twenties by
long enough that the credit for its development cannot be glibly given
to the founders of the *New Yorker* or the members of the Algonquin
Club.

At the risk of overgeneralizing, I hope to suggest here what appears
to be a more valid concept of the origins and the state of the contemporary two-faced laugh.

I

First of all, native humor has not been so much lost as misplaced.
It was always a popular rather than a high-brow literary form. Its
outlets in the late nineteenth century were the lecture platform, the
newspaper, and the subscription book, all calculated to captivate a
commoner market than more artistic literature. *The Carpetbag*, the
Spirit of the Times, the *Laramie Boomerang*, the *Toledo Blade*, and
other such sources of publication were the rule. As the United States
became more and more urban in the late nineteenth century the homespun philosopher, the literary comedian, and the inspired idiot didn't
disappear; they simply channeled most of their activities into different
lines of communication which continued to reach the popular audience.

Native humor, with all its established forms and techniques, flourishes most significantly in such media as radio, television, the phono-
graph record, the cartoon, and sub-literary writing. Charlie Weaver's
letters, for example, follow the tradition of Hosea Biglow and Jack
Downing. Jack Benny's wide-eyed pauses (and the ones in the Peanuts

*Reprinted with permission from *College English*, 25 (December 1963), 170–76.
© 1963 by the National Council of Teachers of English.

comic strip, where frequently three of the four panels will show Charlie Brown or Snoopy in an identical pose) follow the rules set down in Mark Twain's "How to Tell a Story." Andy Griffith's country-yokel description of "Romeo and Juliet" is in the great tradition. Harry Golden's saccharine journalism in the *Carolina Israelite* is a continuation (perhaps, more accurately, a debasement) of the heritage of Mr. Dooley, Josh Billings, and other homespun philosophers. The dialect humor finds its modern parallel in Runyon, Caldwell, Milt Gross, the Hyman Kaplan stories, the Lil Abner comic strip, and the Ma and Pa Kettle series. Burlesque and parody survive in Frank Sullivan's histories, Will Cuppy's almanacs, Don Marquis' archy columns (in part, a burlesque of the form of uncapitalized and unpunctuated free verse), in the "Fearless Fosdick" segments of Lil Abner, in Sid Caesar's versions of the silent movies, even in the recently-popular "First Family" album.

At a more acceptable literary level, these same techniques and devices occur more or less in the novels and stories of Faulkner, Steinbeck, Caldwell, and even Sinclair Lewis. *The Travels of Jaimie McPheeters, Journey to Matecumbe, Taps for Private Tussie, The Reivers,* and *No Time for Sergeants* have all been described as the children—legitimate children—of native humor, because they adapted language, plot situations, stock characters, or comic methods from this heritage.

More important for the present purpose, however, is something more basic, for the "new" humor also capitalizes upon many of the time-tested methods of native humor to get a laugh and it also exploits many of the newer media. Native American humor, though, both in its earlier form and in its contemporary survivals, proclaims an attitude; after a fashion it expounds upon a philosophy completely different from modern humor. It contains, in short, a set of values that affirms common sense, self-reliance, and a kind of predictability in the world. In the gentleman-clown axis of nineteenth-century humor, which Kenneth Lynn has studied in *Mark Twain and Southwestern Humor,* no matter which character was protagonist, he could be counted on to be in control of the situation. This does not mean, incidentally, that native humor must be moralistic. Simon Suggs's shiftiness, Sut Lovingood's and Uncle Remus' amoral worlds, Flem Snopes, Runyon's gangsters, all come to mind as examples. But it does mean that the character who is central in this humor, no matter how sinister, amoral, or reactionary his world might be, believes in its predictability and believes in his own power to remain consistent in it. The protagonist of native humor indeed, is perhaps less neurotic, more competent to face reality simply because he *is* prepared to accept its ugliness and to admit its brutality. Sex, for example, is natural—and fun—in both *Sut Lovingood* and Erskine Caldwell; in Thurber and White's *Is Sex Necessary?* it is the source of nothing but anxiety and frustration. Death is inevitable and a part of life; so both Brer Rabbit and the mourners at Red's funeral in *Sanctuary* accept it as an integral part of their outlook on life, to make the best of. So whether he is a shrewd Yankee peddler, a backwoodsman facing a hostile frontier, or a contemporary, this character faces an *exterior* reality with gusto and exuberance. Even as the "inspired idiot" of the school of literary comedians, laughing at himself rather than the world around him, he was exploiting the "difference between the assumed character and the character of his creator," as Walter Blair points out.[1] Even when he launches forth into his version of fantasy, the tall tale, he is based solidly upon the exaggeration of actual reality, not upon nightmare, hysteria, or delusion.

It would be wrong, then, to call the native streak in American humor "wholesome," but it would be accurate to label it "sane." Assured of the foundations upon which logic and experience rest, it concerns itself with action, characterization, and language. Even when one of its practitioners recognizes the insanity and instability of the world around him (as, say, Will Rogers did), he comments upon that world from a secure, superior point of view, confident of the validity of his own standards and certain of his own stance. He has, in short, as Kenneth Rexroth claims, "a sense of the consistent principle of incongruity on which Nature . . . operates . . . [and] the courage to face and act."[2] Although, as Blair has suggested, growing industrialism and urbanization, the discouragement of controversial ideas in mass media, and and a suspicion of horse sense resulting from mass education have caused native humor at mid-twentieth century to be received not "with great respect but with amiable condescension," the humor itself, as undaunted today as it was a hundred years ago when critics called its writers "mere" humorists, continues to flow in a flood tide.[3]

II

The more modern humor of the twentieth century appears to have evolved as a two-step process. In the late nineteenth century, when the destruction of the small-town newspaper humorist was imminent and techniques of mass appeal began to overwhelm popular taste, the humorists who held control of "polite" magazines captured much of the public attention. Quiet, reserved, sentimental, stuffily proper, these writers were the thinly smiling jesters of the Genteel Tradition. Charles Dudley Warner, E. C. Stedman, and Thomas Bailey Aldrich, for example, were the leaders in the school of sentimental whimsy. Critics were perceptive enough to recognize that a significant shift had occurred. Some lamented the loss of the older forms; others cheered. Some championed the bland wittiness of the newer group; others bewailed the loss of aggressiveness and red-bloodedness. The amazing thing, however, is that so many of them were sensitively aware of a change which they debated in hundreds of articles, of which these titles were representative: "The Passing of the American Comic," "The New Humor," "The Evolution of Whimsicality," "The Humor of To-Day," "Some Figures in the New Humor," "Is American Humor Declining?" "Waning of the Punster," "Slump in Humor," "A Retrospect on American Humor," "A Plea for Nonsense," and "Wit and Humor—Old and New."

The notice that critics took and the influence that the polite humorists had over respectable magazines combined to work vast changes. Humorists decided that humor was literature, that they and it ought to be taken seriously. Burges Johnson pointed out that "as soon as the humorist strains to meet the clamorous demand of a rapacious public, so soon does he drop from the heights of real literature to the lowest depths of space writing."[4] Turned inside out, this meant that the humorist who wrote for a magazine instead of a newspaper, on a monthly instead of a daily basis, and for a cultivated instead of a popular audience, was writing literature, A year earlier, though, Charles Johnston complained that the genteel humorists wrote "that wit which is marred by egotism and vanity, which springs from the desire to shine, to show off, to prove one's self smarter than one's fellows, to air the superior qualities of one's mind. Let us devoutly hope that this mood of self-consciousness . . . is transient only."[5] The school lasted into a second generation in spite of Johnston's hope, and included Gelett Burgess, Oliver Hereford, Carolyn Wells, Peter Newell, and Josephine Dodge Daskam, among others—all long since completely forgotten except Burgess' "Purple Cow."

The Purple Cow School was concerned with pure nonsense. Flip, facile poetry was its major stock-in-trade, slick magazines and Burgess' *The Lark* its outlet, and Lewis Carroll or Edward Lear at least a part of its ancestry. It carried whimsy to the verge of the irrational, and its importance in the line of development for modern humor lay precisely in its tendency to invert, to peer inward into a fantasy world, to play with language—always for fun, but in ways that provided a groundwork for later ramifications. Polished, sophisticated, brilliant, the work of the Purple Cow School aimed at dazzling readers with a kind of froth like Robert Williams Wood's poem "The Tern. The Turnip" from *How To Tell The Birds From The Flowers* (1917):

> To tell the Turnip from the Tern,
> A thing which everyone should learn,
> Observe the Tern up in the air,
> See how he turns, and now compare
> Him with this in-ert veg-et-able,
> Who thus to turn is quite unable,
> For he is rooted to the spot,
> While as we see, the Tern is not:
> He is not always doomed to be
> Thus bound to earth e-*tern*-ally

For "cooked to a tern" may be inferred,
To change the Turnip to a bird.
Observe the Turnip in the Pot.
The Tern is glad that he is not![6]

All that was necessary was for the urbanity and the wit to encounter a world of harsh reality with which it had no equipment to cope, and to assimilate techniques that were becoming fashionable in the serious literature that this brand of humor was striving to emulate.

That the world was a kind of chaos was no news to Sut or Huck, but the surprise that Henry Adams, late Mark Twain, and the literary naturalists unwrapped for America at the beginning of the twentieth century exploded in the face of the genteel tradition. Psychology and psychiatry suggested the unconscious response and associationism, and Gertrude Stein, the Imagists, stream-of-consciousness, Henry James' exploration of a reality dependent upon the perception of the individual, all were literary results of the ideas of Freud, Watson, William James, and Jung about something that might be called *interior* reality. Ultimately, of course, surrealism, Dada, and the cult of the irrational were manifestations of the same trend. Where the native humorist was more readily equipped to deal with a repugnant world, the inheritors of the genteel tradition recoiled in terror. Added to their surface polish, their literary aspirations, their outlet in slick urban magazines, their growing fascination with interior states of mind and neurotic or psychotic conditions, and their shock at coming out into a stark disillusioning sunlight from the honeysuckle and rose bower of Charles Dudley Warner's garden, there was one further ingredient they added—the black humor that had been an undercurrent in Poe, Hawthorne, and Melville, and that began to flourish in earnest in *Pudd'nhead Wilson's Calendar*, Ade's twisted *Fables*, parts of Field's *Tribune Primer*, and Bierce's definitions. Sardonic, bitter, even sour in its outlook on life, black humor's satanic laughter was prompted by its debasement of man. His meanness, pettiness, his inhumanity were sources of macabre delight. In its dehumanization of man it struck a responsive chord in a generation wrestling even in humor with the notion that the human being was an animal controlled by his environment, his genes, and his glands; it survives today in pure form in Charles Addams' cartoons and that humor we call "sick." ("Mrs. Brown, we're playing baseball. Can Jimmy come out?" "You know Jimmy can't play baseball; he has no arms or legs." "Yes, ma'am, but we've got enough players; what we need is a home plate.") The result of these forces is a humor of undependability, unreliability, and the irrational, a humorous world something like Marianne Moore's imaginary garden with real frogs. Man is beset by delusions; he escapes reality in the daydreams of Walter Mitty or in the visceral dream world of the Trojan Horse that Balso Snell visits. Settings have a habit of altering as they do in Herriman's backgrounds for Krazy Kat or in the Thurber cartoon called "Home," showing a house transforming itself into a scowling wife; or they assume the nightmarish aspects of giant drive-ins that look like oranges or peanuts or rocket shops in Perelman's sketches of Hollywood, significantly called "Cuckooland." The naive bride in *Is Sex Necessary?* awaits the roomful of bluebirds and lilies which will mean she will have a child. Robert Ruark discusses a homosexual dog he once owned. Saul Steinberg's cartoon bodies have fingerprints or exit signs for heads. Even an angel, in Bernard Malamud's "Angel Levine," becomes an untrustworthy derelict.

On a recent lecture tour through the United States, Malcolm Muggeridge complained that humor was dying out because the absurdities and the insanity of the real world were so vast, so staggering, and so overwhelmingly ludicrous that no humorist could ever hope to beat the morning newspaper in idiocy. Though Muggeridge's notion might apply most directly to satire, to corrosive and corrective humor, it contains by indirection a certain validity relevant to this discussion. The "new" humorist, overwhelmed by the outside world—by brinksmanship and overkill—reacts in the same way more serious writers have. Faulkner in his Nobel Prize speech and Cummings' insistence that the single secret will still be man, focus microscopically upon the individual unit. Social forces are too enormous and too impersonal, too much like a Juggernaut, for the individual to have any chance against them. As a kind of separate peace, it is what Lewis Leary has called "escape through avoidance of what one wishes to avoid by creation of values of one's own which transcend reality because they seem finally more real than reality." In a similar way, the humorous writer in the dementia praecox school turns inward to that interior reality—or hysteria—which admits by negation the loss of the humorist's role as satirist, his incapability of inventing homespun maxims about hundred-megaton bombs, or of feeling any native self-confidence in the face of uncontrollable fallout.

In consequence, modern humor deals significantly with frustrating trivia, with that tragedy of a broken teacup of which Norris accused Howells' writing. Timid, shy, unconfident of both himself and his world, the typical character knows beforehand that he is doomed to defeat by mechanical forces—pigeons and parking meters, waitresses, french pastry, or vending machines—and his attitude reflects his resignation to his defeat. His weapon and his defense is insanity, his own usually but his antagonist's, instead, occasionally (as in Thurber's "The Catbird Seat" or, less conclusively, White's "The Second Tree from the Corner"). By contrast, sanity, adjustment, or happiness is antagonistic—the lean-jawed guys named David who have their pipes lit by girls named Marsha are, in Holden Caulfield's judgment, phonies. Titles themselves suggest the psychotic nature of the humor: *Benchley Beside Himself, My World and Welcome to It, A Bed of Neuroses*. And as Benchley points out in his schizophrenic "My Subconscious," "my Subconscious makes a much better job of things than I do." Even when modern humor stops short of clinical case history it utilizes the same methods and outlook on life.[7] Much of Ogden Nash's poetry, H. Allen Smith's work, or Max Shulman's current cigarette ads in college newspapers are zany and reflect in a more lighthearted way the notion that the individual and his times are somewhat out of joint. On the stage, the invisible rabbit Harvey comes to mind; in the movies, the Marx Brothers. Even in children's literature, though it evolves from an older heritage of fantasy, such examples as Crockett Johnson's Barnaby, Dr. Seuss's books, and Ruth Krauss's tales border on the insane or at least exploit the irrational. Mr. Magoo's myopia results in a distorted world, but the consequences lack great significance. Long-play records by Jonathan Winters, Dick Gregory, and Lenny Bruce exploit some of the humor of the dementia praecox school.

III

The characteristics of the two schools of humor suggested above are too theoretical, too abstracted from specific humorous writing to apply in very many actual cases. Each "school" of humor has borrowed from the other; dementia praecox humor has invaded the popular media— in *Mad Magazine*, the *New Yorker* cartoonists, and Wally Cox's television character, Mr. Peepers; some ubiquitous humorists like Thurber and Marquis have adapted the conventions of both schools artfully and without difficulty. In spite of this leveling process, though, there are significant enough distinctions that one can spot them without difficulty— the eyes of Dr. T. J. Eckleburg in *The Great Gatsby*, whatever their functions on other levels, are eyes whose vacant, grotesque, exaggerated stare makes them surrealistically humorous.

Perhaps the best way to suggest the distinctions in the two types of humor is to compare briefly two contemporary narratives that are identical in their basic situations but vastly different because one has the characteristics of "native" humor and the other reflects the qualities of the dementia praecox school. One is Chapter IX, "I Learn to Hate Even Baby Chickens," in Betty MacDonald's best-selling novel, *The Egg and I*; the other is Sherwood Anderson's short story, "The Egg." Both narratives deal with the frustrations of chicken-raising. Both catalog the diseases chicks are heir to and the stupidity that kills the ones the diseases miss. Compare sentences from both works: "But I learned to my sorrow that baby chickens are stupid; they smell; they have to be fed, watered and looked at, at least every three hours. Their sole idea in life is to jam themselves under the brooder and get killed; stuff their little boneheads so far into their drinking fountains they drown; drink cold water and die; get B.W.D.; coccidiosis or some other disease which means certain death. The horrid little things pick out each other's eyes and peck each other's feet until they are bloody stumps." That was MacDonald's description, and this is Anderson's: "[A chicken] is born out of an egg, lives for a few weeks as a tiny fluffy thing such as you will see pictured on Easter cards, then becomes hideously naked, eats quantities of corn and meal bought by the sweat of your father's brow, gets diseases called pip, cholera, and other names, stands looking with stupid eyes at the sun, becomes sick and dies. . . . If disease does not kill them they wait until your expectations are thoroughly aroused and then walk under the wheels of a wagon—to go squashed and dead back to their maker. Vermin infest their youth, and fortunes must be spent for curative powders."

Betty MacDonald's chapter, though, never even suggests that the chickens will win their battle; hard work, industry, and ingenuity (in rotating chickens in four chicken yards) prove that in spite of her repugnance she *can* raise chickens, and by the end of the chapter she and her husband "were not too far behind [a] prize flock" in production. In addition, she digresses from her narrative to describe Mrs. Hicks and Mrs. Kettle in terms that would be familiar to any local colorist. Mrs. Kettle castigates a wealthy sister and decides, "You know where I'm going to hang your god-damned pitchur? In the outhouse!" Mrs. Hicks puts disinfectant in her chicken's drinking water so that they were antiseptic "inside and out." With good-natured humor, MacDonald puns, like the literary comedians, when she lists the causes of death in her chicken record book as "Chickenpox-Eggzema." Unhampered by "a lot of traditions or old wives' tales," the MacDonalds succeed.

The family of the narrator of "The Egg," by contrast, is destroyed by the chicken and the egg. The father "from long association with mother and the chickens . . . had become habitually silent and discouraged." He prizes as a family heirloom a collection of deformed chickens with extra legs, wings, and heads, which he preserves in bottles of formaldehyde and believes will make his fortune. Two trivial stunts, making an egg stand on end and boiling one in vinegar until it will squeeze into a small-necked bottle, defeat him, and the spectator to the abortive tricks "decided that the man who confronted him was mildly insane but harmless." The family totters at the brink of insanity, figuratively if not literally, and the inanimate setting revolts and controls the action of the tale. Without reaching the irrational level, Anderson's short story reflects hopelessness, despair, and a lack of control by the characters over external reality; it involves, that is, the philosophical, social and psychological premises of the dementia praecox school without putting them to their ultimate, surrealistic use. At the same time, emphasis is on an internal conflict, and external characterization, language, and physical action are minimal, where they were major devices in *The Egg and I*.

Thus, instead of there being a decline in American humor, there is actually a dual trend, in theory at least. If the branching of humor into two streams means a loss of force and vigor, it also means that humor has adapted itself to shifting points of view and assimilated the social pressures of contemporary society. Humor retains, in one branch, its demotic laughter; in the other, it faces a neurotic anti-hero with a neurotic culture and seeks, though it seldom finds, a solution in the exploration of what one comic has called "inner space." And this two-faced laugh, of course, was what James Thurber referred to when he said, "People can laugh out of a kind of mellowed self-pity as well as out of superiority." That is to say, modern humor releases itself in both the hearty guffaw and the neurotic giggle; it reacts to both the bang and the whimper.

Notes

1. Walter Blair, *Native American Humor* (San Francisco: Chandler Publishing Company, 1960), p. 173.

2. Kenneth Rexroth, "The Decline of American Humor," *The Nation*, 27 April 1957, p. 375.

3. Walter Blair, "Some Values of American Humor," Marshall University, Huntington, West Virginia, 20 March 1962 in The Scott Lectures, No. 6, *Marshall University Bulletin*, Vol. 2, No. 2.

4. Burges Johnson, "New Humor," *Critic*, April 1902, p. 331.

5. Charles Johnston, "Essence of American Humor," *Atlantic*, February 1901, p. 201.

6. Robert Williams Wood, "The Tern, The Turnip," in his *How to Tell the Birds From the Flowers* (New York: Dodd, Mead, 1917).

7. In *Native American Humor*, pp. 171–80, Blair examines the symptoms of insanity in Thurber, Benchley, and Perelman more exhaustively than space will allow here.

[From *The Rise and Fall of American Humor* (1968)]

Jesse Bier*

"Drownd them kittens!" Shillaber's comic heroine, Mrs. Partington, calls out to her nephew. But she has an afterthought. "Stop a minute. . . . I'll take the chill off the water."

She is actually a prim but kindly old lady. Her career now appears dated and ineffectual, existing in a sidestream of benevolent, mild, and harmless American whimsicality. And yet there are these deflections

*Reprinted with permission of the author and of Holt, Rinehart and Winston, from *The Rise and Fall of American Humor* (New York: Holt, Rinehart and Winston, 1968), pp. 1–10. © 1968 by Jesse Bier.

to cruelty and grotesquerie. Meanwhile, the rest of authentic American humor is as we shall find it: caustic, wild, savage. All of our comic expression may be placed along a continuum from irreverence to out-right shock.

The general impulse of our humor is to enjoy life's conquest over all particular systems of values. The paradox of pluralistic American life is that our special history has furnished our humor simultaneously with both its targets and weaponry. One consequence of pluralism is a desperate conformity, of value or status or aspiration, in order to hold our society together at any given time. The other consequence is to safeguard enrichment and to oppose fanaticism by encouraging all dissent and even attack. Humor has accepted that challenge with alter-nate glee and rage, and it has pushed its peculiarly heightened preroga-tives in America to the furthest limits.

Our humor, for instance, employs a great number of nonsense jokes and stories. The phenomenon is like that of "witty" music, of melodic lines that are funny because they do not develop. Such humor lies in our frustrated expectations. "The highest part of this mountain," lectures Artemus Ward, "is the top." We are thwarted, the way we are in watch-ing fizzled firework. A good deal of American humor has its point in not rocketing to glory. But we cannot fully relate the point to purely psychological theories that explain our laughter as a discharge of pent-up tension. There is a philosophical activity, equally reflective. In America we laugh at a visible progress disappearing before our eyes; we laugh at our assumption of utter and sequent control, at our subse-quent and real diminishment.

And we laugh harder, and need to in the United States, where pretense and rhetoric and sentimental shibboleth have been more solidi-fied than elsewhere. When Fred Allen's Senator Claghorn declares, "Ah stand four-square. Sixteen, that is," we laugh at more than the deflated politician. We also laugh at what the particular devices, literalism and circularity, imply for us psychically: the humor of nonadvancement in a nation committed to "progress" everywhere. Indeed, undisguised thematic counterparts of the same nature occur in almost every come-dian's repertoire of jokes. Even benign Will Rogers becomes explicit: "America—a nation that flourished 1900–1942, conceived many odd inventions for getting somewhere, but could think of nothing to do when they got there."

The greatest part of American waggery and comic attitude exists in a magnetic field, and we miss the force of the whole if we separate devices and objects of the humor from potent under-setting. Moreover, this field force of what we may call antitheticism in American humor has repercussions for general theories of humor that, up to now, have not taken the American demonstration into adequate consideration.

In any event, it promotes generalizations of its own, some of them unexpected.

Our humor criticizes all verities and cozy securities, consistently idealized as these have been in America. Its voice is the voice of hard, fresh truth, as the long and popular tradition of the cartoon shows. Moreover, this urge to tell the whole truth lies behind the function of so much cruelty in our humor. This may be the cruelty of Shillaber's drowned cats, where it is rather gratuitous. Or we may find it in Erskine Caldwell's episode of the grandmother who is repeatedly run over by an old Ford car in the gravel driveway, where it is a requirement. Against a nauseatingly prettified ideal of American life, humorists set their cruelty as a particular redressment of reality. The fact that they can go too far is a commentary on the intrinsic difficulties of the approach, as seen often in the extremes of black humor, and also on the proportions which false idealizations of character and prettifications of life have assumed in America.

A leading approach, in these respects, has been that of mockery. The famous Jewish sense of humor has had particular success in the United States. Here is Groucho Marx on Horatio Algerism. "When I came to this country, I didn't have a nickel in my pocket. Now I have a nickel in my pocket." Literalism here serves a comic mockery that would have been intolerable in Hitlerite Germany. There, as John Mander has pointed out, Jewish cabaret humorists became prime enemies of a state dedicated to a self-exaltation so insanely serious that, indeed, only comic ridicule could have successfully withstood or destroyed it. There was a method, then, in the madness of anti-Semitism. Artificial mythmakers know their enemies everywhere. But that pluralism which has led America to similar messianic positions or to a host of social and psychological tyrannies of the mind has also savingly kept open its lines of reactive or subversive attack. Which is to point out how necessary freedom is to humor, a fact that is no less true because it is a commonplace.

But insights into the antithetical nature of American humor must not lead us to define all the humor itself as simple in function. As a matter of fact, since much of the American mentality itself battens on simplifications—on clichés, on shibboleths, on proverbs, on slogans, on fomulas—an equal amount of our humor is in the service of unholy complication. That is not unique in the world either, although a surprising number of European theoreticians ignore the point and attack humor itself as a genre of gross simplification. They need only attend one of their own circuses and watch the impresario clown push the grand piano across the stage to the lightweight stool. This is not only reversalism but complication, more often than not an inherent characteristic of comedy. Indeed, the greater part of American literary, journalistic, and cinematic comedy is humor that makes simple events or situations unforeseeably complex.

The observation, for instance, accounts for the whole career of Rube Goldberg. His cartoon work involves the comedy of wild and unnecessary though ingenious complication. Here are the details for his "automatic" device for keeping screen doors closed:

> House flies (A), seeing open door, fly on porch. Spider (B) descends to catch them and frightens potato bug (C), which jumps from hammer (D), allowing it to drop on pancake turner (E), which tosses pancake into pan (F). Weight of pancake causes pan to tilt and pull cord (G), which starts mechanical soldier (H) walking. Soldier walks to edge of table and catches his head in noose (I), thereby hanging himself. Weight in noose causes string to pull lever and push shoe against bowling ball (J), throwing it into hands of circus monkey (K), who is expert bowler. Monkey throws ball at bowling pins painted on screen door, thereby closing it with a bang.

It is to the point, of course, that at any juncture of levers, strings, shoes, or rolling balls, Goldberg could have simplified and still been funny enough. But his task was aways to pack as much as the cartoon space and comic imagination allowed. The very essence of the comedy was complexity.[1]

Likewise, when Laurel and Hardy appear in their first two-reeler simply to sell Christmas trees to a Scotsman on Vine Street, the chaotic mayhem that follows is a product of pure complication. Not to be denied on their first call, they insist on calling him back to the door, and he finally whisks out a pair of shears and clips their samples. The graduated mayhem builds from there. A simple confrontation turns into a complicated comic war.

Inadvertent humor provides final confirmation. Here is a scene of Ernest Hemingway's partisan group sitting down to eat: "'There are no plates,' Anselmo said. 'Use your own knife.' The girl had leaned four forks, *tines down*, against the sides of an iron dish." It is true that in *For Whom the Bell Tolls* Hemingway is aiming for a particularly significant sense of experience for Robert Jordan. The work is altogether serious, and we are seriously involved, even at this moment. But Hemingway introduces, as I have italicized the detail, an unintentionally funny complication. That is why he is notoriously easy to parody. It is sufficient to our purposes, however, to show how unnecessary complication may disrupt a serious and even powerful work or an absorbing scene, because it is inherently funny.[2]

One is led to conclude that overt American humor is filled with more complication than the humor of other nations. In fact, English and Italian film makers of the post-World War II period learned that lesson from our example, apparently after we forgot it. In any event, the role of complication in successful American humor is primary. Its ultimate function is to complicate our idealized simple modes of customary thought.

But there is a humor of the obvious, too. The overflowing washing machine is a simple cinematic scene, where there is hardly any complication, only inevitability: the sure advance of the suds into the living room in a vast tide of catastrophic foam. But in every use of minimal complication, there is always the hypnotic comic power of disaster, *that* supreme antithetical deflation of smooth-going American living.

If the exception to the rule confirms a yet larger rule, still the lesser rule holds in great part. The humor of exaggeration and tall tales employs techniques of frustration and complication. We might consider all nonsense humor in this connection, especially the American tendency to *non sequiturs*, first epitomized by Artemus Ward. "I knew a man from Oregon once who didn't have a tooth in his head, and that man could play the drums better than anyone I ever met."

This is depthless humor, but effective in the United States. Most foreigners denigrate it out of hand. That is because it exists in a general background field which they, as outsiders, cannot fully detect.

Such observers may miss the force of another trait of our humor as well. It is that element of antic, absurd, comic freedom best exemplified by our movie cartoons. Tom and Jerry are freed of a thousand deaths, exempt from all physical laws and even the worst consequences of unmitigable catastrophe. The largely European theories of comedy as discharge of tension will not quite serve. For the tension itself is annihilated in the wild antics of these movie cartoons and other cinematic comedy. We are liberated from consequence as well as judgment and, indeed, from all biologic purpose itself, even that of discharge. All counter-pressures themselves are blown away in obedience to no rules at all. In our comic heritage there are indigenous sources for these phenomena, such as our frontier comedy, especially the Bunyan and Crockett humor of unbounded extravagance. Other elements and explanations are involved, of course, like the psychic realism of aggression operative under all the fantasy, or of wish-fulfillment, particularly that of immortality. But in any event, social and physical terms of existence are not merely reversed or upset but annihilated in the American contribution, which is an explosion rather than a simple discharge. And what that suggests, as a kind of ultimate comic freedom, is a commentary on the general repressiveness against which American humor is set. Needless to say, in these connections, theories of comic proportion, like Molière's, are not directly applicable to the subject.

The question of comic freedom is related to an even more distinctive feature of American humor, what we may call comic momentum. In a situation or joke of this kind, we are the witnesses and victims not of a sudden change in direction, or even of surprise,[3] but of the sheer momentum involved in going the whole distance. The comic matter goes out of control, as in the vignette where, as a milliner, Groucho Marx tries to sell a hat to Madeleine Carroll on the radio program of the thirties, "The Circle":

> CARROLL: This is a lovely five-dollar hat. How much were you asking?
> MARX: I was asking fifteen. I'll settle for fourteen.
> CARROLL: I'll give you six.
> MARX: Make it thirteen.

She says seven, and he says twelve, she moves to eight. Marx quotes eleven, and she nine. "Ten," he declares, and she cries, "Eleven." He shouts nine, and she twelve. Eight, he insists, and she answers thirteen. "Seven," he bargains doggedly. "Fourteen." His tone rises at, "Six," and there is the slightest pause.

> CARROLL: Fifteen!
> MARX: Five! *Sold.* There, you'll have to get up early in the morning to put one over on me!

We do not have what Koestler has defined as bisociation here, the sudden intervention of another plane of meaning. There is an unstoppable momentum of thought or reflex. It characterizes not only such jokes but a great deal of our movie comedy, as in the custard-pie crescendo portrayed on the American screen. It is another consequence of extreme psychic freedom, a distinctive native technique that only the French approximate on occasion. Inclusive theories of humor must make room for it.

They must also account for another striking American characteristic. That is what we can name comic pertinence, the comic recall to relevance, as in Josh Billings. "The hawk is a carnivorous animal—and a chickenivorous one, every chance it gets." Often the comedy resides in the simple recall to truth, funny only because we have pretentiously hidden or conveniently forgotten it, as when Mark Twain refers to "Authors' Readings, that kind of crime."

Sometimes what is comic, especially in America, where all sorts of interests are at work to conceal all sorts of truth, is the merest statement of truth, without any colorful or hyperbolic style whatsoever. Perhaps this again is a subtle question of comic momentum as applied to ordinary facts. They are supposed to remain in a state of rest; pushing them along a steady line of implication is amusing in itself. Ask the average man, for instance, to remember the architecture of old banks, some of which he can still see in old-fashioned neighborhoods, crenelated, fortress-like, designed visibly to protect and defend his money, which he had deposited there specifically for safekeeping. Then point out the new design of our banks, with their open, fluid driveways around an outside booth, which in a credit age facilitates the public's taking rather than leaving of money. Our audience smiles. But not at our figure of speech, for there is no comic metaphor at all, only the literal, drawn-out truth. If they do not suffer concealment or disguise, facts suffer a kind of inertia in the United States, and giving them a certain natural movement makes for humor.

American comedy is voracious, deflationary, skeptical, cynical, pessimistic, blasphemous, and black, not by turns or accident but in an inevitable sliding scale of function. Its spirit is realistic. Its realism often serves the fiercer hostilities, and the principal risk it takes is to be too highly charged for its own good. It has characteristically taken that risk. In doing so, it has scored phenomenal successes in just hitting a certain line of exposé and comic criticism. Only in contemporary times does it go over that line with a full force. . . .

A list of its leading modes and devices—nonsense, confusionism, reversal, anticlimax, antiproverbialism, undercutting—indicates the predominately negative, penetrative tendencies throughout its history. As such, it is not merely allied with the movement of Realism in American literature and culture, but is part and parcel of it. American humorists have consistently given their minority realist report on American life. It is no coincidence either that a great many of our comics have risen from the lower class, from frontier or immigrant quarters, conditioned to disabusement and resilient clarity. Furthermore, humorists, as in the Local Color movement, spearheaded Realism itself, and figures like Bret Harte and Mark Twain are pertinent in this connection. Moreover, in their advanced use of real speech and dialect (as in the early "southwest" humorists), in all their antirhetorical devices, and in their combativeness, they foreran the Realists by a full generation. They have gone on to pace the Realist movement in a great range of techniques, and they have regularly contributed subject matter others pick up later, such as the frank cruelty and sexuality of George Washington Harris, the political satire of the earlier Seba Smith, and the excoriations of the later Finley Peter Dunne. Struck by such features, the commentator, T. L. Masson, has even made the claims that humorists as gentle as George Ade surpass standard Realists like Theodore Dreiser and Sinclair Lewis in sheer accuracy and consistency of performance, and famous critics like Howells and Mencken have said as much.

In any case, the alliance between American humor and formal Realism is as close as the alliance between American humor and general truthtelling, and the fact counts heavily. There is a strong mutual animus to counter the standard American pronouncements and formulas. On the whole, the element of corrective is far less optimistic in America than in most quarters of Europe. The Civil War and its aftermath appear to signal a decisive turn to corrosive acid and nascent savagery for their own sake. The "literary comedians" of the epoch register not only temporary virulence but a cynicism and contempt which persist afterward. The climactic war resolved too little of the social and moral past and only added northern rapacity and the sins of industrial conquest to a bloody ledger. Probably Professor Leo Marx's statement about "the bitterness present almost everywhere in American humor" rises especially from postbellum morale. It applies to Mark Twain's backward look to the 1840's, sweet humorous nostalgia turned acidic even in *Huckleberry Finn.*

Twain himself signals best the mounting pressures on one's sense of humor in America, where the comedian suffers from too rich a field and too many targets that blunt the comic assault and convert it to frustrated anger. "If I could keep my faculty for humor uppermost," he told Dunne, "I'd laugh the dogs out of the country. But I can't. I get too mad."

Certainly the earliest humorists, including Franklin, are traditionally "corrective," aligning themselves with society against foolish deviators from custom and sense. But the course of American humor is a rapid and accelerating realignment with the non-conformists, the maladjusted even, the hypercritical antagonists of social code and self-deception. Retrenchments from sharp commentary and virulent humor, as in Kin Hubbard or Will Rogers, are secondary and temporary phenomena, though explicable and even inevitable.... They afford the briefest rural respite from that surge to the pith and force of our modern cosmopolitism humor, itself an equally inevitable outgrowth of the latter quarter of the nineteenth century. The subsequent excesses of black or sick humor are the results of both a later sociopolitical development and a built-in tendency of our traditional comedy.[4] Just so long as a national identity is basically unattained and unnatural absolutisms continue, American humor will appear vengefully antithetical and will have to resist a certain over-all momentum that characterizes the whole American genre.

Notes

1. Frequently the nature of a movie gag by W. C. Fields is sheer complication. A man enters a stationery store and asks for a 2¢ stamp, choosing the one in the middle of a huge sheet which Fields places on the counter. Fields gives the stamp to him with the corners of 8 other stamps surrounding it—costing Fields 16¢.

2. We often encounter variations of the phrase, "It's so complicated, it makes you laugh," applied to all fields of advanced investigation—musicology, biophysics, economics, or whatever. Over and beyond the nervous reflex of incomprehension, there is intrinsic amusement in complexity itself.

3. Surprise has been grossly exaggerated as an indisputable or unique characteristic of comedy. The humor of George Ade, for instance, as Mencken was first to point out, contains virtually no element of surprise at all.

4. The banana-peel practical joke, particularly favored in America, indicates

the readiness of antithetic laughter in the United States, the utter and unfailing release of predisposed feeling; the greater the pomposity of the victim as a social figure, of course, the more relevant and effective the comedy. The observation would be banal except that the course of recent sick humor moves in an opposite direction for sadism's sake.

Toward Vernacular Humor [1970]   James M. Cox*

Humor itself is the first problem and had best be faced bluntly. First and last, humor is that form of life and literature which cannot be taken seriously. Whatever the sense of humor is, the non-sense of it is making it serious. Yet making it serious is the preoccupation of most critics—so much so that they evade the reality of humor wherever they confront it by means of shifty prepositional displacement, positing a prior reality "behind," "beneath," "beyond," or "above" the humorous surface. And that prior reality inevitably turns out to be dark, somber, tragic—most of all, serious. The word *serious* is in its way inevitable in discussions of art since it functions as the chief value-giving epithet to forms of pleasure. By calling art or artists or writers *serious*, a person can, without making a single conceptual effort, shift completely from esthetic to moral grounds. Given the inexorable secularization of art and literature after the seventeenth century, the word comes more and more to be a substitute for the term *religious*, and is instinctively mobilized to lend gravity and profundity to objects whose chief end is pleasure. The term can be applied with the utmost complacency to tragedy, epic, and novel. But when comedy, burlesque, farce, and humor are under discussion, the value-giving term is so much at odds with the identity of the object that it denies the reality of the form.

The problem is intensified by the fact that comic forms are considered lower in the genre hierarchy and thus need transfusions of value in order to be elevated into the realm of serious art. Thus book reviews, quarterlies, and academic journals abound with reflexive references to serious art, serious artists, and serious literature. Thus humor is often tricked out as satire in many critical discussions, since satire, having ostensible moral purpose, is a more serious form. And thus current humorists are called black to suggest that they aren't just humorists.

Which brings us precisely to the "just humorous" response to humor. The antithesis of the serious response, it embodies two attitudes: the patronizing attitude, which holds humor as a lower order of creation and as therefore "just" humor; and the defensive attitude, which proudly

*Reprinted with permission of the author and of the *Virginia Quarterly Review* from the *Virginia Quarterly Review*, 46 (Spring 1970), 311–30. © 1970 by the *Virginia Quarterly Review*.

insists that humor, far from being decadently high falutin, is just folks. In the face of the complacency exhibited by both attitudes, the wish to see humor as serious seems, for all its contradictions, not only inevitable but laudable. For the person claiming seriousness for humor is at least trying to bring it within the purview of the intelligence.

But since seeing the seriousness of humor inevitably obscures the humor, such a course, far from being fully meaningful, is a refuge from the meaning of humor. What follows is an attempt to approach American humor by exploring the vernacular forms of Mark Twain, Ring Lardner, and J. D. Salinger. Now I am not at all insisting that vernacular humor is the only humor, though it is well to remember that vernacular, being the "lower" language, offers itself readily as a possibility for the inversions and releases of "low" humor. Even more important, vernacular opens itself to the dramatization of personality, and humor—unlike comedy, burlesque, satire, or even parody—is not a literary genre but emerges from physiological and psychological theories of personality; and for all the changes the term has undergone since medieval times it has never really been dissociated from its sources in the personality of man. Thus, when we say that a man has a sense of humor we are defining his personality, and it is again well to remember, particularly in the light of what follows, that we mean he is a person who can not only tell a joke but take one.

Even so, I do not want to begin with the masters of American vernacular humor but with Chaucer, who seems to me the master humorist. I take it to be one of the world's great jokes that, given the fact that Chaucer is the first distinctly great English writer, the English have been called a people lacking a sense of humor. That howler is equaled only by those who continue to say that the Puritans didn't like imaginative literature in the face of our indisputable knowledge that the one irrevocable epic in English, "Paradise Lost," was written by a Puritan. Though I shall not dwell on Chaucer as a vernacular writer, it should not beforgotten that he was indeed just that. In fact, his choice of the Midland dialect rather than French or Latin as his form of expression was as decisive for English literature and language as Dante's determination to write in Italian was for Italian literature and language. But since we are so deep into the culture and language which Chaucer made possible, his great decision is beyond our immediate consciousness, and I shall therefore begin with what we helplessly begin with—his act of humorous narrative.

II

In his masterpiece of humor, "The Canterbury Tales," Chaucer introduces a frame of reference which removes him from authority and puts the Host in his stead. By depreciating himself and elevating the

Host, Chaucer is able to escape responsibility for, and at the same time release, the whole spectrum of reality which is "The Canterbury Tales."

The Host, at once the representation and embodiment of the audience, demands above everything else to be pleased. But pleasure for this earthly Host does not consist simply of the "lower" pleasures. Being pleased, it turns out, is having the illusion of morality along with the ribaudrye. Thus, the Host wants fables as well as *fabliaux*; he wants the Knight's Tale as well as the Miller's. And Chaucer too, by making himself "helpless" in the pilgrimage, wants the Miller's Tale as well as the Knight's. Indeed, the helpless laughter to which the Miller's tale reduces the pilgrims is the perfect fulfillment which Chaucer's imaginative act makes possible. To be sure, Chaucer reserves a certain amount of ironic license, but it is genial, not satiric, irony. Thus, when Chaucer says that he agreed with the Monk that monks should enjoy hunting, he is not simply exposing the monk but revealing the kind of agreeableness he himself had to have in order to draw the Monk out. This sociability of Chaucer the Pilgrim is not a trick but a trait, a quality and style of consciousness which are not only dramatized within the poem in the person of the pilgrim Chaucer, but are present in the conception of the artist Chaucer and make the poem possible. Chaucer is not rôle-playing but both being his true self and carrying out his poem— and any interpretation which evades this reality about him, whether by seeing him as *persona* or by seeing his poem as allegory, inevitably begins to see the prologue as a device rather than what it is: one of the great imaginative acts of literature.

Chaucer's humorous act of reducing himself in order to enjoy the company gently but unmistakably reorients the whole system of values of the medieval world. Thus, the Pardoner, who is by all odds the worst or nearly the worst pilgrim, tells one of the best tales, whereas the Parson, surely the most virtuous figure in the group, tells the dullest tale. Reading it, we begin to understand—unless we are stricken medieval scholars seeking hidden significance—why Chaucer never got his pilgrims to Canterbury. For Canterbury is the place where the significance, the allegory, the morality, and the unbearable dullness would prevail. Chaucer casually determined to give his audience and all posterity the great tales instead. He even gave one of his greatest to the Nun's Priest, a person denied any characterization in the Prologue. Finally, Chaucer himself had to have sense of humor enough to tell a dull tale and after being rudely, but not unjustly, interrupted, an even duller one. And no amount of scholarly interpretation can make "The Tale of Sir Topas" or "The Tale of Melibee" as marvelous as "The Miller's Tale."

The entire act of "The Canterbury Tales" is a pleasurable revolution in which the aim becomes not to get to Canterbury but to have fun on the road. Not only is Chaucer liberated from the conventional responsibility of finishing the ridiculous number of tales he promises into the freer form of finishing when he pleases, but the most serious activity in the medieval world, the pilgrimage, is beautifully reduced to direct, overt, and earthly pleasure. The cost of it all is there, of course. First, Chaucer does not finish, leaving critics who can't see the humor or those who must see more than the humor the pleasure of plotting serious endings. Second, Chaucer writes his retraction. But if his failure to finish emphasizes the pleasure he has given and not its absence, his retraction is surely a last joke—one which, leaving God the problem of censoring those tales which tend toward sin, parallels his earlier joke of leaving his readers the responsibility of censoring the *fabliaux*.

III

Whereas Chaucer's way of getting into his form is to put himself down as the helpless recorder of the tales, Mark Twain's way—in his masterpiece—is to release a character and a language which will thrust him aside and take over. When that happens, and only when, what has formerly been dialect framed by literary language becomes vernacular. Although Chaucer is able to release with broad freedom the whole impulse of ribaudrye which Mark Twain so scrupulously censors, Mark Twain's vernacular in turn releases a reality which scarcely exists for Chaucer—the reality of childhood. For childhood was, by virtue of Rousseau, Wordsworth, Dickens, and Mark Twain, one of the great expressions, not repressions, of the nineteenth century.

Now the reality of Huck's language and the reality of his character are one and the same; to speak of one is to speak of the other. In its simplest terms, and these are the ones to hold to, Huck's vernacular is incorrect, a "low" language evoking the illusion of illiteracy, yet a written language nonetheless. For Huck is writing his book, not telling it. Instead of being framed by conventional language, Huck's vernacular implies it; his errors, characterized by his excessive double negative and his ignorance of tense distinctions, evoke as much as they deny the norm from which they deviate.

Coupled with Huck's bad grammar is his bad action—freeing a slave in a society based on slavery. Now we can put it as a law that if the bad grammar and the bad boy are not really bad but represent approved morality and attitudes, then both are sentimental fictions instead of the powerful realities they are so often said to be. Yet precisely here the vision of "Huckleberry Finn" seems most conventional. For the entire mechanism of bad grammar and bad conduct operates on a principle of direct inversion, arousing the indulgence and moral approval of the reader. Thus the teacher who would not think of tolerating Huck's "free" language on a student paper (and tolerates it today only because Mark Twain's classic has made it respectable) and the parent who would be indignant to find his child filching a carton of Pepsi Cola from the local supermarket, not only indulge but wholeheartedly applaud Huck's language and action.

The reason for their approval resides in Huck's involvement in a one-hundred-per-cent approvable situation—a situation as safe, to borrow a line from Mark Twain, as a Christian holding four aces. For Huck, though fictively freeing a slave in the Old South, is acquiring all his virtue from an implied post-Civil War morality. The reason the reader indulges him is that, in addition to behaving nobly in terms of anti-slavery morality, Huck is a boy behaving nobly, and his action, by virtue of the inverted perspective, can be totally indulged by the adult reader. It is just this process of inversion which, constantly transforming Huck from bad to good boy, embodies what can best be called the moral sentiment sustaining the action. But this sentiment, even as it evokes approval for Huck, is directly at odds with his identity, for though the sentiment inverts his theft into a liberation, his cowardice into courage, his flight into a quest, and his lies into truth, Huck's identity remains rooted in his profound belief that he is morally and literally bad.

The moral sentiment is nothing less than the powerful wish which Huck's great language and his great journey arouse and which the ending of the novel frustrates. For in those last ten chapters the novel changes its direction from its seeming high purpose to crude horseplay, from great art to mere burlesque. Hemingway, who paid the book its highest compliment by calling it the first and best American book, warned readers to stop short of the ending which was, he said, "just cheating." The reason he so confidently used and we so confidently accept the term is that Tom Sawyer, who indulges the romance of freeing Jim, actually knows that Jim is already free. Tom's private knowledge—the real index to his contemptible and gratuitous pleasure in elaborately setting Jim free—is the reason, or at least the rationale, critics of the ending can use to expose Tom. Yet the ultimate irony is that Tom's action in freeing a free Negro is directly analogous to the reader's moral sentiment. For if Tom knows that Jim is free, so does every reader of the novel, and he has counted as heavily as Tom upon that central security. This crucial irony, which complaints about the ending invariably refuse to acknowledge, is, or at least can be, the means of getting back to the point at which the novel turned against the moral sentiment it had relied upon.

That moment, I hope everyone will reluctantly acknowledge, is when Huck utters his grandest line, "All right, then, I'll *go* to Hell." For this is the moment when Huck makes the choice which the moral sentiment applauds by sending him instead to the heart of heaven. Yet it is also the moment when Huck's identity is fatally threatened. For with his choice his grand evasion ends. He does not, to be sure, go to a fire-and-brimstone hell in this novel which plays endlessly upon the absurdity of superstitious hereafters; he goes instead to the only hell there is: adult civilization. And he is there within five minutes of reading time after his apparently heroic utterance. What has happened is that his decision, a positive choice instead of a doubly negative evasion, represents action based on principle and is actually—in style as well as substance—in the manner of Tom Sawyer, whose rôle Huck is about to assume. The best way to see the transformation at work is to see Jim converted from affectionate friend to image of guilt in the lyrical moment when Huck prepares for his grand line:

> I . . . got to thinking over our trip down the river; and I see Jim before me, all the time, in the day, and in the night time, sometimes moonlight, sometimes storms, and we a floating along, talking, and singing, and laughing. But somehow I couldn't strike no places to harden me against him, but only the other kind. I'd see him standing my watch on top of his'n, stead of calling me, so I could go on sleeping; and see him how glad he was when I come back out of the fog; and when I come to him again in the swamp, up there where the feud was; and such-like times; and would always call me honey, and pet me, and how good he always was; and at last I struck the time I saved him by telling the men we had smallpox aboard, and he was so grateful, and said I was the best friend old Jim ever had in the world, and the *only* one he's got now; and then I happened to look around, and see that paper.

This is the moment when the action of the novel becomes Huck's reflection; it is also the moment when Huck's instinct becomes his conscience.

This new conscience is in reality his Northern or inner conscience in the act of displacing his Southern or social conscience. The Southern conscience had put him in flight from his society; his Northern conscience welcomes him into ours. It is just this new conscience which puts Huck *in* society during those last ten uncomfortable chapters. For the real tyrant of his novel which plays upon Negro slavery is the conscience—any conscience—whether Northern or Southern, whether terrorizing by fear or paralyzing by guilt. The action of the novel discloses that the conscience is at once the tyranny and the pleasure by means of which the adult civilization acts out its endless cruelties. Huck's rejection of this civilization in the closing paragraphs of the novel is the radically negative vision which his doubly negative grammar embodies.

Yet if the book is nihilistic—and surely it is—it is humorously nihilistic, which means that it must neither fulminate, satirize, nor complain, but continue to be acted out under the reader's indulgence, affection, and approval. But the last ten chapters, instead of evoking a wholehearted approval for Huck, initiate a disturbed disapproval of Tom.

With Huck's fatal choice, Mark Twain had reached, though he probably could not afford to know how completely he had reached, the limits of his humor: that point at which humor's necessity to gain indulgent and affectionate approval mortally threatened the very identity and character of his humor. Yet even here the form of his masterpiece saved him. For even as Huck chooses the Northern conscience, there is a dimension, an inescapable dimension, of his character which chooses to act not heroically because it is the best and right course of action, but *helplessly* because it is the easiest thing to do in a tight place. The good life for Huck has been, and remains, life based not on principle but on comfort, and he leaves civilization not because it is a sham but because it is cramped and smothery. Tom and the adult reader are the ones who have all the principle. Moreover, Huck goes into the territory not as an apostle of freedom but as a boy to play. And this is not all. The ending leaves the moralizing reader, if not in approval of the action, in a state of greater self-approval than any point in the novel—complacently superior to the author's "failure" and obtusely scornful of his own sentimental surrogate, Tom Sawyer. If it is not a perfect ending, it is as good as one can easily imagine for this completely humorous novel of reconstruction which brought not the Old South but an entirely new South back into the union, converting in the process the tragic issues of slavery and Civil War into the very sentiment which would so please the mind that Huck's radical vision would pass pleasurably intact beneath the gaze of the rapt censor.

IV

To see how Mark Twain reached the limits of his humor is to see where Ring Lardner had to begin. And he did begin there, coming to his particular vernacular efforts much more quickly than Mark Twain had done. If Mark Twain entered the ranks of successful authors as reporter of the first organized pleasure trip from the New World to the Old, Ring Lardner became successful just at that moment when the playing of games was becoming a profession of entertainment on a national scale. Lardner's vernacular is, on the face of it, much like Mark Twain's. Whether it is the busher Jack Keefe, the young girl in "I Can't Breathe," the old husband in "The Golden Honeymoon," or the evasive correspondents in "Some Like Them Cold," Lardner's characters speak or write a language hopelessly distant from "correct" usage.

Yet it is, on examination, startlingly different vernacular from Huck's. Lardner's characteristic error of grammar is not the double negative, though he employs it abundantly. He evolves a series of errors—misplacement of first-person pronoun (I and Florrie has made it up), case error of first-person pronoun ("Between you and I"), elaborately nonparallel constructions ("I have not got nothing against him though because he married her and if he had not of I probily would of married her myself but at that she could not of treated me no worse than Florrie")—which intrude unassimilated correctness and abortive formality into the primitive illiteracy which Huck had mastered. These errors are not at all the errors of one, like Huck, who don't know no better, but of people who, incipiently straining to be right and proper yet remaining helplessly wrong and awkward, develop a hopeless self-consciousness. Lardner's characters, far from being boy law-breakers in flight from society, are adult failures trying to keep their social and financial balance yet steadily losing it. Caught in the discrepancy between their capacities and their desires, they fabricate larger and larger self-deceptions. Instead of lying to others as Huck does, they lie to themselves in acts of humorous self-exposure. Their styles are the boast, the impotent threat, and the alibi; their ultimate way of escape is quite likely to be the bottle.

Such characters could, of course, be fit objects of satire, but Lardner at his humorous best deflects his own and the reader's impulse toward moral judgment in two ways. First, he gives his characters so much more justice than they deserve that the reader is saved from supplying his own. Their self-deceptions are not therefore pretenses so much as they are humorously resourceful defenses, providing—to follow Freud—a direct gain of pleasure by means of an economy of pity. Second, and equally important, Lardner almost inevitably finds his characters at play—whether at baseball, bridge, horseshoes, a social gathering, or a barbershop interlude. Thus, for all their ridiculous traits, they can never quite be taken seriously. Though Lardner habitually involves these overgrown children in ineffectual and abortive confrontations of courtship or in the hopeless toils of marriage, he displaces erotic content with innumerable variations on popular jokes about nagging wives, awkward adolescents, bumbling swains, impossible children, and defensive husbands.

Neither Lardner's vernacular nor his vision plays upon the complete inversion which Huck so beautifully exploits. Thus, whereas Huck's malapropism for Tom's planned invasion is "evasion," Lardner's busher converts the World's Series into the World's Serious. That deviation, far from meaning that baseball is really serious, discloses that everything serious is really a game. By restricting his action to the world of overt play, Lardner saves himself from the threat of the moral sentiment and maintains a direct correlation between situation and form. But such a restriction denies him the opportunity of being taken seriously. If Mark Twain is likely to be taken too seriously, Lardner is likely always to be treated as a mere humorist. Indeed, there will be readers who question his presence in this discussion, preferring to remember him as a minor writer in the age of Hemingway and Fitzgerald. It was just this identity which Fitzgerald had in mind when, in paying tribute to Lardner's memory, he observed that no matter how richly Lardner managed to develop his world it still retained the dimensions of Frank Chance's baseball diamond. Lardner himself, for all his characteristic, self-depreciation (the humorist's necessary strategy of self-protection), was restive in his limited world and often threatened to convert his play into a nightmare in an effort to extend the range of his humor. This dark side Lardner tended to reveal in two ways: by abusing his characters with satire or by making them abuse themselves to the point of madness. Beyond these dramatizations of sadism and masochism, Lardner moved toward a world of nonsense, writing plays in which the elaborately illogical connections of humor were displaced by absurd disconnections.

But Lardner's satire, epitomized by such stories as "Champion," "The Love Nest," "A Day with Conrad Green," and "Ex Parte," is extremely heavy-handed, depending as it does upon melodramatic structure. Like Mark Twain, Lardner lacked the *mind* for satire and therefore could not displace the anger and indignation which stand behind satire with the wit and analysis which are its constituents. The very reason that both writers descended into the vernacular form was that it freed them from the constraints imposed by conventional morality, logic, and syntax. The "unconscious" vernacular character actually becomes their form, evoking from the reader a corresponding unconscious indulgence of the limitations, inadequacies, *and* the freedom of the "low" language. The conscious superiority to and dissociation from the victim, so utterly essential to the judgment and exposure of satirical narration, are thus suspended in favor of indulgent feelings—the precise emotional equivalents of pleasures felt to be repressed by the correct, mature, and logical syntax of adult society.

Lardner's mad humor ("My Roomy") and his black humor ("Haircut") are products of the satiric impulse working within and against the vernacular consciousness. Instead of fulfilling Lardner's imaginative impulses, the satiric irony invariably threatens to curtail them. Thus, the bitter strain in "Haircut" tends to mechanize the repetition compulsion at the heart of humorous invention. The irony of the story, by working against the narrator, fixes his identity, threatening always to reduce him to a caricature instead of releasing him as a character who is at once the form and narrative—the principle and the invention—of the story. Though such satiric irony exposes the sadistic element in his humor, it runs athwart the creative force of the story, which is the humor. As for Lardner's nonsense plays, though they can be seen as forerunners of the Theater of the Absurd, they are actually extreme forms of withdrawal—and withdrawal not toward but away from a world of invention and imaginative energy. They may be good enough to satisfy critics like Gilbert Seldes and Clifton Fadiman, who are pleased to find Lardner's serious side, but they are not good enough for anyone who believes that Lardner, like Mark Twain, had great moments of complete humor.

Those moments—best represented by "You Know Me, Al," "I Can't Breathe," "Zone of Quiet," "Some Like Them Cold," and "The Golden Honeymoon"—embody much more total criticisms than any of Lardner's satire and much more absurdity than any of his nonsense. For in such stories he rejects adult civilization as totally as Mark Twain had done. Lardner rejects it, however, not in the name of the conscience but in the name of boredom. The adult world—the world of marriage, money, ownership, and work—is a world where people are waiting "like something was going to happen but it don't." That is why they find themselves at ball games, at horseshoes, at cards, at the bar, at play. The play world, as institutionalized by the adult world, is that arena where something *can*, or at least may, happen—where narcissistic fantasies can be fulfilled, where losses are the order of the day but are not final, where hope—however fatuous an illusion—is the helpless dream of the perennially gullible player.

Lardner is at his best when, as in "You Know Me, Al," his characters are professionally located inside that world. For then their work becomes playing for a living, reversing the adult dream of making work the pleasure of the world, and revealing that the true work of the world is play. Baseball is Lardner's glory because, in the world of professional baseball as Lardner beautifully conceived it, the children's game becomes the adult institution offering refuge from adult "reality," particularly marriage. Marriage is, after all, the social institution which concentrates, controls, and utilizes erotic pleasure yet in the process ironically represses the childhood it is designed to produce. But Lardner's ball-players and their vernacular diffuse erotic pleasures and forms into a world of narcissistic play. This does not mean that they triumph over the girls or their wives. They are more often the victims of love and marriage since, in the last analysis, they are provisionally adults. But, because they are essentially baseball players, their courtships and marriages are merely the problems which complicate their careers in the baseball kingdom. For love is the force which imperils the gullible rookie and must be elaborately manipulated into its proper, subordinate rôle by the manager and the old pros. Romance, marriage, and children, instead of being the ends of action, are the means which impoverish the ball-player, keeping him enslaved to his work—which is play.

Lardner's great force in portraying the baseball world lay in his recognition that its essence, instead of being mythical or serious, was indeed play. It was not a play element in culture, but culture as play. Totally comprehending its meaning and fully committing himself to it, he accomplished the difficult task of humorously inverting his language and perspective, thereby equaling the genuine social reality he recognized in the world of sports. Freed from symbolic strategies of representing the serious reality behind the face of the game, Lardner gained the fine economy of having the game as it was. Thus, his players, except for his central characters, are "real," bearing their historic names, personalities, and legends. And his bats, instead of being the phallic symbols which Malamud's characters swing, seem always to be genuine Louisville Sluggers. It is not his world which is fictive, but his narrator, whose language must perpetually render the world of baseball not as his fiction but as his life—that form of childhood pleasure indulged by the adult society where, from within the confines of the ball park, adults both in the stands and on the field helplessly convert loss, despair, and boredom into direct and overt gains of pleasure. In the process of such a major conversion, it is small wonder that Lardner converted, and thereby redeemed, the epistolary novel, which Richardson had boldly used to keep middle-class virgins precarious maidens, into a form for keeping adult children from becoming mere adults.

V

The humorous inversions and conversions of Lardner and Mark Twain provide the background for seeing Salinger's literary heritage and discovery. Like Mark Twain and Lardner, Salinger has established himself as a vernacular writer; like them, he too has been so popular as to have been restive under the threat of his insatiable audience. But whereas Mark Twain and Lardner indulged and exploited their popularity—the one as lecturer, the other as journalist— Salinger has retreated into a self-imposed isolation from the popularity which relentlessly pursues him. Moreover, Salinger—unlike Mark Twain, who announced his humorous identity in his pseudonym, and unlike Lardner, who gained fame as a sportswriter and inventor of the Busher—began his career as a serious writer. By 1948 he had written "A Perfect Day for Bananafish," the story containing the tragic suicide which he has been painfully, patiently, and tediously reconstructing for the past decade. Between the time of its appearance and his extensions of it came his vernacular form, "The Catcher in the Rye," the book which is, for all feelings and wishes to the contrary, his masterpiece, capable of sustaining comparison (which it invited and inevitably received) to "Huckleberry Finn."

Salinger's vernacular is vastly different from Mark Twain's or Lardner's. Though Holden Caulfield, like Lardner's characters, often produces an awkward "I and Allie," or, like Huck, a double negative, what makes his language different from theirs is his insistent use of four-letter words—the words which Chaucer freely used and which Mark Twain and Ring Lardner insistently avoided, at best managing to make jokes of the circumlocution they so assiduously practiced. Yet Holden's language is not rebellious or shocking; rather, it is the new vernacular which can be indulged, just as Huck's "ain'ts" could be indulged in the nineteenth century. As a matter of cultural fact, Holden's language, more than that of any other literary character since World War II, repeats in its rhythm, attitudes, and substance the language of the GI. By making that language the very consciousness of a prep-school adolescent, Salinger, far from being guilty of the class betrayal so-called liberal critics charge him with, actually realized the experience of the war as the consciousness of the new generation instead of treating it as the experience of the old.

Not only can Holden's language be indulged by his readers; Holden himself indulges it to the point of endangering his vernacular, for his indulgence brings him precariously close to slang, the perennial threat to the vernacular. Vernacular is the linguistic struggle of an impoverished character to speak the best he can; slang is the metaphorical excursion of a privileged character indulging his imagination. The one leads, as in "Huckleberry Finn" and "You Know Me, Al," to a powerful illusion of social reality; the other, as in "A Connecticut Yankee," "Henderson the Rain King," or "On the Road," to journeys into fantasy. If the measure of Huck's indulgence of his style is to be found in his tendency to play Tom Sawyer, the measure of Holden's indulgence can be charted in his repeated impulses toward literary or movie fantasy. At such times, both characters move toward the threshold of slang fantasy and are vulnerable to the loss of their essential identities.

But Holden, as much as Huck, is a vernacular character. He is in bad trouble and doing the best he can. The reason that he resembles Huck more than Lardner's creations is that he is in open conflict with the adult world and thus seems involved in a serious rather than a humorous action. But Huck was helplessly against the adult world; Holden seems much more aggressively against it. Yet if the irony of Huck's flight is that the indulgent drift of the great river bears him deeper into the slavery of society, the irony of Holden's criticism is that it carries him forward into adult literary sensitivity. Thus, the more positively rebellious he becomes the more correct and literary his language becomes and the more he is likely to tell us about Old Eustacia Vye and Old Thomas Hardy—the more, in other words, he threatens to be the ultimately good bad boy who grows up. What saves him from that fate is his swearing. Instead of being a rebellious and indulgent slang, his profanity is his instinctive way of expressing himself. It is not so much an aggression as it is a protection, for it serves to convert erotic content into anal joke, and thus endlessly saves Holden from the sexuality of adolescence.

The other significant aspect of Holden's vernacular is his helpless repetition, whether through recurrent epithets ("Old Phoebe" "Old Ackley,"), repeated words and phrases ("phony," "You know"), and habitual emphatic utterance (disclosed in the text by excessive use of italics). These repetitions not only give the illusion of spoken language—

and Holden, unlike Huck, is apparently speaking—but they also reveal Holden's limited linguistic resources at the same time they perfectly reflect the circular dilemma of his life. For Holden, unlike Mark Twain's boy and unlike Lardner's adult children, is an adolescent directly faced with adult sexuality. All the world beckons him to go forward into its pleasure; he even tells himself to enter. Yet confronted by the prostitute in the hotel room, he rejects entry into manhood, and takes instead the pleasure of a beating, imagining even amid the pain of receiving it that he is in a movie scene.

Having rejected adult heterosexuality, he finds himself threatened by the homosexuality and phony maturity of Mr. Antolini, after which discovery he determines simply to run away from the hopeless adult world awaiting him at every turn. But before departing, he returns home in the dead of night for a secret good-bye to his sister Phoebe. At this marvelous moment, what would be the bedroom scene in the novel of seduction, the assignation in the romance, and the erotic, tormented, and incestuous longings in the *bildungsroman* (e.g., "Werther" and "David Copperfield") becomes the pathos of Holden Caulfield. For pathos is, as every nineteenth-century humorist knew, the "high seriousness" of humor. In Holden's meeting with Phoebe, the passion, secrecy, and fatality of erotic and romantic love are converted into the tenderness, fidelity, and helplessness of childhood affection.

But Holden cannot remain with Phoebe and die with her as if they were the Babes in the Wood. Her real function is to elicit from him the true direction of all his wishes. Confronting her stark doubt that he loves *anyone*, Holden finds himself disclosing that, aside from Phoebe herself, his dead brother Allie is the sacred object of his heart's desire. And it is toward Allie, toward Death, that Holden's sentiments lead him as he departs from Phoebe. His visit to the museum—long a place of privileged retreat for him—marks the height of his self-pity. There, in the tomblike depths of the Egyptian section, he arrives at the center of his fantasy of dying. But at the selfsame moment he reaches the destination of his vernacular—the "Fuck you" scrawled as if literally across the tomb he has imagined for himself. That scrawl—surely the same scrawl which Nick Carraway's feet had romantically rasped from the steps of the dead Gatsby's mansion in the distant literary past—is of course the crass reality of the world's sensibility. But much more important, it is the glorious end of Holden's vernacular, the remorselessly inevitable last reach of his profanity. He faces the oldest and surely most common invective in the world's language—that instinctive insult which converts erotic act into anal metaphor—and makes it the climax of the novel, the "poetry" of humor. And it is indeed the poetic moment of this masterpiece of humor, the triumphant interlude when the reality of Holden's language, which has been his life, beautifully saves him from the serious death his and our indulgent sentiments might have brought upon him. Though bringing off such a triumph may have almost killed Salinger as a writer, as "Huckleberry Finn" almost killed Mark Twain, the fact remains that just as Holden's humorous vernacular literally displaced his death wish, it also displaced Seymour Glass's suicide, that elaborately gauzy event which Salinger's super-conscious Jamesian style discovered well before Holden's complete act of life and has been reconstructing ever since.

Released from suicide, Holden emerges from his "ordeal" to go a little mad with delight at watching the essence of the pleasure he cannot leave—his sister whirling on a carousel. I say he goes a little mad advisedly. Although the serious-minded adolescent will want him to have descended into the soul's dark night, it is impossible to tell how serious his malady really is. And although the serious-minded adult may complain that rich little Holden didn't have a real rebellion and didn't go mad enough but sold out instead, the truth is that Holden had a real rebellion all right. Like his forebears in the realm of American vernacular humor, he rejected adult civilization. Not however under the sign of Mark Twain's conscience or Lardner's boredom, but under the sign of sexuality. Though it is of course possible for psychological criticism to lament these rejections as regression, and for theological criticism to moralize them as the dangers of innocence, the point is—if our contentions are somewhere near the mark—that the rejection is the most total criticism of our lives in the form of the greatest gain of direct and overt pleasure.

That pleasure is the miracle of humor, which, far from being serious or evasive, is an invasion into the very temple of seriousness, reducing us, as working adults, to the helpless laughter from which all our seriousness happily cannot save us. To be so reduced is not to be transported back to childhood where play was reality, but forward toward the last possibility of adulthood. For in the adult world, work is reality and play is indeed pure and purposeless play. It remains for the sense of humor to transform the realm of work into the realm of play—and not childhood play, which was real, but adult play, which is pure. Thus, when children disclose a genuine sense of humor, they are not "being" children but are already losing childhood. For it is always and forever the *loss* of childhood play which vernacular humor converts into the gain of purest pleasure. There is no sense of humor in childhood.

NEW ESSAYS

A German Connection:
Raspe's Baron Munchausen

Walter Blair*

I

Soon after alert America-watchers in England noticed that some of our countrymen were trying to be funny and, surprisingly, were succeeding, several of the watchers announced that they had spotted the distinctive ingredient in overseas comedy. After scanning discussions by British critics, Clarence Gohdes summarized their consensus: "By the middle of the [nineteenth] century the critical conclusion was pretty generally fixed that the essence of American humor was exaggeration." For decades, commentators on this side of the Atlantic shared the English belief. In 1899 Bret Harte, for instance, said that our "distinct and original humor" was "delightfully extravagant"; in 1918, Professor Will D. Howe remarked that early comic writers "in the main channel of American humour" developed long-lasting devices," particularly the tricks of gigantic exaggeration and calm-faced mendacity"; and in 1936, Max Eastman noticed that it was "customary to say that American humor is distinguished from British by exaggeration."[1]

By the 1840s common folk were using the word "tall" to describe the talk and the yarns that most obviously made use of magnification. *Knickerbocker Magazine* was announcing that "one of the striking peculiarities of our people is the disposition to talk tall." Colloquial speech called a narrative "that is highly exaggerated or difficult to believe" a "tall tale," and a Sucker from Illinois told a famous raconteur, Jim Doggett in "The Big Bear of Arkansas," that "his stories smelt rather tall."[2]

The popularity of the tall tale as an American genre has been verified by scholars who read acres of pages in books, newspapers, and periodicals, who cornered storytellers and set down their monologues,

*This essay was written specifically for publication in this volume and is included here by permission of the author.

then listed and counted occurrences and types and motifs. A leading compiler, Ernest W. Baughman, needed more than six hundred large pages for his *Type and Motif-Index of the Folktales of England and North America*, which surveyed publications in the two indicated areas until a few years before its issuance, 1966. "The tall tale," he decided, "constitutes the largest segment of our published tales." His list shows that "the tall tale . . . is an overwhelmingly American form (3,710 American variants, 29 English variants)"—a ratio of 128 American tellings of such fanciful windies to every one that Britons told. International listings indicated that other nationalities did no better than the British, if as well.[3]

These facts show why the thesis of this paper merits development: I suggest that an eighteenth-century German author who never visited the United States, and his immediate imitators, were the most important contributors to the plots, motifs, and techniques of American tall tale literature.

Having made this suggestion, I must hurry and do a bit of weaseling. It must be admitted that unassailable proof of this claim will be impossible. A reason will be found in the very nature of the literary corral in which the obstreperous genre, the tall tale, has been stabled—jokelore. For, like germs, viruses, and great ideas, jokelore is all but impossible to confine. As Gershon Legman has said: ". . . jestbooks, . . . which derive mainly from one another . . . are not so much being alimented by folk sources as constituting, themselves, a main source of the jokes in oral transmission. . . . their copying from one another is only one intermediate step in their migrations: from one mouth to another, one book to another, one land to another."[4] Jokelore, in other words, meanders unpredictably and without leaving a clear trail, from age to age, region to region, talk to print, and print to talk, in mysterious ways *ad infinitum*. The best I can do, therefore, is set down available evidence, admittedly inconclusive, in the hope that my suggestion will prove to be worth entertaining.

Rudolf Erich Raspe (1737–1794) appeals to me as a candidate for the kind of recognition I urge because, for one thing, his German education gave him learning quite incongruous for a begetter of yarns told by untutored farm folk who told them by fireplaces or hunters and fishers who told them around campfires. At thirty he became a university professor and museum director. He wrote erudite tomes in several languages about antiquities, geology, mines, mountains, volcanoes, and literary history. A member of Britain's Royal Society by invitation, he contributed scholarly papers and suggested improvements on Benjamin Franklin's glass harmonica so impressive that Ben invited him to visit Philadelphia. His contribution to art history so impressed Horace Walpole, himself an art historian, that Walpole financed its publication.

For another thing, Raspe himself was a most appropriate predecessor of some great American comic characters—Sam Slick, Thimblerig, Simon Suggs, Petroleum V. Nasby, Col. Sellers, the Gentle Grafter, Egbert Sousé and other perpetrators of confidence games. He got his professorship and his curatorship by enlarging upon his qualifications. He puffed up his reputation by browbeating intellectual disputants. Trusted to catalogue and protect a museum's treasures, he pilfered a number, pawned them, tried to bluster himself out of being punished, failed, and absconded to England. There, after a brazen pitch for a Cambridge professorship miscarried, he used his scientific expertise to talk himself into a job as an assayer. In the mines, he again tried some skulduggery—the salting of a Scottish claim—and once more when detected managed to elude punishment.

Pressed for money (as he usually was) in 1785, Raspe hurriedly wrote a one-shilling 42-page booklet about a comic German blowhard and somehow got a London publisher to issue it. *Baron Munchausen's Narrative of His Marvellous Travels and Campaigns in Russia* was a great immediate success. Within a year, impressive sales brought a commission to add materials for a "considerably enlarged" new edition. By 1800, eight "legitimate" English editions, a pirated "sixth" edition, and two editions (1792 and 1796) of a sequel had appeared.

Translated and augmented German editions in 1786 and 1788— *Wunderbare Reisen zu Wasser und Lande, Feldzüge und Lustige Abentheuer des Freyherrn von Munchhausen*—helped deliver the stories to the European continent. Thereafter, bibliographers have ticked off 138 more editions in English and 237 more in German detailing the baron's yarns, pure or adulterated and without added matter or (more often) with it, plus hundreds in other languages and countries. In addition more adaptations have appeared worldwide than even compilers with lusts for lists have been able to record. The problem was complicated because from the start many publishers of these works were careless or deliberately deceitful about dates and publishers. The first English edition, for instance, came out in 1785 but was assigned to 1786, and the German translations of 1786 and 1788 were said to have been published in London, though in fact they were published in Göttingen. In both England and Germany for some years publishers had a good reason for hiding their true identities: a real German Baron Hieronymous Karl Friedrich von Münchhausen of Bodenwerder, plagued by pilgrims to his estate, was doing his damnedest to sue somebody responsible for the libel bringing unwelcome fame, but he was baffled.[5]

II

It appears that the fictional baron's books about his military and hunting exploits did well in the United States. Early editions were imported from England for the enjoyment of American readers; but less than two years after the first edition came out—in 1787—our enterprising countrymen, untrammeled by any copyright laws, began to put out their own printings. One of the most successful versions, initiated in 1793, appeared with Americanizations and updatings of its satirical thrusts in 1813, 1832, and 1845. Henry A. Pochman in his *German Culture in America . . . 1600–1900* toted up 39 appearances of Munchausen's *Narrative*, and undoubtedly the impressive number would have been even larger if he had counted reissues. A title-page of a printing as long ago as 1835 called that edition the twenty-fourth; and though, to be sure, publishers have been notoriously grandiose when counting copies, as a rule they were more accurate when they counted editions.[6]

But since accurate (or even, in fact, inaccurate) sales figures for editions and adaptations of Munchausen's fabrications are not available, anybody who wonders how popular they were must turn to other indications of their notoriety. Three kinds are useful: (1) usages in common speech of the old liar's name, (2) references to Munchausen that manifest general familiarity over the years, and (3) records of oral and printed retellings of the baron's tall tales.

The terms *Munchausens*, *Munchausenish*, and *Munchausened* have invaded the vernacular. From the 1830s on, without bothering to explain, popular writers about local champion liars called them *New York Munchausens*, *Vermont Munchausens*, *Texas Munchausens*, and the like. Even medical doctors, who do not go in for many literary allusions, have got into the habit of saying that sufferers who exaggerate their agony have *Munchausen's Syndrome*.

More impressive, a reader of popular American publications of various kinds can easily find every now and then casual references— without glosses—to Baron Munchausen that take for granted general familiarity. Examples:

1822–23. When Charles Mathews, a noted British comedian, toured the United States in a one-man show, newspaper reports, the program, and the widely circulated printed text identified Major Longbow, one of the characters he impersonated, as "a modern Munchausen."

1833. A newspaper and then a comic anthology titled a joke "One of Jonathan's Munchausens."

1847. The author of an article, "Tough Stories," in *The Yankee Blade*, remarked that in a little town in Maine "all the villagers" agreed that a local storyteller "left Munchausen 'no whar.'"

1856. In his best-selling *Prue and I*, G. W. Curtis made the ghost of the baron a prominent character.

1864. Robert Carter told in a travel book about his encounter with "a marine Munchausen of the first water [whose] adventures were nearly as wonderful as those of the renowned Baron himself."

1870. A burlesque mining prospectus in the Boston *Commercial* offered stock in "the Munchausen Philosopher's

Stone and Gull Creek Consolidated Oil Company"
which was preparing to work its tract for "quinine,
sardines, and the milk of human kindness" under the
guidance of Baron Munchausen, the "company director."

1896.   A St. Louis book, *Arkansas*, issued as an advertisement
for that state, reassured possible migrants: "No, don't
be afraid of Arkansas on account of Munchausen reports
of ignorance and crime."

1901.   The popular humorist, John Kendrick Bangs, published
*Mr. Munchausen, an Account of Some of His Recent
Adventures*, with an Introduction in which he explained
why he became "the medium between the spirit of
the late Baron Munchausen and the reading public":
it was "to render a service to an honest and defenseless
man." The fifteen chapters were excellent addtions to
the tales told in the 1786 booklet.

1913.   William Rose Benét published in *Century Magazine* a
poem, "The Marvelous Munchausen," nostalgically pic-
turing the baron as he tells three listeners several tales
which Benét renders in verse.

1928.   Ginn & Company, a leading publisher of textbooks,
published an edition of the baron's *Narrative* for grade
schools, with an Introduction by the editor, Steven T.
Byington, which held that "Munchausen's modest seat
in the Valhalla of classic literature is undisputed," and
that "the education that does not include knowledge"
of some of his famous stories is "incomplete." "We all,"
said Byington, himself a humorist, "bow to the Baron
as the patriarch, the perfect model, the fadeless frag-
rant flower, of liberty from accuracy."

1931.   Constance Rourke, in her best-selling history, *American
Humor*, told about the time Audubon was called "a
new and greater Munchausen" for telling an unbeliev-
able story about a rattlesnake.

1931–1943.   Jack Pearl (1895–1982), a comedian, playing the role
of Baron Munchausen, was a major radio personality.
After making a hit by telling whoppers on the Ed Sullivan radio show, Pearl headed national network shows
of his own, telling wild tales in German dialect. When
his straight man, Cliff Hall, expressed disbelief, he
would say, "Vas you dere, Sharlie?"—always winning
howls of laughter. The expression became a household
phrase. Pearl, as "Baron Munchausen," also appeared
in two films, one with Jimmy Durante, the other with
not only Durante but also Laurel and Hardy.

1929 and 1952.   The Limited Editions Club published two editions
of *The Travels of Baron Munchausen*, the first with an
Introduction by Carl Van Doren, who said, "Munchausen is the Euclid of Liars," and the second introduced
by John Carswell, Raspe's definitive biographer.

1982.   When Jack Pearl died on Christmas day, newspapers
throughout the country played up his death on obituary
pages. The Associated Press story said that Pearl, after
appearing in vaudeville and in 18 Broadway shows,
"made his greatest impression on radio" when "he lampooned the widely read adventure tales of Baron Munchausen."

> *1983.* In the June issue of *Smithsonian,* James Cox, without elaboration, quoted an editor's request that he write an article about lies: "Just think of Baron Munchausen and Pinocchio's nose."

I list these allusions to Raspe's old liar because they go to prove that his tellings, rather than others, were likely sources of American retellings. Jokelore, as has been said, was widely diffused over time and space, and it is relevant to notice that just possibly Raspe's versions of some were those most likely to be encountered. Raspe himself, however, can serve as a leading witness for the ubiquity of his stories, since the huge amount of reading in many fields that made him a polymath also had acquainted him with oft-repeated windies; he had stored them in his excellent memory and he recalled them when he was writing his booklet. Here, for instance, is one story that the baron tells: During an unusually severe winter—one so cold "that ever since the sun seems to be frost-bitten"—he is journeying across Russia:

> I travelled post day and night, and finding myself engaged in a narrow lane, I bid the postilion give a signal with his horn, that other travellers might not meet or stop us in the narrow passage. He blew with all his might, but all his endeavors were in vain. He could not make the horn speak, which, as he pretended to be a good performer, was . . . unaccountable. . . . Soon after we found ourselves in the presence of another coach coming the other way. It was very troublesome for both parties in this horrid weather, for there was no proceeding either way, without taking the carriages to pieces and putting them together again, past each other. . . . However we reached the much-looked-for stage, and . . . all of us hastened to warm and refresh ourselves.
>   The postilion hung his great coat and horn on a peg and sate down near the kitchen fire. . . . I sat down on the other side. . . . Suddenly we heard a *Tereng! tereng, teng, teng!* We looked around, and now found the reason, why the postilion had not been able to sound his horn. His tunes were frozn up in the horn, and came out now by thawing, plain enough, and much to the credit of the driver, so that the honest fellow entertained us for some time with a variety of tunes, without putting his mouth to the horn.

This little episode, like others in the *Narrative,* had traveled long and far, and there simply is no telling for sure where Raspe had encountered it. In a study of its multitudinous appearances, Otto Weinreich required 144 pages to trace its reincarnations, none of them, it happens, in America. Plutarch, the ancient Greek biographer (46?–120?), who said he was repeating it as a jest of Antiphanes' instead of inventing it, was the earliest teller identified, but thereafter it was retold by such varied storytellers as Calcagnini, Castiglione, Rabelais, Donne, Butler,

Addison, Mandeville, Burger, Jean Paul, Saint-Martin, Balzac, and many others.[7] Such wanderings are typical. As John Carswell says:

> To get at the origins of the stories the Baron tells, we must follow tracks which lead back into the furthest uplands of collective memory, running across one another and finally vanishing into uncertainty, like sheep-runs among the heather. We can chase individual tales through the pages of monkish jest-books and fifteenth-century collections of facetiae, or trace the German tradition of *Lügendichtungen* through its successive phases, until we find that the Bible, or the *Mabinogion*, or the folk literature of almost any country, from the English (and Greek) *Six Sillies* to the Serbian *The Biggest Liar in the World* will give us stories the Baron might have told. The fairy fruit which turns to ashes in more sophisticated hands was safe enough with Raspe.

Carswell suggests that, since Raspe drew upon his "common stock," the characterization of Munchausen and Raspe's storytelling skill are his "only original contribution to the tales," and he may be right. However, in all fairness, it should be noted that those indefatigable folklorists mentioned earlier—the readers of many printed works and recorders of oral yarn-spinnings—so far have been unable to find tellings previous to Raspe's of only four of the tales in the first edition of the *Narrative*.

III

Just the same, the listers of types and motifs in huge indexes and in books about folklore pay an impressive tribute to the contributions of Raspe and his hero. In his great six-volume *Motif-Index of Folk-Literature*, for instance, Professor Stith Thompson recognized the most famous teller, world-wide, of tall tales by calling a group "Münchhausen Tales."[8]

Writing in 1946, Professor Harold Thompson thought it "probable that in the past century Americans have owed as much to the Baron Munchausen as to any English drawer of the long bow ... the cosmopolitan source of American fun [and] a welcome immigrant." He noticed that folklorists "from New England to New Mexico" have collected oral versions of tales told by "that suave and poker-faced master of lies." Having read reports and collected tales in New York state, Thompson said "the favorite" may be one that Raspe might have encountered in Julius Caesar's *Commentary on the Gallic War* (45 B.C.).[9] Here is Raspe's version:

> Having one day spent all my shot, I found myself unexpectedly in the presence of a stately stag. ... I charged immediately with powder, and upon it a good handful of cherries, of which I had partly

sucked the flesh as far as the hurry would permit. Thus I let fly at
at him, and hit him just in the middle of the forehead between the
antlers. It stunned him—he staggered—yet he made off. A year or
two after I was with a party in the same forest—and beheld a noble
stag come out with a fine full-grown cherry tree between his antlers.
I recollected my former adventure; looked upon him as my property;
and brought him to the ground by one shot, which at once gave me
the haunce and cherry-sauce; for the tree was covered with the richest
fruit, the like I never had tasted before.

Thompson noticed that only fourteen American variants had been
written about by 1946 and made a prediction—that "doubtless scholars
will uncover many more." Sure enough, folklorist Leonard Roberts in
1969 cited an additional variant found in New Jersey, one in Wisconsin,
and two each in Indiana and Michigan, and himself printed "The
Peach Tree and the Deer," which he got from an informant in Knox
County, Kentucky, who had heard it back in 1920. An old man, the
story begins, having feasted on peaches from a tree in a forest, shot a
fat deer with a peach stone:

> A few years later he went hunting again in the same woods. This
> time he . . . looked over beside a big log and there was another peach
> tree full of good peaches. He cloomb up in it and begin to eat
> peaches again. The peach tree begin to move. He looked down and
> to his surprise the tree was growing out of a deer's back. He got a
> switch and started whupping the deer and it bolted around through
> the woods. Finally it come out to the big road and run up through
> the church-yard where there was a bunch of chillern playing. He
> shook the tree and a lot of peaches fell off for the chillern to get.
> The deer run on and on and went through a big thorn patch. The
> man looked back and saw the eyes hanging on a thorn winking at
> him.[10]

In spite of the displacement of the cherry tree and the somewhat grisly
fillup at the end, this story's ancestry is quite clear.

Ernest Baughman, whose monumental compilation of American
variants of types and motifs has been mentioned, agrees that the story
nominated by Thompson was one of the most popular Munchausenized
narratives, but he suggests that the tale about the frozen coach horn
quoted a few pages back may have been even more popular, especially
if some close relations are taken into account. He lists eight versions of
the tale in which music congeals and later thaws, then makes what
surely are plausible additions in which other "unfreezables freeze"—
words, dog barks, train whistles, flames, smoke, fog, air, light beams,
and sunbeams—thirty of these in all.

His compilation includes a half a dozen additional descendants of

Raspe's whoppers, each with numerous variants (total: 61). "I don't think," he remarked in a recent personal letter, "you can go far wrong in stressing Raspe's importance, especially in the early part of the nineteenth century."[11] The half a dozen do not include variants of the Raspe concoction that I gather he believes is the most popular of all here. This is the one that the late Richard M. Dorson nominated in his book, *American Folklore* (Chicago, 1959). Dorson, whose research led him to comment on variants in the United States of at least nine of the "Münchhausen Tales," calls attention to some printed in 1808 as told by liars from New York, Virginia, and Vermont. One of these appeared in *The Farmer's Almanac* for 1809, and was headlined "Amusing." A contributor, addressing the editor, Robert Thomas, speaks of "the wonderful feats and extraordinary stories of *Simonds, old Kidder,* and *Sam Hyde*," but hopes "to divert some of your evening readers" with a yarn told by a formidable competitor, George Howell, famous in New England as *the Vermont Nimrod*:

> "I was once," said he, "passing down the banks of the Hudson in search of game, and suddenly heard a crackling on the opposite bank. Looking across the river, I saw a stately buck, and instantly drew up and let fly at him. That very moment a huge sturgeon leaped from the river in the direction of my piece.—The ball went through him, and passed on. I flung down my gun—threw off my coat and hat, and swam for the floating fish, which, mounting, I towed to the bank and went to see what more my shot had done for me. I found the ball had passed through the heart of the deer, and struck into a hollow tree beyond, where the honey was running out like a river! I sprung round to find something to stop the hole with, and caught hold a white rabbit—It squeaked just like a stuck pig; so I thrash'd it away from me in a passion at the disappointment, and it went with such force that it killed three cock partridges and a wood cock."!!!

"This," said Dorson, "is the first recording of America's favorite tall tale, the Wonderful Hunt, also well liked in Europe." Later, in his discussion of Pennsylvania folklore, he wrote:

> Again, the best-known of all American tall tales, the Wonderful Hunt, appears in Montgomery County in more fantastic form than ever. Not only does Beltz, the champion hunter, shoot into a tree trunk to split a limb and clamp the toes of seven pigeons, in a standard feat, but he adds the novelty of exciting the pigeons to pull up the tree and fly off; Beltz jumps on the butt, and by waving his hat from side to side guides the pigeons to his home across the Schuylkill River. True, the butt occasionally dipped into the water. Reaching home old Beltz found his trousers full of suckers, adding to his pigeons and winter's wood.[12]

Although Professor Dorson and other folklorists have given these narratives and variants of them the title, "The Wonderful Hunt," the fact is that they combine happenings that the baron and his followers often tell about in separate episodes. Professor Baughman, who is sure that "Wonderful Hunt" types and motifs were "borrowed from the Munchausen books," discusses them in remarks about one, "The Lucky Shot." (The numbers are those that have been assigned for classification.)

> 1890. *The Lucky Shot*. The discharge of the gun kills the heath-cock which falls on the sprouts of the tree, killing the bear, etc. [X1124.3]. Compare Munchausen . . . (two ducks, four widgeon, two teal.)
> [Note: The accidental discharge of the gun is not a characteristic motif of the English nor of the American forms of the type. In each variant, the weapon is used deliberately, although luckily. There are about seven major subdivisions of the type with considerable overlapping of the subdivisions and of other types, notably 1895. The Man Wading in Water Catches Many Fish in His Boots, 1881. The Man Carried Through Air by Geese, 1900. How the Man Came Out of the Tree Stump, 1894. The Man Shoots a Ramrod Full of Ducks, 1882. The Man Who Fell Out of a Balloon. Buried in the Earth. He Goes for a Spade to Dig Himself Out.][13]

The modification that Baughman mentions—making the shot intentional rather than accidental—is one of several, e.g., the fauna and flora of course are thoroughly localized, and often the domino-like series of happenings are made remarkably elaborate. In general critics agree with Norris W. Yates's comment in his history of America's leading sportsmen's magazine between 1831 and 1858: "A number of hunting stories owed something to Munchausen; for instance, those built around the theme of the 'wonderful hunt'. . . . Variations on the pattern are often ingenious but usually minor."[14]

The above samples, summaries and commentaries show clearly the nature of the pattern that is repeated time after time in "Wonderful Hunt" stories: Thanks to a sportsman's skill and good luck in a country where fish, fowl, and four-legged critters abound, a sportsman slaughters prodigious quantities of game. It is therefore no trick to figure out why this particular tall tale in its several guises has been so popular for so long in the United States, or why its fame is doomed to fade in the future. For centuries, the North America of promotion tracts and in actuality was truly a hunter's paradise. From colonial times on, our Nimrods and anglers did what their ilk always have done everywhere: they enlarged upon their triumphs. Both the boosters boasting about our salubrious climate and the braggarts celebrating their full bags and creels became common objects of derision and, as many critics noticed, satirical exaggerations of exaggerations became favorite materials for comedy. And so the baron's tales about hunting and fishing in Russia, where his claim was that game "abounds more than [in] any other part of the world," were ready made for American appropriation and naturalization. But a likely prediction is that—thanks to environmentalists, defenders of endangered species, and sufferers from cholesterolophobia—jokes about the extinction of great quantities of fauna will decline in popularity in the future.

In numbers of the sportsmen's magazine issued between 1846 and 1856, Professor Yates found several Munchausen stories in addition to those I have mentioned. Twice writers (one with a bow to the baron) adapted one about the fellow who "rammed his arm down the throat of a charging wolf, seized it by the tail, and turned it inside out with a jerk," by substituting a panther for the wolf though "the story remains substantially the same." The baron's tale about the bitch which whelped as she ran was improved upon by adding that the precocious pups immediately fetched game. Finally, the baron's hound "that ran its legs off until it was merely a short-legged terrier" inspired a yarn about a pony that ran its hoofs off in pursuit of a buffalo that ran his legs off. Thus, as Yates points out, "these American cousins" have become "backwoods stories in setting, tone, and atmosphere," but still are easily recognized.[15]

Other scholars have recorded American tellings in other media not only of these three Munchausen stories but of additional ones—about a jumper who turned around part way through his jump; about the split dog reassembled with his back legs pointing upward; about the snakebite or sting that caused an inanimate object to swell; about the indefatigable hound that chased birds or game for days, weeks, or even months; about the fellow who made a wolf jump out of its skin by nailing its tail to a tree then beating the poor beast; about the animals that pounced on horses pulling a sleigh, ate their way into the horses' hides, and kept pulling. All these appeared after the *Narrative* and its sequels had been widely distributed in the United States. Add the recurrences in print of these to those about the Wonderful Hunt, and the total is more than a hundred. And beyond a shadow of a doubt, innumerable oral retellings enlarged the total.[16] So widely have Baron Manchausen's tall tales been retold and re-enjoyed again and again from sea to shining sea that anyone who dares to say that they aren't funny must be labeled unAmerican.

IV

Whether modern Americans (and unAmericans) find the German-made tall tales amusing or not, they have to concede that their popularizer, Herr Raspe, showed remarkable sensibility when he discovered among his wide readings so many plots and motifs that so long would convulse our countrymen. A consideration of his technique provides additional insight concerning taste and artistry unique in the long history of popular jokebooks.

Raspe's contemporary, Horace Walpole, a fine stylist himself, remarked that this emigrant wrote English "much above ill"; and Carswell argues persuasively that "the credit for creating the Baron as a figure belongs to Raspe and to Raspe's English style. . . . the pungency and racy vitality of the Baron's diction that brings him to life"—an achievement "the more remarkable in that it is carried out in a language not the author's own—a *tour de force* accomplished by Conrad and Beckford, but very few others." Carswell cites as proof a fine but quite typical paragraph—one, it happens, for which no source but numerous American retellings have been found—one admirable for its lucid ordering and its economical but apt choice of concrete details:

> "What do you say to this for an example? Daylight and powder were spent one day in a Polish forest. When I was going home, a terrible bear made up to me at great speed, with open mouth, ready to fall upon me, all my pockets were searched in an instant for powder and ball, but in vain—I found nothing but two spare flints: one I flung with all my might into the monster's open jaws, down his throat. It gave him pain, and made him turn about, so that I could level the second at his back door, which, indeed, I did with wonderful success, for it flew in, met the first flint in his stomach, struck fire, and blew up the bear with a terrible explosion. Though I came safe off that time, yet I should not wish to try it again or venture against bears with no other defense."

"There he is," says Carswell, "and as such he has lived, for there is not a word of direct description [of him] in the whole book."[17] True, the completely deadpan and matter-of-fact but efficient style does much to individualize the baron, and true, Munchausen's physical aspects never are indicated. However, both third-person commentaries and his own lengthy monologues further characterize the old prevaricator in ways that the passage does not illustrate.

The publisher's preface and advertisements to early editions, including the 1792 sequel, are third-person frameworks that unfold the baron's family history, compare him with other storytellers, and describe his way of talking—his careful skirting of controversy as he "adroitly turns the conversation so that he may hold the floor," for instance. "A man of great original humor," he has, the tongue-in-cheek publisher announces, a high purpose—"to awaken and shame the common sense of those who have lost sight of it," and to convince those who find his stories "border on the marvellous" that they are true.

So Munchhausen bolsters the purported believability of his tales by carefully tracing logical causal relationships. Why does he succeed as a hunter? "Presence of mind and vigorous exertions" bring many triumphs, "chance and good luck [which] correct our mistakes" bring others. Again, "in a case of distress, . . . try any expedient." Using "the very best implements" will help: "I have always been as remarkable for the excellence of horses, dogs, guns, and swords, as for the proper manner of using and managing them." And be alert in watching for a recurrent peril: "There is a kind of fatality in it. The fiercest and most dangerous animals, generally come upon me when defenseless, as if they had a notion or foresight by way of instinct. . . ." These and other insights based upon long experience acquaint readers with Munchausen's ways of thinking.

Though Carswell is right when he notices Raspe's omission of physical descriptions of his storyteller, illustrators nevertheless eventually agreed pretty well about the baron's appearance. Probably this was because one artist's superb picturings that have been printed some sixty times since they came out in 1862—those of Gustave Doré—have set the fashion. Doré's likenesses as well as those of most subsequent limners are not greatly unlike the description of Raspe in the 1775 German warrant for his arrest for embezzlement—"of middle height, face long rather than round, small eyes, nose somewhat large, beady and pointed, red hair under a short tie wig, wearing a red coat with gold facings." The resemblance (though pretty surely this is a coincidence)[18] is appropriate because, as Carswell perceives, Raspe "may have . . . given away something of himself, the seedy failure, by creating Munchhausen, the fabulous success." Personal tragedy was transmuted into closely related comedy when Raspe supplanted his own overweening arrogance with the baron's patently overblown self-esteem, his own sordid dishonesty with the baron's playful and transparent exaggerations, and his own frustrating, disastrous failures with triumphant, comic successes. Raspe's fantasies, in other words, identify the creation with his creator but with refurbishings that make the old storyteller a sympathetic figure.

Similarly, the American authors of many renditions of our country's (and Raspe's) favorite tall tales empathize with highly individualized, likeable or even loveable fabricators, and the characterizations of the storytellers—the tellers, for a century and a half, of falsehoods, medium tall tales, and very tall tales—vie in interest and in appeal with the monologues unfolding the stories. Let us count a few of the most admired storytellers, listed roughly in the order of their appearances: T. C. Haliburton's Sam Slick, James Kirke Paulding's Nimrod Wildfire, *Crockett Almanack* makers' Davy Crockett, T. B. Thorpe's Jim Doggett, J. R. Lowell's Birdofredum Sawin, Ned Buntline's Jim Bridger, H. E. Taliaferro's Fisher's River storytellers, C. F. Browne's Artemus Ward, G. W. Harris's Sut Lovingood, J. C. Harris's Uncle Remus, A. H. Lewis's Old

Cattleman, Owen Wister's Trampas and the Virginian, E. N. West-cott's David Harum, O. Henry's Jeff Peters, Frank Bacon's Lightnin' Bill Jones, Don Marquis's Old Soak, W. C. Fields's Egbert Sousé, Ed Wynn's Fire Chief, H. L. Davis's Flem Simmons, Jack Pearl's Baron Munchausen, William Faulkner's V. K. Ratliff, Thomas Berger's Jack Crabb, and Richard Pryor's Oilwell.[19] Mark Twain created a goodly series of such story-tellers and made them memorable as characters: Simon Wheeler, Col. Sellers, Jim and Dick Baker, Corpse Maker and the Pet Child of Calam-ity, the King and the Duke, Huck Finn, Hank Morgan and the Paladin come to mind; and this list is only a partial one.

Now quite obviously anyone who hailed Raspe as the sole begetter of all these offspring would be perpetrating a stretcher, and I shan't do anything of the sort. But because of Raspe's priority, his creative literary skill, and the long-lasting popularity of his storyteller and that storyteller's tales, I believe that the German author deserves credit, if not for setting off this American chain reaction, at least for helping it along during a great many years.

For another thing, Raspe early found a way to do something quite a few American humorists would do—to surround his deadpan yarn-spinner with a very palpable, attentive, and appreciative audience.

The baron's remarks about the chase, the chaser, and the chased do something more than show zest for a pastime; they help evoke an attractive ambience—that of a genial entertainer with a receptive group of like enthusiasts drinking, taking its ease, and appreciatively listen-ing to him. As early as the title-page of the first edition, a dedication announces a book-length oral-storytelling session: "Humbly dedicated and recommended to Country Gentlemen; and, if they please, to be repeated as their own, after a hunt, at horse races, in watering-places, and other polite assemblies; round the bottle and fireside." The fore-words describing Munchausen's way of talking and praising his skill as a teacher help body forth not only a yarnspinner but also his amused listeners. And on one occasion after the baron retires, a third-person commentator tells about the group's response: "the company much diverted and in good spirits" one by one comment on "the extraordinary entertainment," and "a near relation" of Munchausen tells a smutty story in which the baron figures.

Every few pages, too, the baron's speeches remind readers of what is going on by having him directly address his listeners: "I shall not tire you Gentlemen with the politicks, arts, sciences and history...nor trouble you with the various intrigues...I shall confine myself...to the greater and nobler objects of your attention, to horses and dogs, of which I have always been as fond as you are, to foxes, wolves and bears....You have heard, I dare say, of the hunters and sportsman's saint and protector, Saint Hubert....But gentlemen, for all that; I was not always successful...."

Writing what Bret Harte called the "distinctly original and novel" American story—"orally transmitted . . . in bar-rooms, the gatherings in the 'country store,' and finally at public meetings," humorists often did what Raspe did to recreate the atmosphere of its telling, including a story-teller and a charmed audience. George Washington Harris for instance introduced a narrative: "By the light of a campfire, after a hunter's supper, enjoyed with a hunter's appetite," and others pictured yarnspinning sessions at political barbecues, on stagecoaches, in steamboat social halls, alongside cowboys' chuck-wagons, around dinner tables, and so forth. Like Raspe, humorous writers told of listeners' interruptions: "Where did all this happen?" "Sam, what do you suppose was in that pot?" "Allow me to interrupt you." "Is it possible?" And like Raspe, authors told about listeners' responses: "When the story was ended, our hero sat some minutes with his audience in a grave silence."[20]

Now of course, without ever reading *Munchausen's Narrative* or its sequels, our humorists could have encountered oral or written versions of the baron's tales told by others, and could have learned from others how to have a deadpan liar spin his yarns amusingly, and how to show him diverting a pleased and attentive audience.

But on the other hand, thanks to Raspe, especially during the early part of the nineteenth century but later as well, there is a good chance that a fair number of them made a valuable German connection.

Notes

1. Clarence Gohdes, *American Literature in Nineteenth-Century England* (New York: Columbia University Press, 1944), p. 57; Bret Harte, "The Rise of the 'Short Story,'" *Cornhill Magazine*, NS 7 (July 1899), 3; Will D. Howe, "Early Humorists," *Cambridge History of American Literature* (New York: Macmillan, 1918, 1936), II, 158; Max Eastman, *The Enjoyment of Laughter* (New York: Simon and Schuster, 1936), p. 90.

2. *A Dictionary of Americanisms*, ed. Mitford M. Mathews (Chicago: University of Chicago Press, 1951), p. 1701.

3. Ernest W. Baughman, *Type and Motif Index of the Folktales of England and North America* (The Hague: Mouton & Co., 1966), p. xvii. References to "Munchausen Tales" cited hereafter are on pp. 51–57, 407–09.

4. Gershon Legman, *The Horn Book* (New Hyde Park, N. Y.: University Books, 1966), p. 462.

5. Details concerning Raspe's biography here and throughout the present essay come from John Carswell, *The Prospector: Being the Life and Times of Rudolf Erich Raspe* (London: Cresset Press, 1950), as do the critical comments of Carswell cited. Bibliographical data concerning early editions of the *Narrative* and sequels are in *Singular Travels, Campaigns and Adventures of Baron Munchausen by Rudolf Erich Raspe and Others* (New York: Dover Publications, 1961); so are quoted passages from these eighteenth-century books. Two volumes containing extensive lists of editions and adaptations in several languages, and accounts

of sources and of the baron's growing fame, frequently drawn upon, are *Münchhaussen und Münchhausiaden*, ed. Werner R. Schweizer (Munich: Francke, 1969) and *Münchhausiana*, ed. Erwin Wackermann (Stuttgart: Eggert, 1969), the latter augmented by a *Supplement 1969–1978*, ed. Wackermann (Stuttgart: Eggert, 1978).

6. Edwin G. Gudde, "An American Version of Munchausen," *American Literature*, 13 (Jan., 1942), 372–390; Henry A. Pochman, *German Culture in America* (Madison: University of Wisconsin Press, 1957, 1961), pp. 327, 346, 677, and Wackermann's bibliography.

7. Otto Weinreich, *Antiphanes und Münchhausen* (Vienna and Leipzig: Holder-Pichler-Tempsky, 1942).

8. Stith Thompson, *Motif-Index of Folk-Literature* (Bloomington: Indiana University Press, 1955–1958), V, 404–08.

9. Harold Thompson, "Humor," in *Literary History of the United States* (New York: Macmillan, 1948, 1953), p. 728.

10. Leonard Roberts, *Old Greasybeard: Tales from the Cumberland Gap* (Detroit: Folklore Associates, 1969), pp. 165–66, 207. The same scholar's *South from Hell-fer Sartin: Kentucky Mountain Folk Tales* (Lexington: University of Kentucky Press, 1955) contains (pp. 144–47) versions of three other Munchausen Tales, with commentaries on other occurrences (pp. 162–63). Other variants, with valuable comments, will be found in the books of Ozark tales by Vance Randolph published between 1955 and 1976.

11. Letter received from Ernest Baughman, 14 October 1921. My thanks to Professor Baughman for many helpful suggestions.

12. Richard M. Dorson, *American Folklore* (Chicago: University of Chicago Press, 1959), pp. 14, 44, 57, 200–01, 227. Professor Dorson notices that many American exaggerations "depend upon stock fictions current throughout the country, which they adopt as authentic personal experiences [in] the manner of the most redoubtable truth twister, Baron Munchausen . . . whose solemn faced *Narrative* . . . made his name synonymous for gorgeous fabrications."

13. Baughman, p. 54.

14. Norris Wilson Yates, *William T. Porter and "The Spirit of the Times"* (Baton Rouge: Louisiana State University Press, 1957), p. 173.

15. Yates, p. 174.

16. Here I can make a modest footnote contribution. In 1911, aged eleven, I first heard a tall tale told. My uncle John W. Merritt told it beside a campfire on the shore of Lake Coeur d'Alene, Idaho—the first one in Raspe's *Narrative*, about the man halted by a bad snowstorm who tied his horse to a "pointed stump," lay down in the snow and slept through a thaw. When he awoke, he saw his horse tied to a weathercock on a steeple, and had to shoot him down. My uncle had heard it told without any recognition of a printed source. Oral tellings, one as recently as 1965, have been recorded by folklorists. In some, sand which has replaced the snow was blown away during the night.

17. Carswell, *The Prospector*, p. 189.

18. A slight possibility is that the artist who drew the frontispiece portrait of the baron for the 1792 edition of the sequel had seen Raspe and pictured him, and that Doré saw this likeness.

19. Most of these are discussed in Walter Blair, "A Man's Voice Speaking: A Continuum in American Humor," *Veins of Humor*, ed. Harry Levin (Cambridge: Harvard University Press, 1972), pp. 185–204, and Walter Blair and Hamlin Hill, *America's Humor: From Poor Richard to Doonesbury* (New York: Oxford Univer-

sity Press, 1978). These treat ways storytellers emphasize relationships with listeners.

20. Bret Harte, "The Rise of the 'Short Story' "; George Washington Harris, "Sut Lovingood Sets Up With a Gal," *Knoxville Press and Messenger*, 29 Sept. 1869; T. B. Thorpe, "The Big Bear of Arkansas" [1841] in *Native American Humor*, ed. Walter Blair (San Francisco: Chandler Publishing Co., 1960), p. 348. The last of these cites other instances, pp. 90–92. Professor Baughman summarized in a letter of 31 May 1983: "Because the Munchausen tales must have served as sources for many tellers in this country, their style probably had its effects also: what I call the yarning style—first person narrator, deliberate manner of telling (poker-face), digression, insistence on veracity, etc."

Colonial Humor:
Beginning with the Butt   Robert Micklus*

The two indispensable works on American literary humor, Constance Rourke's *American Humor* and Walter Blair's *Native American Humor*, have promoted a common bias about colonial humor implicit in their titles: for a humorous work to deserve much attention, it needs to possess certain "American" qualities. This obviously excludes most colonial humor. Rourke, in fact, snubbed colonial humor completely in her book, warning us against the "beguiling pedantry"[1] of digging up pre-Jacksonian texts and making greater claims for them than they deserve. No one knows more about American humor than Blair, so when he tells us that there really was no American humor prior to the Revolution because colonial authors were not able before then to recognize "the comic possibilities of the American scene and American character, and the development of a fictional technique which would reveal them,"[2] we can bet our houses that he is right. It is aggravating, though, to hear someone saying thirty years after Rourke and Blair that "too much is made of our earliest humor,... [which is] indecisive and confused, *highly derivative* and labored, severely topical, and otherwise inexpert"[3] —aggravating not because loyal colonialists like me cannot stomach such stuff, but because we can see the old bias still sneaking in: colonial humor is not bad because it is bad; it is bad because it is not "American."

We might as well surrender: colonial humor is not "American," and it is possible to make too much of it by insisting on its "Americanness." But I have trouble understanding why we make such a fuss about its Americanness in the first place, and why we cannot accept it and appreciate it for what it is—*colonial* humor. Once we do, perhaps we will be able to get beyond treating it as though it were merely a building block

*This essay was written specifically for publication in this volume and is included here by permission of the author.

in the development of American humor, beyond making the standard remarks about the dearth of New England humor and the wealth of Southern humor and discussing them as though they existed in different hemispheres, and start focusing our attention on what makes colonial humor colonial humor. In a rudimentary way, this essay attempts to take a step in that direction by addressing the primary question in any study of colonial humor: what did our earliest humorists, north and south, laugh at? Throughout the colonies, there was a sort of unspoken agreement that the butt of the joke always had to be "out there" among the British, the Indians, or, perhaps, some country bumpkin, but, before Franklin's time, rarely was it the author himself or even his persona. Obvious as that answer might seem, no point about colonial humor deserves more attention, for nothing aids us more in interpreting the tone and meaning of our earliest humorous works, and nothing reveals more about the level of sophistication of early American—rather, colonial —comic literature.

The Simple Cobler of Aggawam in America is early New England's most intriguing humorous work, not simply because of its delightful wordplay, but because it entices us into questioning the credibility of its speaker. It is indeed tempting to write an essay demonstrating that the ultimate butt of Ward's humor is the cobbler—and, by implication, Ward—himself, the guardian of truth who frequently takes us on the most circuitous path toward truth imaginable. Although de la Guard pronounces from beginning to end of his treatise that his humble mission is to promote the simple truth, he repeatedly obscures the truth behind his odd vocabulary, confusing syntax, and mazy reasoning. Surely anyone who has read The Simple Cobler has been at least a bit puzzled by de la Guard's "excessive fondness for antitheses; [his] untempered enjoyment of quirks and turns and petty freaks of phraseology; . . . [his] blurring of its sentences with great daubs and patches of Latin quotation; [and his] employment of outlandish and uncouth words belonging to no language at all, sometimes huddled together into combinations that defy syntax."[4] If the truth is so plain and simple, one wonders, why does the cobbler chronically toy with it and embellish it? "Not to tolerate things meerly indifferent to weak consciences," he says during one of his more lucid moments, "argues a conscience too strong: pressed uniformity in these, causes much disunity: To tolerate more then indifferents, is not to deale indifferently with God?"[5] It is amusing to follow de la Guard through these twists and turns, but surely he could find a simpler way of expressing the truths he is after.

It is not just his penchant to manipulate the truth, however, that makes it difficult to accept the cobbler as a reliable mender of souls. From the outset of his harangue, it is hard to view him as a prophet of truth when his opening remarks seem so blatantly to introduce us to a *mock*-jeremiad of the degenerate times; to trust him when he insists that he "speak[s] seriously, according to [his] meaning," then immediately babbles out something about how "the whole conclave of Hell can so compromise, exadverse, and diametricall contradictions, as to compolitize such a multimonstrous maufrey of heteroclytes and quicquidlibets quietly" (pp. 22–23; cf. p. 29); or to take him at all seriously when he directs us down the road to truth by arguing that

> The wisest way, when all is said, is with all humility and feare, to take Christ as himselfe hath revealed himselfe in the Gospel, and not as the Devill presents him to prestigiated fansies. I have ever hated the way of the Rosie-Crucians, who reject things as Gods wisedome hath tempered them, and will have nothing but their Spirits. If I were to give physick to Spryts, I would do so too: but when I want Physick for my body, I would not have my soule tartared: nor my Animall Spirits purged any way, but by my Naturall, and those by my bodily humours, and those by such Ordinaries, as have the nearest vicinage to them, and not by Metaphysicall Limbeckings. I cannot thinke that *materia prima* or *secunda*, should bee good for me, that am at least, *Materia millessima sexcentesima quadragesima quinta.* (pp. 19–20)

What should we make of a speaker who begins a paragraph by instructing us to follow Christ as our example, then degenerates into a discussion on how to rid the body of waste, and finally ends up with some nonsense about the 1645th order? Simply put, how can we accept as truth a treatise so full of artifice, and how can we accept as guardian of truth a speaker who continually undercuts his own truths at every turn?

Ward's most perceptive readers, Robert D. Arner and P. M. Zall, have helped to address, yet not put to rest, these and similar questions. In what is still the best essay on *The Simple Cobler*, Arner suggests that the obstacles cluttering the cobbler's rhetorical pathway to truth are in keeping with "the appropriate style for satire, . . . [which] was necessarily obscure."[6] Along somewhat different lines, Zall argues that the sometimes bewildering language and reasoning in *The Simple Cobler* are in keeping with the tradition developed by Democritus of Abdera, "the laughing philosopher," and other Greek Cynics who were "sometimes criticized for mixing serious subjects and humorous tone," and whose "strategy was to assume roles as eccentric preachers . . . carrying their message to common farmers and fishermen in language they could understand."[7] Satire, no doubt, is often purposefully obscure; and Democritus laughed his way well into the eighteenth century in the works of many colonial authors. Still, it is tempting to argue that by placing de la Guard in one tradition or another we have perhaps gone out of our way to account for his sometimes confusing prose and purpose. When the cobbler says, "It is a most toylsome taske to run the wild-goose chase after a well-breath'd Opinionist: they delight in vitilitigation: it is an itch that loves . . . to be scrub'd: they desire not satisfaction, but satis-diction" (p. 17), perhaps Ward is suggesting that anyone who seeks the truth from this man who delights in "satisdiction" will be engaged in a fool's errand, and that the arch-Opinionist in the treatise—and con-sequently the arch-fool—is the cobbler himself.[8] Perhaps he means to imply that de la Guard is "simple" not in the sense that all students of American humor like to interpret that word—plain, unlettered, unaf-fected (he is actually none of these)—but "simple" in the sense that he is foolish and, indeed, idiotic.[9]

If only it were so. Our earliest humorous literature cries out for an author who had the sophistication and the security to create an idiot in his own image, and it is tempting to offer Ward as a candidate for that honor. But to do so would be to misconstrue Ward's purpose in writing *The Simple Cobler* and to misinterpret the role de la Guard plays. As Jean F. Beranger points out, "Behind the mask of Theodore de la Guard we cannot help noticing the face of Nathaniel Ward. The man needed to get rid of his obsessions. He was deeply involved in the political and religious history of the Bay Colony. . . . And precisely because he was so much involved, he could not simply write a pamphlet, a bitter satire upon the times. He needed the sort of protection as well as liberation which a comic discourse could provide."[10] Ward's religious and politi-cal life in England, America, and then again in England shows that he took quite seriously many of the complaints that the cobbler humor-ously voices against the Church and State. Fortunately for us, though, Ward had the good sense to realize that his misguided countrymen would be more likely to mend their souls if instructed by a comic cob-bler than by a pouty preacher. So he hid behind a comic mask. More than that, he created a persona who hides behind his own mask by playing the fool. The cobbler is no simpleton; he plays the fool so that he can not only chastise his audience with impunity but also exhibit his scorn for his foolish readers, who he supposes "are uncapable of grave and rationall arguments" (p. 29). He speaks to his readers on their level—as a fool—because, he implies, they are too ignorant to under-stand him otherwise, and by masquerading as a fool and pulling one gag after another from his rhetorical fool's cap he continually reminds them of their ignorance of the truth.[11]

The Simple Cobler, then, is more than just a humorous treatise on the virtues of intoleration. It is a rhetorical truth hunt. The full brunt of Ward's humor is directed not merely against false enthusiasts, af-fected women, or his deluded king, but against the reader who cannot see that the cobbler is only playing the fool and who cannot sort the truth from the foolishness. From beginning to end, the butt of Ward's humor is not himself, not even the cobbler; it is always out there among all the "phrantasticks" who think "they have discovered the Nor-west passage to Heaven" (p. 20), all the ladies who parade about like "ill-shapen-shotten-shell-fish" (p. 26), the king who has "take[n] up the Manufacture of cutting [his] Subjects throats" (p. 51), and any ignoramus who fails to smoke the truths beneath his jests.

Like the cobbler, Thomas Morton expertly plays the fool in the *New English Canaan* only to expose the foolishness of those around him. Unfortunately, the frequently anthologized Merry Mount selections encourage the notion that Morton regarded himself as little more than a practical joker, and that he wrote his narrative to poke fun not only at the Separatists but at himself. But the first two books of the *New English Canaan,* in which Morton soberly records the customs of the natives and the features of the land, show that he considered his position in the New World and his role as its historian no laughing matter. In these sections Morton rather humorlessly presents himself as a man at home in his adopted country and genuinely appreciative of its natural abundance. In the third book, however, his role and the tone of his narrative radically shift as he "puts on an antic disposition and becomes the outcast jester, fool, or satirist whose apparent madness is his best protection from persecution"[12] as well as a reflection of the disruptive forces at work in the New World. Into the edenic world of the first two books have entered the Separatists, whose name alone implies their disruptive nature, and whose social and religious laws have disturbed the natural order of things. In a land ridden with fools, Morton, like the simple cobbler, merely plays the fool to address the lunacy he sees threatening his sense of order. Especially in the Merry Mount episodes he makes it clear that he is only donning a mask. Lest the reader miss the jest by failing to see that the real man of culture and virtue is "mine Host" and the real "salvages" are the Separatists who treat our gracious host so monstrously, Morton sprinkles his narrative with asides to let us know that he is a fool only in the eyes of the beholders. The Separatists were extremely delighted, he says at one point, that they had captured their "capitall enemy (as they concluded him)"; or, in another instance, he writes that the "nine worthies" stopped before "the Denne of this supposed Monster (this seaven headed hydra, as they termed him)."[13] Rather than allow the comic situation he has created to speak for itself, Morton feels obliged to remind us that he is not, after all, the butt of the joke. All the monsters, all the fools, are out there.

The straight man of books one and two, therefore, makes it apparent that the narrator of book three is only playing the fool, and that Morton's ridicule in book three is directed not against the supposed clown running the revels but against the clowns tampering with the natural order of things in the New World. Once set in motion, the outward thrust of Morton's satiric jibes against the clownish Separatists becomes more and more pronounced as book three progresses. In the early chapters of book three the tone is relatively light, appropriately culminating with the sections on "Master Bubble," the ignorant, long-winded, incompetent go-between appointed by the "Brethren" to deal with the natives. By the middle chapters of the Merry Mount escapade the tone of Morton's humor begins to darken. However ridiculous "Captaine Shrimpe" and his bunch might be, there is something rather humorless about their falling upon Morton "as if they would have eaten him: some of them were so violent," Morton reports, "that they would have a slice with scabbert, and all for haste; untill an old Souldier . . . that was there by accident, clapt his gunne under the weapons, and sharply rebuked these worthies for their unworthy practises" (p. 287). The exaggeration and punning keep us from ever fearing for Morton's life, but the stakes have gotten higher than the plight of Master Bubble. And by the time Morton relates the misfortunes of "Innocence Fairecloath" his early mockery of the Separatists has turned into invective. For claiming that "the Divell was the setter of their Church," Faircloath is brutally whipped until his back looks "like the picture of Rawhead and blowdy bones, and his shirte like a pudding wifes aperon" (pp. 318, 320). "Loe," Morton bitterly moralizes, "this is the payment you shall get, if you be one of them they terme, without" (p. 320).

The greatest irony in the *New English Canaan*, of course, is that the Separatists, not Morton, are the ones who exist "without" the natural laws and customs of the New World. Although the Separatists regard him as a savage, Morton is no more a renegade than any good satirist. As the first two books demonstrate, Morton and the Indians follow the norm; the Separatists are the renegades in the new land, and, like any good satirist, Morton directs his ridicule against those who are violating the established norms. We expect that. But we also expect any good satirist to let his satire speak for itself rather than constantly remind us that its central character is only a fool in someone else's eyes. Ward, at least, allowed us to figure out for ourselves that his fool is no fool; Morton was too afraid that the joke might fall on his own head to take any chances.

Other New England humorists found it as difficult as Ward and Morton to laugh at themselves. Even among the writers who kept travel journals—a more private form of writing in which we might expect a greater degree of self-humor—only Sarah Kemble Knight found much time to laugh at herself.[14] Although she sometimes resorts to a humorous scapegoat when she finds herself in an awkward predicament,[15] Knight often manages to poke fun at her own naiveté. Having to cross a river by canoe, for instance, she observes that it was "very small and shallow, so that when we were in she seem'd redy to take in water, which greatly terrified mee, and caused me to be very circumspect, sitting with my hands fast on each side, my eyes stedy, not daring so much as to lodg my tongue a hair's breadth more on one side of my mouth then tother" (p. 9). Knight's ability to depict a greenhorn in an awkward situation such as this is nothing unusual in colonial literature; what is unusual this early on, however, is that she does not mind allowing that the greenhorn is herself.

More typically, though, Knight projects her humor outward at the uncouth rustics and crude conditions she encounters. Like Ward and Morton, but without playing the fool,[16] Knight repeatedly expresses her scorn for those who do not meet her standards of propriety. She establishes herself as a barometer of decorum on the first day of her narrative when she reports her interrogation by the innkeeper's inquisitive daughter: "I told her shee treated me very Rudely," she says, "and I did not think it my duty to answer her unmannerly Questions" (p. 6). Knight's inquisitive rustic is not only nosey but annoyingly pretentious: "Perhaps to gain the more respect," she appears before Madame Knight wearing her finest jewelry; "But her Granam's new Rung sow," Knight observes, "had it appeared would have affected me as much" (p. 7). Similarly, as if her portrayal of the rustics "Bumpkin Simpers" and "Jone Tawdry" is not unflattering enough, Knight ends it with a heavy-handed moral about "the great necessity and bennifitt both of Education and Conversation; for these people have as Large a portion of mother witt, and sometimes the Larger, than those who have bin brought up in Citties; But for want of emprovements, Render themselves almost Ridiculos" (pp. 43–44). Despite her good intentions, the only thing that keeps remarks like these from appearing condescending to today's readers is the fact that Knight sometimes had the good grace to laugh at herself, too.

Most colonial humorists were less gracious than Knight about laughing at themselves, especially in the South. The reasons why humor was more plentiful in the cavalier South than in Puritan New England have been discussed so often that it is needless to rehash them here.[17] The point I wish to stress is that even though it is true that wit flourished more in the South than in the North, in one important respect attitudes about humor were very similar in both regions. Regardless of their region or religion, all colonial humorists enjoyed a good joke—as long as they were playing it on someone else. Southerners simply seem to have enjoyed it more. Like Knight, William Byrd employs humor in the *History of the Dividing Line Betwixt Virginia and North Carolina* to cope with the many uncouth shapes and situations he encounters. But whereas Knight sometimes manages to relieve her anxieties by laughing at her own foolishness, Byrd habitually seeks comic relief by directing his abuse at others. His entry for October 31 is a typical case in point. After admitting that he found "Miry Creek" "an uncomfortable place to lodge in,"[18] Byrd reports that

> Our hunters killed a large doe and two bears, which made all other misfortunes easy. Certainly no Tartar ever loved horseflesh or Hot-

tentot guts and garbage better than woodsmen do bear. The truth of it is, it may be proper food perhaps for such as work or ride it off, but, with our chaplain's leave, . . . I think it not a very proper diet for saints, because 'tis apt to make them a little too rampant. And, now, for the good of mankind . . . I will venture to publish a secret of importance which our Indian disclosed to me. I asked him the reason why few or none of his countrywomen were barren. To which curious question he answered, with a broad grin upon his face, they had an infallible secret for that. . . . [H]e informed me that if any Indian woman did not prove with child at a decent time after marriage, the husband, to save his reputation with the women, forthwith entered into a bear diet for six weeks, which in that time makes him so vigorous that he grows exceedingly impertinent to his poor wife, and 'tis great odds but he makes her a mother in nine months. (pp. 277–78)

Rather than display his anxiety by mocking his own discomfort, Byrd fidgets about for someone else to laugh at, mocking first the crude backwoodsmen, then the intemperate clergy, and finally the barbarous heathens. In passages such as this, Byrd usually appears in perfect control of his scorn, whimsically bouncing his wit from one butt to another, but, as Donald T. Siebert, Jr., points out, beneath the "controlled contempt" in the *History of the Dividing Line*—indeed, because of it—"Byrd's wit [often] fails to give the impression of naturalness and ease. It lacks the warmth, the lightness of touch, the self-humor which truly disinterested, playful writers of burlesque convey. . . . Byrd's is severe, relentless, . . . and at times rather heartless and cold."[19] Byrd's response to the commissioners from North Carolina in *The Secret History of the Line* serves almost as a veiled confession of his general inability to mask his disdain for those who vex him: "For my part," he says, "I was not courtier enough to disguise the sentiments I had of them and their slavish proceeding and therefore could not smile upon those I despised" (pp. 94–95). Although Byrd often manages to mask his scorn behind his casual gentlemanly wit, equally as often he is not dissembler enough to wear a smile, and his scorn frequently breaks forth undisguised in *The Secret History*, where he annihilates his enemies with ridicule, and in the *History of the Dividing Line*, where,—as his famous attack against the "Lubberlanders" attests—he "usually manages to devastate his enemies with satire."[20]

Byrd's contempt for the swinish common folk of Lubberland is surpassed only by Robert Bolling's contempt for the swinish gentlefolk of Virginia in "Neanthe," a bawdy "heroitragicomic tale"[21] about the struggle between the noble Dolon, son of a bullfrog salesman, and the equally distinguished Euphenor, son of a plunderer, for the hand of the eminent Neanthe, illegitimate daughter of a maidservant. Of all the genteel ladies in the land, Neanthe is the fairest of the fair:

Her Hair, whose Color rivall'd Jett,
(With her own Bear's Oil dripping wet)
So matted hung her Face upon,
That, as to Forehead, she had none.

 .   .   .   .

Her Mouth, from Ear to Ear display'd,
Discovered every Tooth, she had:
And they were polish'd, white and strong,
As Juniper's, and quite as long.
Upon her Lip a reverend Beard,
That claimd the Barber's Aid, appear'd . . .
A vast Profusion! but her Chin
A noble Tuft was smother'd in.   (ll. 83–102)

As if that is not enough to bewitch any doting young lover,

One Quality Neanthe had,
Which almost ran her Lovers mad.
A most divine and powerful Scent
She scattered round, where e'er she went,
Which, smelt by them, gave such keen Twitches,
They scarce containd them in their Breeches. (ll. 117–22)

As J. A. Leo Lemay suggests, Neanthe is perhaps "the worst slut . . . in American literature,"[22] and Bolling's assault against her and her suitors, who, among other indications of their fine breeding, vie for her affection by ejaculating at the moon and setting off rockets from their anuses, is relentless. No other pre-Revolutionary work makes it more apparent than "Neanthe" that the colonial humorist lives in a world of ignorant clods—excepting, of course, the humorist himself.

The frequency with which colonial authors direct their humor outward against a world of fools has perhaps contributed to problems in interpreting Ebenezer Cooke's *The Sot-Weed Factor*. We become so conditioned by authors who castigate their audiences either directly or through their personas that it is easy to assume, as one critic has, that the factor voices Cooke's opinions, and that Cooke's satire is aimed at the people and manners of Maryland.[23] But Cooke's satire is aimed—I think exclusively—at the character he draws our attention to in the title. Like other colonial humorists, Cooke directs his satire outward—but with a refreshing twist. Whereas other humorists such as Ward and Morton create personas who play the fool to rail against a foolish world, Cooke creates a persona whose railing accentuates his own foolishness.

Probably the best place to begin in interpreting *The Sot-Weed Factor* is the curse that concludes the original version. In discussing the poem as a "double-edged satire,"[24] critics have pointed to the promotional literature, such as George Alsop's *A Character of the Province of*

Mary-land, that might have led the factor astray. To be sure, much promotional literature was misleading, and much of it would have warranted a hearty curse from disappointed travelers. But be that as it may, it seems to me more pertinent that we ask ourselves what internal evidence there is in the poem to substantiate the factor's claims. By focusing upon the discrepancy between the factor's expectations of America and his disillusionment at what he finds,[25] we have overlooked the fact that the indictments he levels against Maryland, calling it "This Cruel, this Inhospitable Shoar, . . . Where no Man's Faithful, nor a Woman Chast,"[26] are all disproven by his own testimony. Aside from losing some useless accoutrements to a thief in the night (useless in Maryland) and being hustled by a Quaker that he is trying to hustle and a quack lawyer that he employs to do his dirty work, the factor is treated more hospitably than he probably deserves. The first "surley Peasant" (l. 84) he meets takes one look at him and assumes he is running away from something, which he is (probably from debt), but, after being reprimanded by the factor, who indignantly "lugg'd out [his] Sword; / Swearing [he] was no Fugitive" (ll. 87–88), the young man humbly apologizes and offers to take him home. The boy's father also wonders whether the factor might not be on the loose but nevertheless gives him free food and lodging. After his first frantic evening in the orchard, where he is his own worst enemy, the factor returns to have breakfast with the planter, then remarks,

> I took my leave of Host so kind;
> Who to oblige me, did provide,
> His eldest Son to be my Guide,
> And lent me Horses of his own,
> A skittish Colt, an aged Rhoan. (ll. 246–50)

The horses might not be much alongside English thoroughbreds, but, like everything else the planter provides the factor, they are free. The planter's son, moreover, proves to be a boon companion, discoursing with the factor like any romantic hero's sidekick, and a faithful one, too, until he sensibly goes off to track down his horse. Left alone, the factor falls in with another kind soul who takes him home and treats him to a sumptuous dinner. All in all, the factor has not fared too badly—until he starts wheeling and dealing.

The factor's second accusation, that Maryland is a land of unchaste women, is nothing but a bad case of sour grapes. During his third night in Maryland, the factor goes to bed drunk and wakes up in a haze before stumbling upon some women playing cards. At first he imagines they are witches, then Indians, and finally prostitutes. He is likely mistaken on all counts, and the last suggestion especially is probably just wishful thinking, for the factor is a lecherous man. Earlier in his narrative, while again in a fog (this time from tobacco fumes) so that he "scarce could find [his] way to Bed" (l. 146), he tries to corner a chambermaid who has gone through bad times: "I prest her to declare her Name," he says; "She Blushing, seem'd to hide her Eyes" (ll. 152–53). The poor girl is genuinely embarrassed, since the sotted factor is literally pressing against her. When he supposes she is really nothing but a whore, she instinctively recoils from him: "Quick as [his] Thoughts, the Slave was fled" (l. 174). Throughout his account, too, the factor sneaks in lecherous asides whenever possible. While watching the planter pack his pipe with tobacco, he remarks that this "Indian Gun" is "scarce longer than ones Finger, / Or that for which the Ladies linger" (ll. 123–25); while describing the noble savage he encounters, he cannot help pointing out that "Thus naked Pict in Battel faught, / Or undisguis'd his Mistress sought; / And knowing well his Ware was good, / Refus'd to screen it with a Hood" (ll. 275–78); while debating the first settlement of America, he litters his analysis with sexual innuendoes, talking about how "a Chinese Host, / Might penetrate this Indian Coast" (ll. 342–43) and how "Phoenicians old, / Discover'd first with Vessels bold" (ll. 350–51), before saying outright that the Phoenicians returned regularly with "Lasses kind, / To comfort those were left behind" (ll. 354–55); and even while berating his quack lawyer in the midst of his fury at the end of the poem, he compares the scoundrel to a "Maid upon the downy Field" who "Pretends a Force, and Fights to yeild" (ll. 690–91). If only some kind lass would come along and relieve the poor factor's sexual frustration, he might have a lot less to say about the unchaste women in Maryland.

His being a lecher is just one of several characteristics that destroy the factor's credibility. He has a terrible persecution complex, regularly informing us that he is cursed, plagued, and besieged by fortune and fate; he is an ignorant greenhorn who, by his own account, has come to America on a ship "Freighted with Fools" (l. 10), and who, among other examples of his prowess, crosses a river standing up in a canoe and spends a night in a tree being tormented by mosquitoes; and he is a miserable coward who is put into "a pannick Fright" (l. 73) when he mistakes cattle for wolves or when he supposes a peaceful Indian is after his scalp. Of course, he behaves with uncommon valor when a flock of geese enter his room: "Raging I jump'd upon the Floor," he boasts, "And like a Drunken Saylor Swore; / With Sword I fiercely laid about, / And soon dispers'd the Feather'd Rout" (ll. 194–97); or when he seeks vengeance after learning that his hat, wig, and stockings are missing:

> Vext at the Loss of Goods and Chattel,
> I swore I'd give the Rascal battel,
> Who had abus'd me in this sort,

> And Merchant Stranger made his Sport.
> I furiously descended Ladder;
> No Hare in March was ever madder. (ll. 448–53)

What a commanding figure this factor is, especially since he is perpetually sotted in one form or another. How appropriate that the man who sells the sot-weed is habitually in a stupor, and that the incidents he relates occur to him once while he is reeling from tobacco fumes, twice while he is drunk, and once while he is recovering from a fever. His presence virtually commands us to ignore him.

The sot-weed factor is an incompetent ass, not because he has been reading too much promotional literature, but because he simply does not have the mettle it takes to survive in the world of "Battle-Town." During his first day in Battle-Town, he witnesses two lawyers wrangling, "strongly bent, / In Blows to end the Argument" (ll. 397–98), while all the interested parties "fight like earth-born Gyants" (l. 408). When the court adjourns "In Battle Blood, and fractious Clamour" (l. 415), the factor retreats to an inn, but there again he finds planters "fighting and contending" (l. 424). Rather than join the battle as his guide does, he slips off to a corn-loft, "Glad that I might in quiet sleep," he observes, "And there my bones unfractur'd keep. / I lay'd me down secure from Fray, / And soundly snoar'd till break of Day" (ll. 440–43). All that Cooke really seems to be saying here and throughout the poem is that life is a constant struggle in Maryland, and anyone who comes to its shores unwilling to fight had better stay at home—or find a nice, quiet corn-loft. The factor's refusal to roll up his sleeves and join the fray leads us only to relish his getting swindled and to scorn his contempt.

In effect, the sot-weed factor is a classic example of what Robert C. Elliott calls "the satirist satirized,"[27] and as such he signals an increased sophistication in colonial humor. But it was not until nearly fifty years later that another Marylander, Dr. Alexander Hamilton, realized the potential of self-humor in "The History of the Tuesday Club."[28] In "The History" Hamilton mocks just about everyone and everything he can think of, but he especially enjoys mocking his own circle of friends, the members of the Tuesday Club. Such distinguished Marylanders as Jonas Green, Thomas Bacon, and Alexander Malcolm appear in "The History" under the names of "Jonathan Grog," "Signior Lardini," and "Philo Dogmaticus" as the targets of Hamilton's humor. The greatest butt of Hamilton's wit, however, is the character who plays his own role as club secretary and orator, "Loquacious Scribble," a mischievous, conniving rabble-rouser who will stop at nothing to advance himself in the club or, if frustrated, to raise a commotion among the members. In his constant pursuit of self-aggrandizement, Scribble delivers numerous bombastic speeches to the club "under pretence of checking the grouth of Luxury, and arbitrary power in the Club" (I, 192), and by the time he delivers his ninth anniversary speech he has become a parody of himself. Lamenting the "great decline and falling away, of the wonted Glory and magnificence of this here Club," he contends that

> Luxury has in a great measure got footing in this here ancient and honorable Club; Luxury, in the opinion of all wise men has been the bane and ruin of States and nations, and therefore must at last be the ruin of Clubs, where it has been admitted; are there not long standing members here present who have seen, the primitive times of this here ancient and honorable Club, did they not in alittle time see an end to that virtuous and heroic frugality, that prevailed in it, at its first Institution, have they not seen Luxury, peeping from behind the Scene, and preparing for her pompous entry upon this Clubical Stage, have they not seen this bold actress, take one great Stride at her first advance, and proceed afterwards, with a *grand pas*, to expell Simplicity and plainness from the Club, and introduce pomp, Show, and extravagance, her constant pages and attendants, while [Ceremony], her Companion and Coactor, with the like buskined pride, playd the part of a Momus or mimic, . . . introducing certain fantastical punctillios, forms and modes, by which, he has so disguised and intoxicated the behaviour and manners, of the L[ong] St[anding] memb[rs] . . . that they now seem not to be the same persons that they were at their first Institution.
>
> Happy, thrice happy, in those heroic times of Innocence & Simplicity, were the Long standing members of this here anc[t] & hon[ble]: Club, for then, without molestation, . . . they might rise up, go to the Side board, & after having taken their Sliver of Gammon or Slice of Cheese, standing, return again to their Compotation, Jocosity or Clubical Conversation; how charming, how regular, and how like the simple frugality of the Golden age was this and how different from the present luxury, and profuseness that prevails in most Clubs. . . .
>
> In fine, honorable Sir, and Gentlemen, I have presumed to lay all those matters before you, that you may have a clear view of the present deplorable State of this here ancient and honorable Club, and the ruin that threatens it, if proper means are not used to prevent it, therefore, you will remain without excuse if you do not . . . reinstate the Club in its ancient simple constitution . . . (III, 355–57, 364).

Scribble's speech fills fourteen manuscript pages. Those club members who have endured his harangue without dozing off are simply annoyed that he would cast a pall over such a joyous occasion as their anniversary with his gloomy babbling.

Hamilton's ability to mock himself shows how far colonial humor had come since the days of Morton and Ward. With the exception of *The Sot-Weed Factor*, most colonial humor seems immature today, not because it borrows from British conventions or is in some other way "un-American," but because it is so defensive. Living in insecure times, our earliest humorists were understandably too insecure to enjoy any other than an infrequent laugh at their own expense. By laughing at the manners and beliefs of those who did not meet their standards, they were perhaps able to convince themselves that all was right in their own private worlds or, at least, in their own minds. Consequently, we can almost predict that a colonial humorist will strike a superior pose and that he will ridicule the people and customs that run counter to his own way of life. That, of course, is the traditional pose of any satirist, and many of the works discussed above do contain satiric passages. But few of them can in any strict sense be called satires, and few of our earliest humorists, I am sure, consciously thought of themselves as satirists. What I have tried to stress in this essay, therefore, is not so much the tendency among colonial humorists to express themselves in the lowest forms of satire—ridicule and invective, which they did—but the pervasive attitude among all our earliest humorists—satirists or not—to locate the butt of their ridicule anywhere but in their own mirrors. Robert C. Elliott's remark that "it is a measure of the greatest satirists (perhaps the greatest men) that they recognize their own involvement in the folly of human life"[29] can be applied to great humorists in general. A piece such as *Androboros* makes such tedious reading today not because it lacks the basic ingredients of "American" humor, but because it is so obvious and its author seems so determined to make fools of everyone but himself. In *The Sot-Weed Factor* and "The History of the Tuesday Club," however, our more sophisticated humorists began to turn the joke upon their personas and, finally, upon themselves. If authors such as Hamilton and, later, his friend Franklin learned the art of self-humor by reading such British authors as Addison, Fielding, Gay, and Swift, then we should be grateful rather than lament the fact that colonial humorists borrowed from the British. Their borrowings might have been a small step for "American" humor, but they were a giant step for colonial humor. And, I suspect, for American humor, too.

Notes

1. *American Humor: A Study of National Character* (New York: Harcourt, Brace & Co., 1931), p. ix.

2. *Native American Humor (1800–1900)* (New York: American Book Co., 1937), p. 10.

3. Jesse Bier, *The Rise and Fall of American Humor* (New York: Holt, Rinehart & Winston, 1968), p. 32 (my italics).

4. Moses Coit Tyler, *A History of American Literature* (1878; rpt. New York: G. P. Putnam, 1897), I, 238.

5. Nathaniel Ward, *The Simple Cobler of Aggawam in America*, ed. P. M. Zall (Lincoln: Univ. of Nebraska Press, 1969), p. 8. Subsequent page references to this edition are provided in parentheses.

6. *"The Simple Cobler of Aggawam*: Nathaniel Ward and the Rhetoric of Satire," *Early American Literature*, 5 (1971), 14.

7. Introduction, *The Simple Cobler of Aggawam in America*, p. xv.

8. The cobbler adds to our suspicions when, only two pages later, he warns us to "have an extraordinary care also of the late Theosophers [followers of the German mystic—and cobbler—Jacob Boehme], that teach men to climbe to heaven upon a ladder of lying figments" (p. 19).

9. The cobbler himself plays upon both meanings of the word (see, e.g., pp. 56 and 31).

10. "Voices of Humor in Nathaniel Ward," *Studies in American Humor*, 2 (1975), 98.

11. The cobbler's awareness of his role as fool surfaces throughout the treatise, but see esp. the poem on p. 25 and the first of his "errata" on p. 72.

12. Robert D. Arner, "Pastoral Celebration and Satire in Thomas Morton's 'New English Canaan,'" *Criticism*, 16 (1974), 224.

13. Thomas Morton, *New English Canaan*, ed. Charles Francis Adams, Jr. (1883; rpt. New York: Burt Franklin, 1967), pp. 284, 287. Subsequent page references to this edition are provided in parentheses.

14. Two examples of the earnestness with which colonial authors recorded adventures similar to Knight's are the *Journals of Charles Beatty, 1762–1769*, ed. Guy Soulliard Klett (Univ. Park: Penn State Univ. Press, 1962), and the "Journal of James Kenny, 1761–1763," ed. John W. Jordan, *Pennsylvania Magazine of History and Biography*, 37 (1913), 1–47, 152–201.

15. See, e.g., the entry for October 5th, where Knight reports that after she and her party boarded the New London ferry "our Horses capper'd at a very surprizing Rate, and set us all in a fright; especially poor Jemima, who desired her father to say so jack to the Jade, to make her stand.... She Rored out in a Passionate manner: Pray suth father, Are you deaf? Say so Jack to the Jade, I tell you. The Dutiful Parent obey's; saying so Jack, so Jack, as gravely as if hee'd bin to saying Catechise after Young Miss, who with her fright look't of all coullors in ye RainBow" (*The Journal of Madame Knight*, ed. Theodore Dwight [1825; rpt. New York: Peter Smith, 1935], p. 28. Subsequent page references to this edition are provided in parentheses.)

16. One could argue that Knight sometimes plays the fool by posing as a frightened woman, but I doubt very much that there is any conscious role-playing involved when she offers her social commentary. (Faye Vowell, however, views the social commentator as one of four separate roles that Knight plays in *The Journal* in "A Commentary on *The Journal of Sarah Kemble Knight*," *Emporia State Research Studies*, 24 [1976], 44–52).

17. A good summary of the different "humors" of New Englanders and Southerners appears in Richard Beale Davis, *Intellectual Life in the Colonial South, 1585–1763* (Knoxville: Univ. of Tennessee Press, 1978), I, xxi–xxxi.

18. William Byrd, *History of the Dividing Line Betwixt Virginia and North Carolina*, in *The Prose Works of William Byrd of Westover*, ed. Louis B. Wright (Cambridge: Harvard Univ. Press, 1966), p. 277. Subsequent page references to this edition are provided in parentheses.

19. "William Byrd's *Histories of the Line*: The Fashioning of a Hero," *American Literature*, 47 (1976), 542. Siebert's discussion of Byrd's humor is the best I know. Rather than merely parrot Siebert, I have kept my remarks on Byrd at a minimum.

20. Siebert, "William Byrd's *Histories of the Line*: The Fashioning of a Hero," p. 540.

21. Robert Bolling, "Neanthe," ed. J. A. Leo Lemay, in "Southern Colonial Grotesque: Robert Bolling's 'Neanthe,'" *Mississippi Quarterly*, 35 (1982), 113. Those interested in Southern humor will want to consult Lemay's fine introduction. Subsequent line references to this edition are provided in parentheses.

22. "Southern Colonial Grotesque: Robert Bolling's 'Neanthe,'" p. 107.

23. See Louis B. Wright, "Human Comedy in Early America," in *The Comic Imagination in American Literature*, ed. Louis D. Rubin (New Brunswick, N. J.: Rutgers Univ. Press, 1973), pp. 21–23.

24. J. A. Leo Lemay, *Men of Letters in Colonial Maryland* (Knoxville: Univ. of Tennessee Press, 1972), p. 78. Both Lemay and Robert D. Arner ("The Blackness of Darkness: Satire, Romance, and Ebenezer Cooke's *The Sot-Weed Factor*," *Tennessee Studies in Literature*, 21 [1976], 1–10) argue that Cooke's satire is directed against the factor and against America. In developing his argument, Arner especially focuses upon the promotional literature that presented a distorted view of colonial life.

25. Given the emphasis that has been placed on the factor's expectations of life in America, it is worth noting that we actually learn little about his expectations from his own mouth. All we know is that he came to Maryland hoping to set up shop and, perhaps, to make an easy buck.

26. Ebenezer Cooke, *The Sot-Weed Factor* (1708 ed.), reprinted in *American Literature: Tradition and Innovation*, ed. Harrison T. Meserole, Walter Sutton, and Brom Weber (Lexington, Mass.: D. C. Heath, 1969), I, 222–38, ll. 703, 712. Subsequent line references to this edition are provided in parentheses.

27. This is the title of chapter 4 of *The Power of Satire: Magic, Ritual, Art* (1960; rpt. Princeton: Princeton Univ. Press, 1972).

28. The Tuesday Club, a gentleman's club consisting of many of the most prominent people in the Chesapeake Bay area, met in Annapolis from 1745 to 1756 under the direction of Dr. Alexander Hamilton, a Maryland physician who had emigrated from Scotland in 1738. Best known as the author of *The Itinerarium* (1744), Hamilton was the club's secretary and chronicler, and in "The History of the Tuesday Club" he transformed the minutes he had taken as secretary into a fictionalized mock-epic of the club's proceedings. For years, colonialists such as J. A. Leo Lemay, Richard Beale Davis, and Elaine G. Breslaw, who calls "The History" and Hamilton's minutes "probably the most important unpublished colonial literary manuscripts in existence" ("Wit, Whimsy, and Politics: The Uses of Satire by the Tuesday Club of Annapolis, 1744 to 1756," *William and Mary Quarterly*, 3rd Ser., 32 [1975], 296, n. 3), have been calling for an edition of "The History." It just so happens that my edition is scheduled for publication by the Institute of Early American History and Culture in 1985. (Page references to "The History" in this essay, however, are to Hamilton's manuscript, located at the John Work Garrett Library, Baltimore, Maryland.) For a more complete discussion of Hamilton's humor, see my essay, "'The History of the Tuesday Club': A Mock-Jeremiad of the Colonial South," *William and Mary Quarterly*, 3rd Ser., 40 (1983), 42–61.

29. *The Power of Satire: Magic, Ritual, Art*, p. 222.

The Grotesque Body of
Southwestern Humor   **Milton Rickels***

The most significant esthetic achievement of the humor of the Old Southwest is its language. Such writers as Augustus Baldwin Longstreet, Thomas Bangs Thorpe, Johnson Jones Hooper, and George Washington Harris realized their characters, settings, and actions in versions of regional dialect. "I am often amused," wrote Longstreet of the talk of old women, "and have amused *them* with a rehearsal of their own conversation, taken down by me when they little dreamed that I was listening to them."[1] Thorpe, too, creates as first person narrator an attentive gentleman steamboat passenger bemused by the language and experiences of Jim Doggett, the Big Bear of Arkansas. Perhaps only after the stylistic analyses of Richard M. Bridgeman, Richard Poirier, and Henry Nash Smith can we begin to see the art of this colloquial style.

The rhythm, sound, and emphasis of the American language were a significant part of the pleasure experienced and communicated by the writers of this native literature. For the twentieth-century reader, what remains in rich detail is its diction and imagery. In this esthetically created talk, anciently traditional comic forms and meanings arise. Various writers include social and political satire, but the dominant tone seems positive and celebratory. The expressed values are the human adventure of encountering the new, the excitement of danger, the pleasure in sensation, in revelation, in the play of wit, and most grandly the human yearning for triumph and freedom.

But the responses created by this literature are neither pure nor simple. A common technique among these writers for achieving tone and meaning is the employment of the grotesque as structure: juxtapositions, diction, and images that present "the unresolved clash of incompatibles in work and response."[2] The fundamental vehicle for the grotesque in this literature is the body. Inherent in the grotesque image of the body are an extraordinary realism and a wealth of meaning. For the present essay, I intend to focus on this one element of technique: the imagery of the body.

The bodies traditionally appearing in the world of humor are not the bodies of classic esthetics—devoted to the presentation of youth, beauty, harmony, and balance. Instead, these bodies are too fat or too thin, too short or too tall to represent that stability and completion of being represented by Vitruvian man. Simon Suggs's mock biographer presents him with a "head somewhat large and thinly covered with coarse silver white hair,"[3] scanty eyebrows, eyes which "twinkle in an aqueous humor which is constantly distilling down the corners," a long,

*This essay was written specifically for publication in this volume and is included here by permission of the author.

low, overhanging nose, an abundance of "loose and wrinkled" skin cover-
ing his throat and chin, set on the skinny frame of a fifty-year-old man.
George Washington Harris's Sut Lovingood is a "queer looking, long-
legged, short bodied, small headed, white haired, funny sort of a genius."[4]
Minor characters appear in the comic impressionism of folk humor: Pete
Whetstone's Old Thorp "is one of your *crane* built fellows, and walks
with his head hung down as though his mammy weaned him too early."[5]
Pete's comic songs are rich in images of the body:

> Oh, where did you lay last night—
> Oh, where did you lay last night?
> I lay behind the bed
> To see the *fat gal* shake her leg—
> Oh, little boy—little boy, get out the way. (p. 99)

This is the body of grotesque realism, an essential element of the
culture of folk humor, according to Russian critic Mikhail Bakhtin, the
leading theorist to work with the forms and functions of western European folk humor.[6] Bakhtin separates the imagery of the folk grotesque,
a dominant mode in the Medieval and Renaissance periods, from the
Romantic and Modernist grotesque. What the folk grotesque seeks to
grasp and express in its imagery is "the very act of becoming and
growth, the eternal incomplete unfinished nature of being." At its
summit, the grotesque of folk realism seeks to grasp simultaneously "the
two poles of becoming: that which is receding and dying and that which
is being born . . ." (p. 54). It is at least arguable that many of the humorists of the Old Southwest valued this complex implication of the imagery
of the culture of folk humor. This bodily imagery, as used by the
writers and behind them their folk story-tellers, is not the inspired
creation of a moment, but utilizes the expressive forms of a very old
tradition. Folk humor is neither artless in its forms nor naive in its
concepts.

Harmoniously composed beautiful bodies rarely appear in Southwestern humor, and when they do, their individual impermanence
usually appears also. George Washington Harris's beautiful Sicily Burns,
created in images of breast, buttocks, and thigh, in images of naked
temptation, excites and baffles Sut; but as he tells the story of her wedding from a later vantage point, he can open by calling attention to
her pregnancy: "Durn her, she's down on her heels flat-footed now."
The handsome village heroes of Longstreet's "The Fight" are graphically
presented in imagery of swift maiming. After the first blows, the two
young men fall to the ground in each other's grasp, head to head. Pres-
ently they rise and a disembodied voice from the crowd cries, "Didn't
I tell you so! He hit the ground so hard it jarred his nose off. Now
ain't he a pretty man as he stands? He shall have my sister Sal for his
pretty looks." The gentleman observer's voice tells his reader, "I looked,

and saw that Bob had entirely lost his left ear and a large piece from his left cheek. . . . Bill presented a hideous spectacle. About a third of his nose at the lower extremity was bit off . . ." (p. 50). The scene records a complex set of responses. In addition to the moral horror of "hideous spectacle," the voice from the crowd exults in Bill Durham's sudden ugliness, and connects it at once with a former sexual attractiveness— now destroyed in an instant. Both by the shouts of the crowd and by the narrator's observations, the encounter achieves communal significance. Even after Bill bites off his middle finger, Bob gathers a handful of dirt to grind into his adversary's eyes, and Bob cries "enough." Longstreet adds, "Language can not describe the scene that followed; the shouts, oaths, frantic gestures, taunts, replies, and little fights . . ." (p. 51).

This encounter of champions seems closer to ritual combat than to sport. It is a very deep, brutal play, involving potentially fate and life itself. The community participation is intense; the transport of the winning side ecstatic, the suffering of the losers grave. The humor of dismemberment opens to our view deep human joys and sorrows. We recall Achilles's terrible jocosity when, pointing to the fallen Hector, he asks:

> Tell me you heav'ns, in which part of his body
> Shall I destroy him? Whether there, or there,
> > or there,
> That I may give the local wound a name . . .
> > > (*Troilus and Cressida*, IV, ix).

Such taunts, as Geoffrey Hartman points out, touch a "deeply human anxiety. In ordinary mortals the Achilles heel is everywhere."[7] This privileged looking into the secret of the body's mortality is imaged in surreal fantasy by Harris in "Sut Lovingood at Bull's Gap." In this tale, a huge Dutchman feeds so grossly on beef and chicken that in his sleep he has nightmares and runs across his tavern bedroom with such violence that he bursts his belly open. To repair the wound, Sut sews him up with an old bridle rein: "While I wer makin the holes in the aidges of the tare, he axed me to look inside fur the spurs of 'tat tam schicken cock and cut dem off,' but all I could see wer his paunch, and hit looked adzadkly like the flesh side ove a raw hide."[8] Sut's glance into the corporeal interior reveals that man is exactly like an animal. Humor finds in dismemberment, glimpses of man as flesh, impulses to live intensely, to sew the body up, to eat and drink again.

What happens in the humor of the Old Southwest after the mutilation of the body? With a few repairs, more life, more excitement. One of the great bear stories, echoing Thorpe's "Big Bear of Arkansas," is Henry Clay Lewis's "The Indefatigable Bear Hunter."[9] As the Swamp Doctor opens the story, the reader learns that Mik-hoo-tah, the hunter, lost a leg in an earlier encounter. It was badly mangled by a bear, but he consented to amputation only when told that otherwise he would die. In a few weeks the doctor visits him again: "I made him a wooden leg, which answered a good purpose, and with a sigh of regret for the spoiling of such a good hunter, I struck him from my list of patients" (p. 167). But in time a messenger comes to tell the doctor that Mik's leg is broken "worse than the other." Returning through the darkening swamp to Mik's cabin, the doctor learns Mik broke his *wooden* leg and wants a new one. Relieving himself "by a satisfactory oath," the doctor spends the night to hear Mik's tale.

To questions about why his great frame is so wasted, Mik offers his own diagnosis: "No, Doc, it's grief, pure sorrur, sorrur, Doc! when I looks at what I is now and what I used to be" (p. 170). From this point on the doctor abandons his own framing voice to create Mik's vernacular for the mock oral tale. Mik knows the medicine he needs is not doctors' truck, but a bear hunt, which he anticipates in terms of excitement, danger, and death: "The music of the dogs, the fellers a screaming, the cane poppin', the rifles crackin', the bar growlin', the fight hand to hand, slap goes his paw, and a dog's hide hangs on one cane and his body on another, the knife glistenin' and then goin' plumb up to the handle in his heart—Oh! Doc, this was what I needed, and I swore, since death were huggin' me, anyhow, I might as well feel his last grip in a bar-hunt" (p. 172). The passage teems with the imagery of sound, movement, and the visualization of dismemberment and death. For Mik, in the midst of death is intense life. Stirred out of his wasting quietude, Mik asks "the boys" to take him along on a hunt. At first they laugh at him, but in time agree.

Unable to run in the chase, Mik decides to hunt from stand, and chooses "the singularest place in the swamp"—the middle of a canebrake, in a deep sink. "I knew it war a dangersome place for a well man to go in, much less a one-leg cripple..." (p. 172). The boys drive an old he to the stand where Mik is alone, with no knife and only one shot. When that bullet glances off the bear's skull, Mik clubs his rifle and stuns the bear, but as he tries to follow the blow, he discovers he is stuck fast: "my timber toe had run inter the ground, and I cuddent git out." Before he can unscrew the leg, the bear is upon him: "Bar but little hurt—no gun—no knife—no dogs—no frens—no chance to climb—an' *only one leg that cood run* " (p. 174). He jerks at the wooden leg, which comes loose just as the bear rises. Using it as a club, Mik struggles with the bear all around the hollow.

Just as the boys and dogs come up, Mik delivers a good blow. "The way that bar's flesh give in to the soft impresshuns of that leg war an honor to the mederkal perfeshun for having invented sich a weepun!" (p. 175) The boys hand him a knife to finish the bear he has whipped in a "hand to hand fight." Regenerated through violence, he asks the doctor to make him another leg: "Bar-meat is not over plenty in the cabin, and I feel like tryin' another!" (p. 175) As in Longstreet's "The Fight," mutilations are one consequence of action. After mutilation, one wastes or lives. The extraordinary realism of this scene is rich in meaning: out of the simultaneously fearful and exultant struggle with death, life and abundance are reborn.

Harden Taliaferro's cripples are not heroic, but pursue a life of earnest domesticity: old John Senter's son "Sol took it into his head to marry. Dwarfish-looking and crippled as he was. . . ."[10] His feeling is returned by Sally Spenser, whose "left leg had been broken, which made her equally lame" (p. 175). Sol's father is not sympathetic. On the wedding day, he complains sullenly about "fixin' so much fur them crippled creeturs, that had 'bout as much business a-marryin' as two 'possums" (p. 179). Bob Snipes, who recounts the wedding, describes the couple's coming to meet the squire: "We looked up the hill toward the Blue Ridge and we sees Sol and Sally, dressed in thar best, a-comin' down the hill afoot, side and side, and the old lady a-traipin' along after 'um, Sol throwin' his game leg around one way, from right to left, and Sal a-throwin' hern around t'other way, from left ter right" (p. 180). Such high spirited accommodation expresses a joy as real as it is unnerving. The tone of Bob Snipes's imagery conveys neither the shrinking of disgust nor the condescension of pity. It pictures a deformed but joyous motion of life. The world of grotesque humor expresses a disquieting but thorough-going humanism, and creates an inclusive community.

Mark Twain understood the complex possibilities of the imagery of deformity. Attempting to tell the story of his grandfather's old ram, Jim Blaine recalls that the one-eyed Miss Wagner had no glass eye but used to borrow Miss Jefferson's to receive company in: "It warn't big enough, and when Miss Wagner warn't noticing, it would get twisted around in the socket, and look up, maybe, or out to one side, and every which way, while t'other one was looking as straight ahead as a spyglass. Grown people didn't mind it, but it most always made the children cry, it was so sort of scary. She tried packing it in raw cotton, but it wouldn't work somehow—the cotton would get loose and stick out and look so kind of awful that the children couldn't stand it no way. She was always dropping it out, and turning up her old dead-light on the company empty, and making them oncomfortable, becuz *she* never could tell when it hopped out, being blind on that side, you see. So somebody would have to hunch her and say, 'Your game eye has fetched loose, Miss Wagner, dear.' "[11] The permutations of trouble with the borrowed glass eye are followed in their social consequences with astonishing inventiveness. The narrator's concern for the affright of the children, the company's homely courtesy to Miss Wagner all serve to reduce, humanize, and domesticate the consequences of her physical loss.

With unobtrusive virtuosity, Mark Twain extends the dismemberment: we learn that Miss Wagner has lost a leg. "When she had a quilting, or Dorcas S'iety at her house she gen'ally borrowed Miss Higgins's wooden leg to stump around on; it was considerable shorter than her other pin, but much *she* minded that. She said she couldn't abide crutches when she had company, becuz they were slow. . . ." From the point of view of middle class wholesome appearance, charm, and fashion, so ugly a hostess is impermissible. But Jim Blaine's grotesque realism expresses the ongoing flow of human activity, individual and social. This humor balances for a moment fear, horror, and disgust at dismemberment and disability against human vitality, inventiveness, and persistent sociability.

Jim Blaine's wandering story does not abandon Miss Wagner without one more revelation of physical loss: "She was bald as a jug, and used to borrow Miss Jacob's wig. . . ." The images parallel those of Swift's "A Beautiful Young Nymph Going to Bed," but the meaning is profoundly different. This piling on of details pictures a richly chaotic world, chancy, in which everybody suffers losses. Miss Jacobs is bald, Miss Higgins has lost a leg, and Miss Jefferson an eye. What the humor celebrates is not the beauty or intelligence of their lives, but their "oncomfortable" mortality, their unquenchable vigor, and their cherishing community.

The grotesque realism of Southwestern Humor includes, in addition to whole bodies, and the body undergoing accident, mutilation, and death, clusters of images around bodily processes: sexual activity; eating, drinking, and digesting; and defecation. Although the literature of Southwestern humor was freer than respectable literature, its sexual images are customarily veiled and indirect; and when compared to the images in the *Carmina burana*, the French *fabliaux*, and particularly to Chaucer and Rabelais, very rare. In Longstreet and Harden Taliaferro, human sexuality hardly exists. In Thorpe's "Big Bear of Arkansas," it is briefly celebrated when Jim Doggett praises his favorite hound in an image of human sexual skill: "Strangers, that dog knows a bar's way as well as a horse-jockey knows a woman's."[12] Hooper allows his Simon Suggs to comment even more on the ways of the flesh: " 'Wonder what's the reason these here preachers never hugs up the old, ugly women? Never seed one to do it in my life—the sperrit never moves em that way! It's nater, tho'; and the women, *they* never flocks round one o' the old dried-up breethring—bet two to one old splinter-legs thar,'—nodding at one of the ministers—'won't git a chance to say turkey to a good-looking gall today. Well! who blames 'em? Nater will be nater . . .' " (p. 115). Of all these writers, however, Harris is the most varied and clear in his erotic imagery. Of tempting Sicily Burns, Sut says, to picture her lavish buttocks and narrow waist: "She cudent . . . sit in a common arm-cheer, while yu cud lock the top hoop of a chun [churn] . . . roun the huggin place" (p. 76).

In his suppressed writing, Mark Twain used sexual imagery from the culture of folk humor more openly. Although not in the common vernacular, his *1601* (ca. 1876), a fanciful reconstruction of Elizabethan language, frees him to employ a fair number of the common sexual images.[13] The piece suggests how generally liberating these writers found dialect to be. Mark Twain's later Stomach Club Address, a public speech delivered in his own voice, employs the strategy of indirection.[14] But in *1601* he writes "quiff-splitters," "cod-piece," "prickes," "prickers," and for the fifteen year old Master Beaumont, the queen says "a little birde." For testicles the queen says "bollocks." The young Lady Helen, in defense of her maturity, claims her pubic hair has sprouted "two years syne; I can scarce more than cover it with my hand now." Master Beaumont, in an elegant euphemism, calls this a "downy neste of birdes," but old Lady Margery freely says "cunt." Even the most amateur student of the vernacular is aware how rich it is in sexual imagery.

Even rarer than sexual imagery in the humor of the Old Southwest, is excretory imagery, but it is there, and in sufficient quantity to add significantly to the tone and therefore meaning of this world's body. Sometimes the imagery of defecation, particularly animal dung, is simply used as common, realistic description. Noland's Pete Whetstone frequently uses "sign" as a hunting term to refer to old or fresh or abundant bear droppings (pp. 63, 157, 185). Sometimes the vernacular tone is one of excitement and pleasure: "I was looking for sign, and . . . soon found plenty right fresh and soft bar sign."[15] Sometimes it is satirical, as when Harris has Abraham Lincoln befoul himself; or grandly deflating, as when Mark Twain has Queen Elizabeth, "with vaste irony, mincing," reply to Lady Alice's Euphuistic speech with "O shitte!"

The farts of Mark Twain's *1601* expand in the plot from the silent inadvertent to the triumphant expression of manly vigor. Harris utilizes this imagery, but the word cannot be printed. Squire Hanley's pious old horse was "never hearn to squeal, belch, ur make eny onsightly soun" (p. 288). The sound of farts, in Sut's impressionistic accounts, may even express trouble with pain. When Pap Lovingood, disguised in a bull's hide to teach his dog to attack and hang on, is helpless in the dog's jaws, Mam takes the opportunity to wallop him across the back with a bean pole. In mock perplexity, Sut speculates that "the wind somehow gethered atwix the hary side of dad's hide, an' the raw side ove the yearlin's" and at every lick "it wud bust out at the sowin, pow'ful sudden, soundin loud an' doleful" (p. 295). Like Mark Twain, Harris commands expressive virtuosity.

The most magniloquent example, however, appears in "Sut Lovingood's Daddy, Acting Horse." In this tale, the poor family's only horse dies. About "strawberry time" Pap, feeling his responsibility, decides to be horse himself and pull the plow so that his family can plant the year's crop. As Sut and Mam harness him, the "complicated durned old fool" begins to feel like a horse. He whinnies, drops on his hands, and kicks at Mam's head. Then, just before he is led into the field, "He jis' run backwards on all fours, an' kick'd at her agin, an' ——— an' pawd the groun wif his fists" (p. 23). In this context only the plain word will serve; the reader is required to supply "farted" for the blank.[16] In Medieval folklore in France, the bear's resounding fart of dehibernation announces his re-vivication, the coming of spring, and is therefore joyous and triumphant.[17] The thirteenth-century "Sumer is Icumen In" images the joyous "Bulluc sterteth, bucke verteth" in English. Such a traditional meaning is not absent from Pap Lovingood's expressive fart. It asserts his vigorous animality, his preparation of the land for planting, and thus celebrates his own rite of spring. The narrator's blank space for Sut's word signals that Harris's response included pleasure enough to impel him to smuggle the word in through Victorian conventions.

Perhaps the most richly ambiguous of these excretory images is the defecation scene in Thorpe's "Big Bear of Arkansas." By the time the tale was published, the *Spirit* had already established a tradition of bear-hunt tales in the vernacular. The encounter between man and bear was becoming a representative legend for the frontier and the American character. Thorpe's Jim Doggett and the biggest bear in Arkansas were recognized at once by the *Spirit's* editor and the readers as embodying the central myth.[18]

The image of defecation appears as a brief passage, crucially placed in the structure of the tale. The opening setting is a steamboat salon, a microcosm of America, as described by a gentleman narrator. Into the salon comes Jim Doggett, who quickly forms and commands an audience through his power as a story-teller. He introduces himself as an Arkansas hunter and squatter. First he celebrates Arkansas as an untamed earthly paradise of abundance and adventure. In New Orleans a gentleman had asked him about hunting "and laughed at my calling the principal game in Arkansas poker and high-low-jack." The ignorance is theirs, he roars: "If you'd asked me *how we got our meat* in Arkansas, I'd a told you at once, and given you a list of varmints that would make a caravan, beginning with the bar, and ending off with the cat; that's *meat* though, not game" (pp. 338–39). There are two worlds to be bodied forth here, one the gentlemen's world of game, and the other the world of meat.

When the gentleman narrator asks for the story of a hunt, Jim Doggett tells the tale in which "the greatest bar was killed, that ever lived, none excepted" (p. 343). He hunts the great bear for two or three years, but, emboldened by many escapes, the bear begins to help himself freely to Jim Doggett's hogs, the buzzards eating whatever he leaves: "and so, between *bear and buzzard*, I rather think I was *out of pork*" (p. 345).

He begins to waste away; his loss of power as a hunter is killing him. His spirit shrinks and becomes mean. He quarrels with his neighbors.

"I grew as cross as a bar with two cubs and a sore tail" (p. 347). (The traditional expression Thorpe echoes is "as mean as a sore-assed bear"). This portion of a bear's anatomy seems of some interest to pioneers as a source of images for disabling sensitivity. As one 1840s hunter put it, "an Old She or a bar of any kind, indeed, could not bear to be fingered behind much. . . ."[19] His foul temper grotesquely imaged in the old she, Jim Doggett determines to catch the bear, "go to Texas, or die." He makes his preparations for a Monday morning. But the day before the "great day . . . I went into the woods near my house, taking my gun and Bowie-knife along, just *from habit*, and there sitting down also from habit, what should I see getting over my fence but *the bar!*" (p. 347). Thus very indirectly, Thorpe pictures for the *Spirit's* audience Jim Doggett telling his room full of silent listeners that he was squatting down at his morning defecation when the great bear came over the fence toward him.

To be caught with his pants down does not disconcert the frontiersman. "I raised myself, took deliberate aim, and fired. Instantly the varmint wheeled, gave a yell, and *walked through the fence*, like a falling tree would through a cobweb. I started after, but was tripped up by my inexpressibles [euphemism for trousers] which, either from habit, or the excitement of the moment, were about my heels, and before I had really gathered myself up, I heard the old varmint groaning in a thicket nearby, and by the time I reached him he was a corpse." The great hunter's culminating shot is taken as he stands up from his morning defecation.

Neither Greek nor Renaissance esthetics nor academic humanistic values provide vocabulary or ideas to help much in interpreting the scene. In Thorpe's tale, Jim Doggett himself reveals these details to his listeners, to whom he shows no sign of deference or humility. The scatological humor draws no amusement from the audience.[20] However, in the culture of folk humor scatological imagery is not rare, may have both positive and negative connotations, and finally, Doggett's rising from defecation to shoot a bear is a traditional motif in comic hunting lore.[21]

The grotesque bodily imagery of Southwestern humor is always the language of human reduction or human enlargement, and usually the latter. The respectable Thoreau, who kept an utterly secret privy at Walden Pond, could see excrement as an image of praise only when it was earth: "Few phenomena gave me more delight than to observe the forms that thawing sand and clay assume. . . . As it flows . . . you are reminded of coral, of leopard's paws or birds' feet, of brains or lungs or bowels, and excrements of all kinds" (*Walden*, "Solitude"). Such images Thoreau associates with the creation of the world and of man. He was affected, he writes, as if he stood watching the creator "still at work, sporting on this bank, and with excess of energy strewing his fresh designs about." In comparable wonder Pete Whetstone once pictured his own body recovering from the ague as steam rises from manure: "I am rising agin like smoke from a new-laid improver of the airth" (p. 167)—a grotesque kenning for the body's liberation from suffering.

In discussing Thorpe's scene, perhaps unique in the written literature of its time, it seems best not to divorce it from the positive meanings that excremental imagery may have in the culture of folk humor. Jim Doggett's account of his sitting down *from habit*, then standing up to take deliberate aim at the on-coming bear memorializes an act of great self-possession. The scene does not violate human reality; it only violates conventions of high literature. It goes beyond the earthly pleasure of Sancho Panza, who must conceal from Don Quixote his simple need and enjoy only a constrained and secret defecation. The Big Bear's presentation of himself is open and free. The image is liberating and expansive. The plot itself, and its informing system of images, is primarily celebratory. Its dominant mode is in praise of the power and freedom of man and nature. Even the death of the creation bear is, for Jim Doggett, not only the death of his brother in nature but also a great protecting furry hide and a staggering load of meat.

Scatological imagery within the culture of folk humor retains with notable frequency this basic ambiguity. Indeed, one legend has it that to question a human turd is an impertinence, a "disrespect" to oneself.[22] Its modern specialized function of expressing or evoking disgust or "bitterness" seems strongest in the urban middle class cultures of America and Western Europe.[23] In the city and suburbia, human and animal excretory products are a harrassing problem; but on the farm, whether Indian, Japanese, or American, or in the wilderness they may be problem, or neutral fact, or valuable asset—they may be horrifying or marvellous "sign." The Queen's mincing "O shitte!" not only satirizes Lady Alice's finicking talk, it also expresses her Majesty's majesty. In the culture of humor, the excretory word retains the magic power of taboo violation and a complex resonance of meaning.

For the hunter to see his quarry while he is defecating is a traditional folk motif. Twentieth-century hunters' lore continues so rich in these tales that the motif becomes a cliché. The common pattern is that the hunter always stands his rifle within reach when he goes to defecate. His quarry (in the twentieth century ordinarily a deer) approaches, the hunter stands up, fires, and usually kills the animal. The story is invariably reported as true, is sometimes told by the hunter himself, or, more often about a notable hunter, and always with the greatest satisfaction. It seems a motif with images that combine self-deprecation with self-praise.[24] Unbookish heirs of Jim Doggett expand themselves even yet with his image of rising to the definitive occasion.

To argue that the grotesque images of the body in Southwestern humor are largely celebratory is not to deny that these images also include dark and negative implications. The grotesque by definition presents a clash of incompatibles, and esthetic categories are notoriously rooted in ineffable experiences. But our oldest comic tradition has found in images of the body, food, drink, defecation, and sexual life the occasion for joy and a way of expressing our passion for life, growth, fertility, and abundance.[25]

Notes

1. Augustus Baldwin Longstreet, *Georgia Scenes* (New York: Sagamore Press, 1957), p. 172. Subsequent references to this ed. First ed., 1835.

2. Philip Thompson, *The Grotesque* (London: Methuen, 1972), p. 27.

3. Johnson Jones Hooper, *Adventures of Captain Simon Suggs* (Chapel Hill: University of North Carolina Press, 1969), p. 6. Subsequent references to this ed. First ed., 1845.

4. *Sut Lovingood* (New York: Dick and Fitzgerald, 1867), p. 19. Subsequent references to this ed.

5. Pete Whetstone's Letters, created by Charles Fenton Mercer Noland, appeared in the *New York Spirit of the Times*, 1837–56. They have been collected and edited by Leonard Williams as *Cavorting on the Devil's Fork* (Memphis: Memphis State University Press, 1979), quotation from p. 80. Subsequent references to this ed.

6. *Rabelais and His World* (Cambridge: Massachusetts Institute of Technology Press, 1968), p. 52. Subsequent references included in the text.

7. *Saving the Text* (Baltimore: Johns Hopkins University Press, 1981), p. 96.

8. *High Times and Hard Times*, ed. by M. Thomas Inge (Nashville: Vanderbilt University Press, 1967), p. 154.

9. Madison Tensas, *Odd Leaves from the Life of a Louisiana "Swamp Doctor"* (Philadelphia: T. B. Peterson [1850]), pp. 164–75. Subsequent references to this ed.

10. *Fisher's River (North Carolina) Scenes and Characters* (New York: Harper and Brothers, 1859), p. 174. Subsequent references to this ed.

11. *Roughing It* (Berkeley: University of California Press, 1972), p. 345. Imagery of mutilation and deformity, popular in nineteenth century American newspaper humor, was frequently used by Mark Twain. See "Frightful Accident to Dan De Quille," *Early Tales and Sketches* (Berkeley: University of California Press, 1979), pp. 360–61, and elsewhere. *Adventures of Huckleberry Finn* powerfully uses the esthetics of the grotesque.

12. J. A. Leo Lemay has convinced me that the best text of Thomas Bangs Thorpe's "The Big Bear of Arkansas" is that of the *New York Spirit of the Times*, March 27, 1841, pp. 43–44. The present essay will cite Walter Blair, *Native American Humor (1800–1900)* (New York, 1937; rpt. San Francisco: Chandler Publishing Co., 1960), pp. 337–48.

13. For a recent evaluation of *Conversation as it was by the Social Fireside in the Time of the Tudors*, see Sholom J. Kahn, "Mark Twain as American Rabelais," *Hebrew University Studies in Literature*, 1 (Spring 1973), pp. 47–75.

14. *The Mammoth Cod and Address to The Stomach Club*, introd. by G. Legman (Milwaukee: Maledicta, 1976), pp. 23–25.

15. Sulphur Fork, "Old Long John and the Bear," *With the Bark On*, ed. John Q. Anderson (Nashville: Vanderbilt University Press, 1967), p. 86.

16. For the folk expression see Vance Randolph, *Pissing in the Snow* (Urbana: University of Illinois Press, 1976), p. 50.

17. Emmanuel LeRoy Ladurie, *Carnival in Romans*, trans. Mary Feeney (New York: George Braziller, 1979), p. 99.

18. See Walter Blair and Hamlin Hill, *America's Humor* (New York: Oxford University Press, 1978), pp. 200–212; J. A. Leo Lemay, "The Text, Tradition, and Themes of 'The Big Bear of Arkansas,'" *AL*, 47 (November 1975), 321–42; and Katherine G. Simoneaux, "Symbolism in Thorpe's 'The Big Bear of Arkansas,'" *Arkansas Hist. Q*, 25 (Fall 1966), pp. 240–47. Lemay's is the fullest study of the tale. My briefer survey here argues that his conclusions about the scatological imagery are too negative: "disgust" and "bitterness" seem not the tone of traditional excretory imagery from Chaucer to Randolph's *Pissing in the Snow*. However, G. Legman's *Rationale of the Dirty Joke, Second Series* (New York: Breaking Point, 1975), pp. 810–987, would support Lemay in the tone rising from psychological interpretations of such imagery in many jokes. Partly such "seriousness" seems a contemporary middle-class cultural phenomenon.

19. "Old Long John and the Bear," *With the Bark On*, p. 87. A rare passage. Cf. Jones Tracy, "The Bunghole Story," in Richard M. Dorson, *Man and Beast in American Comic Legend* (Bloomington: Indiana University Press, 1982), pp. 147–48.

20. Sonia Gernes, "Artists of the Community: The Role of the Storytellers in the Tales of the Southwest Humorists," *Jour. Pop. Culture*, 15 (Spring 1982), pp. 114–28.

21. See Frank Hoffmann, *Analytical Survey of Anglo-American Traditional Erotica* (Bowling Green: Bowling Green University Popular Press, 1973), esp. pp. 253–58; particularly Randolph, *Pissing in the Snow*; Legman, *Rationale*, II, Chap. 15.

22. Hoffmann, Q395.1.

23. Stephen Greenblatt, "Filthy Rites," *Daedalus*, 111 (Spring 1982), pp. 1–16, for an examination of disgust. See also Eric Partridge, *A Dictionary of Slang and Unconventional English*, 7th ed. (New York: Macmillan, 1970), "shit" for a sketch of the history of the word.

24. I cannot locate the motif in print. My collection of oral tales over the past ten years includes informants from California, Alabama, Florida, and Louisiana, all hunters themselves or the wives of hunters. For a curious parallel see Patrick McManus, *They Shoot Canoes, Don't They?* (New York: Holt, Rinehart & Winston, 1982), "Reading Sign," pp. 150–58.

25. For a grandly comprehensive synecdoche of the body in the life of man, see the Togo-Tim legend which concludes, "That is why the ability to read the thoughts of others was acquired, not by the hunter's head, but by his penis." "The Hunter and the Snake Woman II" in *African Nights*, ed. Leo Frobenius, trans. Peter Ross (New York: Herder & Herder, 1971), p. 189.

Those *Literary* Comedians

David B. Kesterson*

In his impressive two-volume study, *Mark Twain's Library: A Reconstruction*, Alan Gribben has totally deflated the once popular myth that Twain was essentially an "unlettered humorist" who had little interest in what he called "fiction or story-books."[1] In "reconstructing" Mark Twain's library, Gribben tracked down more than 700 books once owned by Twain that still exist, and he believes there were some 2,500 volumes in the total collection. Fond of libraries other than his own, Twain enjoyed browsing in public libraries, hotel libraries (customary in the nineteenth-century), ship libraries, and the private collections of family and acquaintances, among others. Though perhaps not as bookish as his friend William Dean Howells, who considered Twain less "literary" than Howells' other literary acquaintances, Twain obviously did enjoy a wide knowledge of literature. Gribben concludes that he was familiar with "nearly 5,000 books, stories, essays, poems, plays, operas, songs, newspapers, and magazines" (p. xxxii).

Twain's unliterary pose that cleverly camouflaged a substantial literary background is in many ways characteristic of that whole group of later nineteenth-century humorists that we know as the "literary comedians," such figures as Charles Farrar Browne (Artemus Ward), Henry Wheeler Shaw (Josh Billings), George Horatio Derby (John Phoenix and Squibob), David Ross Locke (Petroleum Vesuvius Nasby), Robert H. Newell (Orpheus C. Kerr), Charles Henry Smith (Bill Arp), James M. Bailey (the Danbury *News* Man), Edgar Wilson Nye (Bill Nye), and—later on—Finley Peter Dunne (Mr. Dooley), to name only the more significant writers in this group. Often viewed erroneously as so many clones—a group or school without much individuality in their humor, all delighting in the use of mispellings and other verbal chicanery—these humorists evoked the same non-literary image as that associated with Mark Twain. They have often been taken too lightly as mere literary funny men (with emphasis on the *funny*) who trifled with writing as an avocation while involving themselves more seriously in their actual professions of journalism, the military, politics, real estate, school teaching, or whatever. It has taken such noted critics of American humor as Walter Blair, Hamlin Hill, Jesse Bier, James C. Austin, David E. E. Sloane, and Brom Weber to separate the "school" of literary comedians into individual components, defend their merit, show the serious purposes of their writing, and re-evaluate and appreciate anew their viable presence in the development of American humor.

To view these humorists properly as *literary* comedians is the purpose of this essay—to further the line of thought introduced by Blair,

*This essay was written specifically for publication in this volume and is included here by permission of the author.

Weber, Hill, and others that the literary comedians were artists in their own right, far more touched by the mainstream of Western World literature than has generally been thought. In an important essay entitled "The Mis-spellers," Brom Weber points out perceptively that these writers were "distinctively different one from the other, demonstrated a considerable degree of literary sophistication, and taught and exhorted their audiences with commendable substantive seriousness."[2] He reminds us that these were educated men—some formally—that they were conscious artists, and that they were writers "familiar with English and American literature of their own and earlier periods" (p. 130). What remains to be examined are the specific literary backgrounds of each of the major literary comedians: their education, their grounding in literature, the influences of authors and literary works on them, the literary allusions in their writings and the use of their reading in their humor. In short, the literary comedians demand a much closer look as literati than has ever been accorded them. Though it would be too ambitious to do here for each comedian what Gribben has painstakingly done in reconstructing Mark Twain's library, one can readily establish the fact that each of these figures enjoyed a remarkable familiarity with literature, often both classical and contemporary, and that their literary knowledge played an important part in their humorous writings.

Probably the most influential of the literary comedians, Charles Farrar Browne (Artemus Ward), was born in Waterford, Maine, in 1834. He experienced little formal education since his father died when Browne was thirteen, causing him to seek work as a printer. He had a short stay at the Norway, Maine, Liberal Institute in 1850, where he participated in the Lyceum debates and was active in the Thespian Society,[3] but Browne's real education was gained through journalism. Browne himself claimed that being a journalist afforded him "a contact with literature."[4] When he went to work for Benjamin P. Shillaber on *The Carpet-Bag* in 1851, as James C. Austin has pointed out, the magazine was publishing the best humorists of the day and would soon print the first writings of Samuel Clemens, George Horatio Derby, and Browne himself (p. 24). In the course of his career, Browne came to know such fellow humorists as Clemens, Melville D. Landon, Henry Wheeler Shaw, and Bret Harte, and he also developed a friendship with William Dean Howells. Austin posits that Browne probably influenced Howells' attitude towards American humor, remembering that Browne published some of young Howells' verse in *Vanity Fair* in 1861 (pp. 110–11).

Browne's Artemus Ward letters are not replete with literary allusions. Browne obviously wants his persona to appear as the unlettered showman concerned more with his wax works than with subjects literary. However, he cannot resist spicing some of the "genial showman's" talk with literary allusions, especially to Shakespeare. In *Artemus Ward: His*

Book,[5] Shakespeare is the author most often referred to. Ward brags in the essay "Wax Figures Vs. Shakespeare" that his traveling show is more moral and elevating than the plays of Shakespeare. How, after all, can Shakespeare be so great when King Lear curses his daughters and makes "an ass of hisself ginerally," when "Mrs. Mackbeth" prompts Duncan to murder, when "Jack Fawlstaf" is an "immoral old cus," when "Hamlick" is "crazy as a loon," when "Richard the Three" is a "monkster" who kills, and when "Iargo" is "ornery"? (p. 83). Ward will hold up his "wax figgers and snakes" as superior to such questionable stage presences anytime. In another letter, "Edwin Forrest as Othello" (pp. 111–16), he chooses not so much to review Forrest's performance as to spend several pages retelling the plot of Othello comically. There are other references to Shakespeare, as in the letter "Thrilling Scenes in Dixie" where Ward measures the trials of his harried trip South against Hamlet's " 'swings and arrers of outrajus fortin.' " They "waren't nothin in comparison to my troubles" (p. 198). In "The Show is Confiscated" he wonders if a prolonged absence from the stage will cause his audiences to think he has gone to the "Tomb of the Cappylets, tho I don't know what those is. It's a popler noospaper frase" (p. 189). There are also references to Shakespeare in Artemus Ward: His Travels[6] and Artemus Ward: His Works, Complete,[7] but little that is different in tone from the earlier volume. In Travels Ward reviews a production of Othello and announces that all the "conventionalities" were adherred to: "Othello howls, Iago scowls, and the boys all laugh when Roderigo dies. I stay to see charming Mrs. Irwin (Desdemona) die, which she does very sweetly" (p. 185). In "At the Tomb of Shakespeare" Ward is tricked by an English boy into believing Shakespeare's grave is outside the church; then he launches into a diatribe against Shakespearean scholars and their constant disagreements over Shakespearean lore. In Works, Ward feels that if scholars persist in investigating every little detail of Shakespeare's life and career, "we shall not, in doo time, know anything about it at all" (p. 239).

Though Dickens was the greatest influence on the picaresque mode at middle century, according to Austin's Artemus Ward (p. 79), there is little in Browne's writings by way of direct reference to him. The most obvious instance is Ward's quoting Joseph Gargery to underscore a point in Travels. Ward is discussing an aged Revolutionary soldier who drinks a glass of liquor a day. But he warns young readers: "But because a man can drink a glass of liquor a day, and live to be a hundred years old, my young readers must not infer that by drinking two glasses of liquor a day a man can live to be two hundred. 'Which, I meanter say, it doesn't follow,' as Joseph Gargery might observe" (p. 108). Elsewhere, in Works, Ward refers to a waterfall in the Rocky Mountains as the "Laughing-Water alluded to by Mr. Longfellow in his Indian poem—'Higher-Water' " (p. 294), and he delightfully spoofs his own misspelling by saying he had received a copy of Chaucer's poems and found Chaucer a talented poet, but one who could not spell: "No man has a right to be a lit'rary man onless he knows how to spel. It is a pity that Chaucer, who had geneyus, was so unedicated. He's the wuss speller I know of" (p. 240). Elsewhere Artemus parodies current romances. The stock devices of popular, sentimental fiction fill the "Romances" in *Travels*, the "Stories and Romances" in Part III of *Works*, and the " 'Vanity Fair' Romances" that Don C. Seitz includes in the last part of his book on Artemus Ward.[8] Obviously, then, Browne was well versed in the trends of popular fiction of his day.

In all, though Artemus Ward is characterized as an uneducated traveling showman, Browne, who is pulling the strings, cannot help but make references to literature and literary trends that he was aware of, if usually in a humorous manner befitting the nature of his protagonist and the situation at hand. Though references are sparse, it is obvious that Browne was well read, if largely self educated, and brought knowledge of English and American literature to the creation of his own characters, situations, and themes.

Browne's friend Henry Wheeler Shaw (Josh Billings), 1818–1885, was born into a prominent family in Lanesboro, Mass. His grandfather, Dr. Samuel Shaw, of Vermont, was a physician and for years served as a United States Congressman. Shaw's maternal uncle was chief justice of New York for many years. His father, Henry Shaw, a close friend of Henry Clay, was active in politics, serving in Congress and also in the Massachusetts legislature for twenty-five years. Young Henry thus grew up in an active, enlightened environment. Though his formal schooling was spotty (a prankster, he was expelled from Hamilton College during his sophomore year for climbing a lightning rod on the chapel wall), he did learn Latin and Greek in a college prep school in Lenox and acquired there a respect for learning, always remembering mentor John Hotchin's pedagogical admonition, "Whatever you get, get it got."[9]

Aside from his famous *Josh Billings' Farmer's Allminax*, which ran for ten years, Shaw was most famous for his aphorisms and pithy essays which appeared in his newspaper columns, books, and lectures. Despite the image of Josh Billings as ingenuous cracker-box philosopher, Shaw's ties were strongly literary. Though his finely chiseled aphorisms show great originality and his essays are his own in subject and style, the classical tradition is discernible in his works. If Billings' misspellings are overlooked, the aphorisms are far more attuned to those of Franklin, La Rochefoucauld, Bacon, Dryden, Pope, and Swift than are those of most of his contemporaries. The economy, balance and graceful turn of phrase are the very model of classical and neo-classical style. Josh himself admits that "fine writing konsists in gitting the most thought into the shortest and simplest form."[10] Examples of classical balance and economy of wording abound in the "affurisms":

Poetri, tew be excellent, wants tew be
like natur, but about 4 times az big. . . .
　　　If yu are handsum, cultivate yure boots;
if you are hoamly, hoe yure branes.[11]
　　　Don't borry nor lend, but if you must
do one, *lend*. . . .
　　　Tew enjoy a good reputashun, giv pub-
lickly, and steal privately.[12]

Working in a rich literary tradition, in fact, caused Josh to reflect in *Ice* that "originality in writing is as diffikult as gitting a fishpole by the side ov a trout brook—aul the good poles hav bin cut long ago" (p. 104), and "About the most originality that enny writer kan hope tew arrive at honestly, now-a-days, is tew steal with good judgment" (p. 138). Critics have pointed to the similarity between Shaw and Franklin as epigram-matists. S. S. Cox wrote long ago that "there is much of Franklin's shrewd, practical humor under the mask of Josh Billings' sayings,"[13] and Cyril Clemens remarked that Shaw and Franklin are "surprisingly alike in their outlook on life: at once shrewd, philosophic, and humorous" (p. 168).

In the genres of the essay and sketch Shaw leans on the tradition of Aesop, Montaigne, and Addison and Steele with his economy of language, ease of expression, clarity of style, and carefully modulated tone. Walter Blair has called Shaw "primarily an essayist" of the "Addi-son-Steele-Goldsmith tradition" because he wrote about "all subjects in a fashion which was formal."[14] Throughout his essays, Shaw refers to noted writers of Western literature. He quotes from them to substan-tiate points, addresses some aspect of their literary art, or comments on their literary success. If frequency of reference is a reliable measure of his favorites, then Shaw was especially fond of Shakespeare, Dickens, Burns, and Bryant. Josh writes of Burns, "I dew consider him the most Poet that ever lived. I had rather be the author ov one poum i kno ov, that he rit, than tew be king and queen of England, and keep a hoss and carriage. . . ."[15] He also frequently alludes to Goldsmith, Pope, Gray, Byron, Bunyan, Defoe, and Ben Jonson. Classical and world literature favorites were Homer, Virgil, Ovid, and Boccaccio. One of Josh Billings' aphorisms from *Ice* clearly explains his fealty to Homer: "I don't read enny boddy else's poetry but Homer's, upon the same principle that i alwus drink, when it is just as handy, out ov a spring, instead ov the outlet" (p. 104). Aside from Bryant, Shaw does not allude much to the classic American writers. There is more interest in his contemporary fellow humorists, especially Ward and Twain. The Franklin connection is obvious, however.

In the miscellany of writings that appears in Shaw's New York *Weekly* columns, Shaw emerges as a knowledgeable man of letters com-fortable with his trade. He writes the essay-length epistle, tries his hand at narrative fiction, experiments with an occasional short dramatic piece, and pens some original poetry. His "answers to correspondents" (either actual or contrived by Shaw) sometimes touch on literary subjects, such as one column that shows his interest in English poetry. In *Sayings* Josh explains to a fledgling contributing poet that there just might be a case or two of plagiarism in the lines submitted for publication:

> This line in your produkshun strikes us as very butiful and original; "And larn the luxury of dewing good." Gold smith [sic] hisself mite hav bin proud ov sich a line. And again; "Oh would sum power the gifty give us, ov seeing oursels as uthers cee us;" yure idee ov introducing the skotch acksent into yure stile, is verry happee. If yu never hav red Robert Burns, yu will be surprised to larn that his style verry mutch resembles yures. Onse more yu sa: "If ignoranse is bliss, tis folly tew be wise." This sentiment is jist as tru as tis common. Pope, I think, has sumthing similar; but awl grate minds sometimes express theirselfs alike. (p. 110)

Again, Shaw's grounding in eighteenth-century English literary classics is evident. His knowledge of literature and his sensitivity to it assert a noticeable presence in his collected writings. Josh Billings' reflective, philosophical nature, of course, was compatible with the enjoyment of literature; thus his familiarity with authors and works is more credible than that of some of the more philistine personae created by other literary comedians.

Probably the most brilliant of the literary comedians, George Horatio Derby (John Phoenix or Squibob) won his fame in the American West, as did Charles Farrar Browne. Born in Dedham, Mass., in 1823, Derby was a "precocious and brilliant" youngster according to biographer George R. Stewart.[16] His schooling was extensive and included four years at West Point, from which Derby graduated in 1845 and became a career officer in the army. A gentleman by birth, he became a well-educated gentleman by training. He knew natural science, was versed in French and Latin, and was a master of Spanish. He was a lieutenant in the Corps of Topographical Engineers while he was writing his humorous essays and contributing to San Diego and San Francisco newspapers. He was commissioned in 1850 to survey the Gulf of California area for proposed navigation of the Colorado River, and he prepared a sizeable technical report on the project for the government.[17]

Derby's major book, *Phoenixiana; or Sketches and Burlesques* is written in vigorous, quick style and exudes Derby's wide-ranging intelligence. While essentially a humorist in his writings, Derby shows an impressive grasp of a host of subjects, from astronomy to the principles of language study. He is frequently allusive to literature. He knew the Bible so well that, according to Stewart, "He could amaze friends by reciting whole chapters" (p. 41). In the Phoenix and Squibob essays there are references to Sappho, Virgil, Horace, Shakespeare, Milton, Defoe, Richardson, Dr. Johnson, Boswell, Smollett, Coleridge, Macauley, Dickens, Emerson, Poe, Agassiz, Harriet Beecher Stowe, G. P. R. James, and others. Many of his character names show eighteenth-century and Dickensian influence, e.g., Professor Heavysterne, Dr. Bigguns, William Boulder, Lt. Zero, Dr. Dunshunner, Prof. Weegates, and others.[18] Derby writes several learned discourses on classical mythology, especially in the selections entitled "Lectures on Astronomy" (pp. 51–66, and 241–53). He relates the mythological figures and stories to astronomical signs and formations. Though they have a facetious air about them, these essays display sound learning on Derby's part. His essays in general address the subjects of the theatre, books, authors, language, and journalism, among other important topics. These pieces are generally longer and more fully developed than the essays of most of the literary comedians. They are impressive because of the amount of knowledge shown.

Many of Derby's references to authors, works, or literary characters are barely more than brief mentions. Others are more substantive, however. Derby adroitly uses a passage from *Paradise Lost*, for example, to describe a reunion between his persona John Phoenix, who had been acting editor of the San Diego *Herald*, and returning editor Judge John Judson Ames. As Ames re-enters the editorial office, he seems to stand before the almost quavering Phoenix like Milton's Satan: "In shape and gesture proudly eminent, stood like a tower: . . . but his face deep scars of thunder had intrenched, and care sat on his faded cheek; but under brows of dauntless courage and considerable pride, waiting revenge" (p. 113). Drawing on his Biblical knowledge, in an earlier reference to Judge Ames, he compares the editor's frenzied coach driving to that of Jehu, son of Nimshi, "for he driveth furiously" (p. 93).

In other essays collected in *Phoenixiana*, Derby takes on the role of critic through the eyes of Phoenix and John P. Squibob, who is presented as the poetry editor of a San Francisco newspaper. He blasts the stereotyped fiction of G. P. R. James, accusing James of assigning to all beautiful women the same degree of beauty (proof of Derby's facetious linguistic argument that the English language needs a more satisfactory adjectival system such as numbers to indicate intensity).[19] He uses Shakespeare as a yardstick for measuring the competence of a fledgling poet from Arkansas (p. 131), has Squibob speak of his racial prejudice being overcome after reading *Uncle Stowe's Log* (p. 154), shows his interest in theatre by detailing Squibob's reaction to stage productions (pp. 165–71), and denigrates Edgar Allan Poe as poet. On this last subject, he cites a faulty image in the poem "*Al Aaraaf*" as an example of how poets are sometimes forced to contrive a rhyme to complete a line, then defend the contrivance as integral in the poem. The passage and image in question are these:

Ligeia! Ligeia!
My beautiful one!
Whose harshest idea
Will to melody run:
Oh is it thy will,
On the breezes to toss;
Or capriciously still,
Like the lone Albatross,
Incumbent on Night,
(As she on the air),
To keep watch with delight
On the harmony there?

Observe that note: "*The Albatross is said to sleep on the wing.*" Who said so? I should like to know. Buffon didn't mention it; neither does Audubon. Coleridge, who made the habits of that rare bird a study, never found it out; and the undersigned, who has gazed on many Albatrosses, and had much discourse with ancient mariners concerning them, never suspected the circumstance, or heard it elsewhere remarked upon.

I am inclined to believe that it never occurred to Mr. Poe, until having become embarrassed by that unfortunate word 'toss,' he was obliged to bring in either a *hoss*, or an albatross; and preferring the bird as the more poetical, invented the extraordinary fact to explain his appearance. (p. 76)

Derby concludes his defaming by denouncing Poe for believing he was "the *only* living original Poet, and that all other manufacturers of Poetry were mere copyists, continually infringing on his patent" (p. 75).

Soldier, engineer, editor, satirist, humorist, George Horatio Derby was an urbane, enlightened writer who read widely and was interested in all the arts, from drama to music (most memorable, of course, is his famous "Musical Review Extraordinary"). His satire and irony are a blend of eighteenth-century urbane wit and the more exaggerated new humor of the American West. His knowledge of literature is among the most impressive among the literary comedians and his use of it appropriate to character and situation.

Three of the literary comedians—Robert Henry Newell, David Ross Locke, and Charles Henry Smith—are closely associated with the Civil War since their writings concentrate heavily on that event and its attendant conditions.

New York-born Newell (1836–1901) was editor of the *American Mercury* during roughly the first half of the war. Later he wrote for the *New York World*, as did Edgar Wilson Nye, and in the middle 1870s was editor of the weekly journal *Hearth and Home*. He is known mainly for the Orpheus C. Kerr papers, though he also wrote novels and several volumes of poetry. He was obviously well read in literature, especially

American writers. In the Nasby letters there are numerous references to the classic American authors, mostly poets, of the nineteenth century— along with mentions of Shakespeare, Milton, and other English authors.

In the Kerr papers, Orpheus is a staunch Unionist, a member of the Mackerel Brigade, a group which Newell uses, as Jennette Tandy has pointed out, to burlesque the campaigns of the Union army. "The absurd adventures of the Mackerel brigade are written in flamboyant newspaper style. . . . His eloquence sets off very well the comic soldiering of Captain William Brown Eskevire, High Private Samivel Green, Colonel Wobbles, Colonel Wobert Wobinson of the fat German cavalry from the West, Captain Bob Shorty and Samyule Sa-mith."[20]

Newell legitimates his literary references by presenting Orpheus as a would-be writer, early in his life at least. Kerr tells in one letter of a literary aunt who gave him "a longing and determination to be a writer."[21] The aunt names the family plough horse "Lord Byron." At her inspiration, Orpheus gets a job on a publication, the *Lily of the Valley*, writing puffs.

The theme of American literary nationalism is evident in the *Kerr Papers*, even if slightly in jest. At one juncture, Orpheus reads an essay in the *Lily of the Valley* on the superiority of British over American literature, becomes irate, and retaliates by writing a "distinctive" American poem (pp. 26–28). In a counterturn, a letter entitled "The Rejected 'National Hymns'" (pp. 54 ff.), Orpheus spoofs the composition of the best national anthem, quoting from examples supposedly written by famous American writers and telling why the songs are failures. Among the writers parodied are Longfellow, Whittier, Holmes, Emerson, Bryant, Willis, Aldrich, and Stoddard. In another set of burlesques, "Balloon Ballads" in *Studies in Stanzas*[22]—a book of poetry by Orpheus—Newell parodies the "inflated" poems of Julia Ward Howe, Bret Harte, Swinburne, Carlyle, and Rossetti. The titles, such as "Balloon Him of the Republic," are clever spoofs.

Two other pieces show Newell's reflections on literature. One is serious. Stepping out of the role of Orpheus C. Kerr, Newell wrote a novel, *There Was Once a Man.*[23] Though there are few literary allusions in the book, in an author's note at the end Newell delineates the distinctions among novel, romance, tale, and story; the essay demonstrates convincingly that he carefully considered such elements of fiction as form and structure, and articulated basic literary theory. In a much lighter vein, reassuming the role of Orpheus, Newell wrote an essay on romantic literature and female authorship that was collected in *Papers.* Kerr's main point is that female authors enjoy creating "an unnatural and unmitigated ruffian for a hero," who invariably attracts and wins the affections of virtuous young girls. He uses Rochester of *Jane Eyre* as a main example, a type of hero who is "harder to understand than Hamlet, when he falls into the hands of our school-girl authoresses" (p. 65).

Kerr follows his observations with a short sample novel of the kind under discussion (pp. 66–73). A simple-minded Galushianna Crushit is infatuated over one Sir Claude Higgins, a wild, unprincipled fellow who specializes in destruction and in doing harm to others. He poisons his only sister, loses a fortune at gaming, sets fire to churches, and crushes the sexton underfoot, but these actions merely attract Galushianna to him all the more. In the concluding scene, where the lovers finally reveal their feelings for each other, our heroine writes: "My bliss was more than I could endure. Tearing all the hair-pins from my hair and tying my pocket handkerchief about my heaving neck, I flung myself upon his steaming chest" (p. 73). Kerr concludes that "the intellectual women of America draw it rather tempestuously when they try to reproduce gorgeous manhood" (p. 73).

Aside from these full discussions and satires of literary trends and movements, there are a number of brief allusions to authors and works in Newell's writings, usually just one-line references. Poe, "The Raven," *The Last of the Mohicans*, Longfellow, Scott, Burns, Milton, Homer, and, of course, Shakespeare, serve as grist for Newell's mill. In representative letters from the *Papers*, Kerr improvises on the final stanza of "A Psalm of Life" (p. 104), decides that one fellow poet's verse reminds him of Longfellow's (p. 146) and another's of "Shakespeare's happier efforts" (p. 191), wishes he himself possessed the "fiery pen of bully Homer" (p. 214), and quips, from his Unionist perspective, that even Shakespeare spoke unfavorably of the South, quoting three lines from Shakespeare to prove his point: "The sweet South, That breathes upon a bank of Violets, *Stealing* and giving odor" (p. 329). In all these references and others, Newell reveals his easy familiarity with the literature of the past and his own times. He was indeed one of the most truly *literary* of the comedians.

With only a common school education, the important learning of David Ross Locke (1833–1888), according to biographer James C. Austin, took place during the five years Locke worked on the Courtland, N.Y., *Democrat* as journalist and printer. Not only did he learn the printing craft thoroughly, but he developed "a powerful and idiomatic writing style and the ability to write on almost any topic of current or antiquarian interest."[24] Locke remained primarily a newspaper man throughout his life, but he had an insatiable appetite for literature and a flair for writing. John M. Harrison mentions that Locke and his son amassed a library of more than 20,000 volumes.[25] As Harrison has noted (p. 5), Locke tried his hand at writing novels, plays, essays, short stories, poems, and hymns, and he published or helped finance at least three magazines. Above all, of course, he is known for the satiric letters of Petroleum Vesuvius Nasby.

Nasby is a narrow-minded, small-town preacher who, after moving from Washington, D.C., to Confederate X Roads, Kentucky, also becomes postmaster. The rascally Nasby is a Copperhead, an unabashedly prejudiced Southern sympathizer who has nothing but testy impatience with Lincoln's policies and outspoken intolerance of Negroes and their emancipation. He is an unlearned, crude bigot who rails against the very philosophy to which Locke himself subscribed.

It is not surprising, then, that there is little by way of literary allusions in the Nasby papers. With the kind of character Locke creates in Nasby and the subject being largely that of the Civil War, there is simply not much need or justification for literary references. It would seem contrived if there were many. Most of those that do exist are to the Bible, but as Joseph Jones has pointed out, Nasby's interest in the scriptures "originated in the politics of the day and not in the realm of religion. The Bible provided him and other Americans with a defense of slavery."[26] A good example of Nasby's general ignorance in the realm of letters is a statement he makes about poets in his last essay in *Swingin Round the Cirkle*: "Poets hev remarked a great many times, too tejus to enoomerate, that 'farewell' is the saddistist word to pronounce wich hez to be pronounst. It may be so among poets, wich are spozd to be a continyooally carryin about with em a load ov sadnis, and sensibilities, and sich; but I hev never found it so."[27]

One has to look to Locke's other, non-Nasby writings to find anything of substance about literature. Even then there is not much, possibly because Locke does not take his satirical protagonists seriously enough to associate them with great literature to any extent. Nevertheless, there are a few examples of literary topics. In *The Morals of Abou Ben Adhem*, Abou is a counterfeiter and charlatan from Maine who comes to New Jersey to impart "the wisdom of Persia and Egypt to simple folk in need of advice."[28] In "How to Win Success in Literature," he tells what it takes for a writer to be popular with the people: one should always write for suffering humanity, always have a moral in the story, always have happy or satisfying endings, eliminate vagaries, and avoid naturalness in writing because it does not attract readers (p. 103). On the last point, Adhem says of Dickens: "The attractiveness of Dickens' sweet little female children consists entirely in the startling fact that children of that style are not lying around loose. They are seen only in his pages and in Sunday-school papers, where the precocious prigs propound heavy questions in theology to their gratified parents, and save up their pennies for the heathen. If you write for children, draw all your portraits from this class" (p. 108). Another satirical piece excoriates the quality of American literature found in the magazines. Abou thinks the tone of American literature needs elevating:

What have we, in the way of magazines or papers, that are proper exponents of the best thought of the country? What kind of an idea would the *literati* of the Old World have of American literature, if they saw only the issues of the periodical press of the country? Echo answers. "The 'Atlantic Monthly' has, as a rule, some good things in each number, but is too light, too airy, too frisky. The 'North American Review' suits, of course, a certain class of readers, but its levity is unendurable. It lacks that weight, that dignity, that a quarterly ought always to possess; and as for the other magazines—well, I will say nothing about them, but I have my opinion." (p. 105)

In such essays as these, Locke mixes seriousness with jest, of course. If Abou's advice to writers is philistine and superficial, his appraisal of American periodical literature is at least aimed towards advocating the best possible writing in this country, thus propounding the theme of American literary nationalism that Robert Henry Newell voiced.

Newell's and Locke's Southern counterpart during the Civil War era was Charles Henry Smith (1826–1903), creator of Bill Arp. Arp is a Georgia cracker, an avid Southerner who, like his creator, feels little but enmity towards the Union. With his backwoods dialect, exaggerative speech, and blatant racism, Arp has been called the brother of Nasby, "except that Nasby is the author's devil's advocate, whereas Smith, the spokesman of the Southern poor whites, meant every word he said."[29]

Like Derby, Smith was well educated. He attended Franklin College (later the University of Georgia) and studied law under his father-in-law for three months before being admitted to the bar. James C. Austin says of his college experience:

> There he had met the future political giants Alexander Stephens, Robert Toombs, and Joseph H. Lumpkin, as well as the poet Henry Timrod. There, in debate, he had formed views on slavery and the Southern cause that he argued throughout his life. There he had received the education that served him well in law, politics, and literature. There, too, he achieved the polish necssary for him to marry into one of the wealthiest families of the region.[30]

Smith practiced law in Rome, Georgia, from 1851–1861, served as a major in the Confederate Army from 1861–1865, was elected in 1865 to the state senate of Georgia and resumed his law practice. If his creation is a rabid, caustic defender of slavery, Smith himself was urbane and mild, a genteel man who, as Austin has observed in *Bill Arp*, "did not look like a comedian": "his manner in public was usually dignified and reserved, and only the gentleness of his eye and occasional inward smile betrayed his humor beneath" (p. 23). Smith's own education and his interest in that of others is manifested in his writing *A School History of Georgia* in 1893, a text that covers Georgia history from 1733 to 1893.

The Bill Arp letters were first published in the Rome newspaper, *The Southern Confederacy*, and then after the war in the *Atlanta Constitution* for some thirty years. Smith wrote more than 2,000 Arp letters between 1861 and 1903, more than two-thirds of them appearing in the *Constitution*. Although Smith's persona is a barely literate cracker who talks in heavy dialect and misspells the most common words, there are a surprising number of literary allusions, a fact that shows Arp as a thinly disguised Smith at times. Shakespeare, the Bible, Cervantes, Boswell, Dr. Johnson, and Harriet Beecher Stowe are mentioned with familiarity. It may be out of character for Bill Arp, but Charles H. Smith emerges through the character as a knowledgeable man in the realm of letters.

Smith's first book, *Bill Arp, So-Called; a Side Show of the Southern Side of the War* is a series of letters by Arp, many addressed to President Lincoln. Austin has pointed to Smith's sensitivity to language and folklore in the letters: "His figures of speech, his folk sayings, and his explicit references to games, songs, and superstitions were as authentic as his vocabulary, idiom, and syntax" (p. 86). There are also literary references. In his letter to the publisher, Smith, in delineating his persona, writes that he is "playing Boswell to an uneducated and humorous man, whose name is not Johnson, but Arp."[31] In a letter to Lincoln, Arp applauds Lincoln's wit and proposes, facetiously of course, that he become Lincoln's Boswell and follow him about (p. 26). In another letter he tells Lincoln he has heard the North has enough cotton "to make as many shirts as Falstaff had in his company" (p. 22). He once quotes Shakespeare as saying, "sweet are the juices of adversity," but concludes that Shakespeare never witnessed a struggle as devastating as the Civil War or "he wouldn't have written that line" (pp. 84–85). Referring to the best, yet most controversial, seller of the day, *Uncle Tom's Cabin*, he writes Lincoln:

> Sir: A Poet has said that "Time untied waiteth for no man." To my opinion it is untied now and hastens on to that eventful period which you have fixed when Africa is to be unshackled, when Niggerdom is to feel the power of your proclamation, when Uncle Tom is to change his base and evaluate his cabin, when all the emblems of darkness are to rush frantically forth into the arms of their deliverers, and with perfumed and scented gratitude embrace your Excellency and Madam Harriet Beecher Stowe. (p. 24)

Elsewhere Arp refers to a man under discussion as being "as fat as old Falstaff" (p. 89), calls one Winter Davis, who is a political foe, "the Winter of our discontent" (p. 156), and speaks of an army officer who will "put just such fellows as me in the front ranks, where David put Goliah [sic] . . ." (p. 42). He hopes that the firm resolve of Socrates and Cato will serve as models for Southerners when they seek justice from the Yankees.

It is obvious that Smith could not resist referring to his literary learning, even if such allusions were out of character with his unlearned persona. His firm grounding in literature was a major part of his experience.

The latecomer to the group of eight men designated by Willard Thorp as "the best and most popular of the literary comedians,"[32] was Maine-born, Wisconsin-raised Edgar Wilson Nye (1850–1896), the "Bill" Nye who rose to fame in Laramie, Wyoming, as editor of the Laramie *Boomerang* and who spent the last part of his life in New York City and the North Carolina mountains writing nationally syndicated humorous newspaper columns.

Nye's formal education was more like Browne's and Locke's than Derby's and Smith's. He matriculated for a nominal sixteen-week term at an academy in Hudson, Wisconsin, and spent two terms at a military school in neighboring River Falls. As a young man in Wisconsin he taught school for a while, and he read law and passed the bar examination in Wyoming. Like so many other American humorists, however, he completed his education in the newspaper office. Reporter, editor, and humorous columnist, Nye learned his trade well and became versed in letters, especially in nineteenth-century literature, while practicing it.

Always interested in literature, Nye tried his hand at writing plays, poetry, short and long burlesques, and even a novel. He had a skill for narration that leaves readers all the more regretful that the manuscript of his only novel, "Thelma," was lost in a shipwreck. He showed a good sense of timing in his narratives, and above all a keen sense of character delineation. Two of his plays, *The Cadi* and *The Stag Party*, appeared on Broadway in the 1890's, the first one meeting with some measure of success.[33] His two long burlesque histories, *Bill Nye's History of the United States* (1894) and *Bill Nye's History of England from the Druids to the Reign of Henry VIII* (1896) were both popular sellers.

Nye's success with the pen was not happenstance or accomplished without having ample literary background. Calling himself "a great bookworm and an omniverous reader,"[34] he read substantially in nineteenth-century English and American literature and acquired a sizeable library by the time he settled at his North Carolina estate, "Buck Shoals," near Asheville. His collection contained Emerson's essays, the works of Dickens, and volumes by Thackeray, Hawthorne, Macaulay, and Victor Hugo, among others.[35] In his newspaper columns he frequently commented on authors and their works. At different times he praised the dialect poetry of lecture partner James Whitcomb Riley,[36] discussed William Dean Howells' realism,[37] commented on the traits and merits of Whitman's and Lowell's poetry,[38] and compared Oliver Wendell Holmes' humor to Riley's.[39] He wrote character sketches of Eugene Field, Bret Harte, Joel Chandler Harris, and James M. Bailey.[40] (It was from the "Bill Nye" in Harte's poem "Plain Language From Truthful James," incidentally, that Nye took his penname.) At other times he refers to such American writers as John Greenleaf Whittier, Mary

Catherwood, Charles Dudley Warner, Rose Terry Cooke, R. H. Stoddard, and, of course, Mark Twain. He was sharply critical and satirical of the Julia A. Moore school of lugubrious verse (as was Twain, of course), coming down heavily on their promiscuous use of poetic license: "A poetic license, as I understand it, simply allows the poet to jump the 15 over the 14 in order to bring in the proper rhyme, but it does not allow the writer to usurp the management of the entire system of worlds, and introduce dog-days and ice-cream between Christmas and New Year. . . ."[41] Of writers across the Atlantic, he was critical of Robert Browning (a "fifteen-puzzle poet," an "over estimated man").[42] He jested that had Pope still been living Nye could have "corrected his essays for him."[43] He was amazed at the energy and vast production of members of the London Author's Club—such men as Walter Besant, Douglas Sladen, Gilbert Parker, and Conan Doyle.[44] The crème de la crème of nineteenth-century authorship, however, was Charles Dickens, Nye's "favorite author." In Nye's own words, he got "more juice out of the works of Mr. Charles Dickens than anybody else. Instead of reading new books, as I suppose I ought, I go back over 'David Copperfield' and the journey of little Nell when I presume I should read 'Robert Elsmere.' But it don't hurt me to rinse off my soul, now and then, with a few tears such as Mr. Dickens calls forth. . . ."[45] Nye defended Dickens against William Dean Howells' attack: "In fifty years from now let us ask the timid little touch-me-not who sells books on the train how William and Charles are standing as to sales of books."[46] Though he championed realism in letters as represented by Howells, Nye marveled at Dickens' depiction of character—not a surprising affinity given Nye's chief interest, people, an interest that unquestionably accounted in a large way for his fondness of literature.

One could go on to discuss still more literary comedians and their awareness of literature and the influence of literature on them. James M. Bailey in *Life in Danbury* discusses Walt Whitman's poetry and refers to Homer and John Bunyan.[47] The last in the line of literary comedians, Finley Peter Dunne, creator of Mr. Dooley, was brought up in a middle class family "with subscriptions to magazines in the home and with a good supply of scholarly books, from which, at the age of eight, [he] read aloud to his mother," and was a devotee of Thackeray and enjoyed such standard Victorian works as Macaulay's *History of England*.[48] But suffice it to say that with the literary comedians we have a group of writers who were serious literary men, grounded in the great literature of the past and present, hide as they did behind personae who themselves were sometimes far removed from learning. Far from being platform funny men, they were sophisticated, cultured men who were ensconced in the literary traditions of the Western World. To paraphrase Bill Nye, most of them were—like him—great bookworms and omnivorous readers. They were the *literary* comedians.

Notes

1. *Mark Twain's Library: A Reconstruction* (Boston: G. K. Hall & Co., 1980), I, xvii.

2. "The Misspellers," in *The Comic Imagination in American Literature*, ed. Louis D. Rubin, Jr. (New Brunswick: Rutgers Univ. Press, 1973), p. 130.

3. Don C. Seitz, *Artemus Ward: A Biography and Bibliography* (New York and London: Harper & Brothers, 1919), p. 10.

4. Quoted by James C. Austin, *Artemus Ward* (New York: Twayne Publishers, 1964), p. 21.

5. *Artemus Ward: His Book* (New York: Carleton, 1862). Hereafter cited in the text as *Book.*

6. *Artemus Ward: His Travels* (New York: Carleton, 1865). Hereafter cited in the text as *Travels.*

7. *Artemus Ward: His Works, Complete* (New York: G. W. Carleton & Co., 1875). Hereafter cited in the text as *Works.*

8. See note 3.

9. Cyril Clemens, *Josh Billings: Yankee Humorist* (Webster Groves, Mo.: International Mark Twain Society, 1932), p. 9.

10. *Everybody's Friend, or Josh Billings' Encyclopaedia and Proverbial Philosophy of Wit and Humor* (Hartford: American Publishing Co., 1874), p. 571.

11. *Josh Billings on Ice and Other Things* (New York: G. W. Carleton & Co., 1868), pp. 25, 111. Hereafter cited in the text as *Ice.*

12. *The Complete Works of Josh Billings* (New York: D. W. Dillingham Co., 1888), pp. 226, 274. Hereafter cited in the text as *Works.*

13. "American Humor," *Harper's Magazine*, 50 (April–May 1875), 698.

14. *Horse Sense in American Humor* (Chicago: Univ. of Chicago Press, 1942), p. 222.

15. *Josh Billings: Hiz Sayings* (New York: G. W. Carleton & Co., 1865), p. 121. Hereafter cited in the text as *Sayings.*

16. *John Phoenix, Esq.: The Veritable Squibob* (New York: Da Capo Press, 1969), p. 7.

17. See *Derby's Report on Opening the Colorado, 1850–1851*, ed. Odie B. Faulk (Albuquerque: Univ. of New Mexico Press, 1969).

18. "Official Report of Professor John Phoenix, A.M.," *Phoenixiana; or Sketches and Burlesques*, by John Phoenix (New York: D. Appleton & Co., 1856), pp. 13–31. All subsequent references are to this edition.

19. See "A New System of English Grammar," *Phoenixiana*, pp. 32–41.

20. *Crackerbox Philosophers in American Humor and Satire* (New York: Columbia Univ. Press, 1925), pp. 118–19.

21. *The Orpheus C. Kerr Papers* (New York: Blackman & Mason, 1862), p. 23. Hereafter cited in the text as *Papers.*

22. *Studies in Stanzas* (New York: Useful Knowledge Publishing Co., 1882), pp. 154–62.

23. *There Was Once a Man* (New York: Fords, Howard, & Hulbert, 1884).

24. James C. Austin, *Petroleum V. Nasby* (New York: Twayne Publishers, 1965), p. 21.

25. *The Man Who Made Nasby, David Ross Locke* (Chapel Hill: Univ of North Carolina Press, 1969), pp. 319–20.

26. *The Struggles of Petroleum V. Nasby* (Boston: Beacon Press, 1963), p. 162.

27. *Swingin Round the Cirkle* by Petroleum V. Nasby (Boston: Lee and Shepard, 1867), p. 291.

28. *The Morals of Abou Ben Adhem* (Boston: Lee and Shepard, 1875), [p. iv].

29. F.C.S., "Charles Henry Smith," *Bill Arp's Peace Papers* (Upper Saddle River, N.J.: Literature House, 1969), [p. iii].

30. *Bill Arp* (New York: Twayne Publishers, 1969), p. 20.

31. *Bill Arp, So-called; A Side Show of the Southern Side of the War* (New York: Metropolitan Record Office, 1866), p. 6. All subsequent references are to this edition.

32. Thorp lists Derby, Newell, Browne, Locke, Charles G. Halpine, Shaw, Smith, and Nye as the major eight. See *American Humorists* (Minneapolis: Univ. of Minnesota Pamphlets on American Writers, No. 42, 1964), p. 17.

33. *The Cadi*, an autobiographical drama, ran for 125 performances in 1891; the less successful *Stag Party* survived for twelve days.

34. "Jay Gould and Tolstoi," *New York World*, 12 October 1890, p. 26.

35. Bill Buncombe, "A Visit to Bill Nye's Home," *Asheville News and Hotel Reporter*, 19 December 1896.

36. "All About a Genuine Poet," *New York World*, 17 June 1888, p. 17.

37. "Bill Nye's Hen Tracks," *San Francisco Examiner*, 5 June 1892, p. 17.

38. "A Good Night's Sleep," *San Francisco Examiner*, 19 June 1892, p. 18, and "Bill Nye by Special Wire," *San Francisco Examiner*, 8 July 1894, p. 13.

39. "Hard to Stay on Pegasus," *San Francisco Examiner*, 16 December 1894, p. 18.

40. See "William Visits Eugene," *San Francisco Examiner*, 28 February 1892, p. 17; "Bill Nye and Royalty," *New York World*, 18 August 1889, p. 9; "Bill Nye Visits Atlanta," *New York World*, 23 December 1888, p. 13; "People Nye Has Met," *New York World*, 22 June 1890, p. 28.

41. "The Muse," in *Bill Nye and Boomerang* (Chicago: Belford, Clarke, 1881), p. 99.

42. "Browning Is Not the Man," *New York World*, 11 November 1888, p. 17.

43. "Just Off Piccadilly," *San Francisco Examiner*, 5 November 1893, p. 17.

44. "The Lights of London," *San Francisco Examiner*, 31 December 1893, p. 18.

45. Edgar Wilson Nye, "Bill Nye's Favorite Novels," *Belford's Magazine*, 4 (January 1890), 254.

46. "Bill Nye by Special Wire," *San Francisco Examiner*, 8 July 1894, p. 13.

47. *Life in Danbury* (Boston: Shepard and Gill, 1873), pp. 75–76, 221–22.

48. Grace Eckley, *Finley Peter Dunne* (Boston: Twayne Publishers, 1981), p. 17.

On or About December 1910:
When Human Character—and
American Humor—Changed   Sanford Pinsker*

"On or about December 1910," Virginia Woolf announced in her essay-manifesto "Mr. Bennett and Mrs. Brown," "human character changed."[1] She had several things in mind: the death of Edward VII on May 6, 1910 (which Woolf discusses more fully in *The Years*), the post-impressionist exhibition of Cézanne, Van Gogh, Picasso and Matisse held in London on November 5, 1910, and, of course, a more generalized sense that only a Modernist imagination could adequately address the "facts" of twentieth-century life. As Irving Howe points out: ". . . Woolf meant to suggest that there is a frightening discontinuity between the traditional past and the shaken present; that the line of history has been bent, perhaps broken. Modernist literature goes on the tacit assumption that human nature has indeed changed, probably a few decades before the date given by Mrs. Woolf. . . ."[2]

1910 was also the year in which Mark Twain died, and while I would not claim that his death on April 21, 1910, *changed* American humor in quite the ways Woolf had in mind, I do think Twain simultaneously exhausted the best possibilities of nineteenth-century American humor and made it painfully clear that they would no longer suffice. One has only to compare the lighthearted illustrations E. W. Kemble provided for *Adventures of Huckleberry Finn* (1883) or even the darker, more satirical ones Dan Beard added to *A Connecticut Yankee in King Arthur's Court* (1889) with, say, the cartoons of James Thurber or those of other *New Yorker* zanies like Charles Addams, George Price or Saul Steinberg to feel the difference. There was a time when "human character" had recognizable outlines, representational shapes, but modernity changed the rules by which an artist, in Joseph Conrad's famous words, makes you hear, makes you feel, before all, makes you *see*.[3]

Although the final destination may have been inevitable, Twain came to his embittered, solipsistic vision gradually. There are hints of it in *Adventures of Huckleberry Finn* (one thinks, for example, of Colonel Sherburn's insistence that "The average man's a coward") and in the louder, more ominous rumblings of *The Tragedy of Pudd'nhead Wilson* (1894), *The Man That Corrupted Hadleyburg* (1900) and *What is Man?* (1906). Increasingly, Twain began to think of himself as a serious philosopher rather than as a humorist "preaching" on the lecture platform. He wrote of large matters largely, in part because he was ill-equipped for the twentieth century, in part because his burlesques of rough-and-tumble Southwestern humor had used-up his most congenial

---

*This essay was written specifically for publication in this volume and is included here by permission of the author.

material. Who could work up even a modicum of that willing suspension of disbelief necessary for the tall tale to do its magic after "The Raftsmen's Passage"? In Twain's hilarious confrontation between the stylized rhetoric of Sudden Death and General Desolation (e.g. "the wails of the dying is music to my ears") and the Pet Child of Calamity (e.g. "the massacre of isolated communities [is] the serious business of my life"), he deflated the swaggering ring-tailed roarer forever, at one and the same time providing us with an apotheosis of the form and its epitaph.

Granted, one makes generalizations about a complicated, deeply divided writer like Twain at great risk. A study like Hamlin Hill's *Mark Twain: God's Fool* (1973) documents in painful detail what we have come to call Twain's "dark period," that mixture of sophomoric nihilism and disenchantment which perplexes those readers who identify Twain with boyhood adventures and American Innocence. Consider, for example, Satan's concluding lines from *The Mysterious Stranger*, a book first published, in Albert Bigelow Paine's "edited" version, in 1916:

> "It is true that which I have revealed to you: there is no God, no universe, no human race, no earthly life, no heaven, no hell. It is all a dream—a grotesque and foolish dream. Nothing exists but you. And you are but a *thought*—a vagrant thought, a useless thought, a homeless thought, wandering forlorn among the empty eternities!"[4]

This is precisely what I had in mind when I claimed earlier that Twain wrote of large matters largely. If a humorist gives metaphysical speculations an inch, they will take over the entire book. In Twain's case, as the distinction between being famous—the "most recognizable face on the planet"—and being wise began to blur, he plowed more and more of his energy into projects (his *Autobiography*, the fragments published posthumously as *Mark Twain in Eruption*, etc.) that spoke more eloquently to his uncompromising "private" stance than they did to his public genius as a folk artist and master story-teller.

By contrast, James Thurber describes the humorist as one who "talks largely about small matters and smally about great affairs": "His ears are shut to the ominous rumblings of the dynasties of the world moving toward a cloudier chaos than ever before, but he hears with an acute perception the startling sounds that rabbits make twisting in the bushes along a country road at night and a cold chill comes upon him when the comic supplement of a Sunday newspaper blows unexpectedly out of an areaway and envelopes his knees."[5] These words—which might serve as a touchstone for the modernity of modern American humor—were written in 1933, the year Adolph Hitler came to official power and the world teetered on the edge of a nightmare from which it has not yet managed to awaken. It was also, of course, the year when the Great Depression gripped our country and writers divided about an appropriate response, some throwing their lot with social reform, radical politics and proletarian sympathies while others stuck to their humorous guns, crafting sentences that depended less on droll timing than they did on precision and a relentless sophistication.

As Thurber would have it, "the damp hand of melancholy" set the wheels of his fellow *New Yorker* humorists into motion.[6] In effect, they explored that internal world Twain could only rant about, and, in the process, they discovered techniques by which their protagonists could triumph over Modernity itself. Thurber's "The Unicorn in the Garden" is such a tale, at once a fable and a projection, a sly reversal in the ongoing battle of the sexes and an allegory of the Artist.

But I am getting ahead of myself: In the beginning was the Word— and that testament holds for humorists every bit as much as it does for theologians. Twain's contemporaries put great stock in unusual coinages (a standard boast of the ring-tailed roarer was "if I ain't [the best man] . . . may I be tetotaciously exfluncated") and eccentric spellings: "I see in the papers last nite [Petroleum V. Nasby begins one of his sketches] that the Government hez institooted a draft, and that in a few weeks sum hundreds uv thousands uv peeceable citizens will be dragged to the tented field. I know not wat uthers may do, but ez for me, I cant go."[7] Alas, what once struck their audience to the quick, now seems dated if not dead. Even if one points out the similarities between Nasby's reasons why he should not be drafted in 1862 (e.g. "I hev verry-kose vanes, hev a white-swellin on wun leg and a fever sore on the uther . . .") and those advanced in Phil Ochs' "Draft Dodger Rag" (e.g. "I'm seventeen, got a ruptured spleen and I always carry a purse . . ."), the antics of the Phunny Phellows (comic misspellers like Artemus Ward [Charles Farrar Browne], Josh Billings [Henry Wheeler Shaw] and, of course, Petroleum V. Nasby [David Ross Locke]) no longer amuse. Their heritage is carried on, if at all, in the "humor" issues of high school newspapers, or other bastions of officialdom where mangled spelling is equated with a daring, subversive act. Read aloud, of course, the impact of phonetic spelling disappears; only on the printed page can it seem eye-catching. The rub, or course, is that the eye adjusts to dialect and avalanches of local color. What Twain wielded with a deft stroke (there is more *illusion* than actual dialect in *Adventures of Huckleberry Finn*), others laid on with a thick hand. Still, as Walter Blair points out, there were Phunny Phellows by the handful between 1855 and 1900, and their readers were legion.[8] Writing them down, in their own style, might go something like this: "*Sick Tramp Sit Gloria's Monday.*"

If we continue to imagine a new decade will be markedly different from the preceding ones, our expectations for a new century raise to the tenth power. A novel like Joseph Conrad's *Lord Jim* (1900) is dazzling enough in attitude and execution to strike us, even now, as an important watershed, a definable moment separating the Victorian novel from its Modernist counterpart. American literature is not so fortunate. Granted, 1900 was the year of Theodore Dreiser's *Sister Carrie* and Sarah Orne Jewett's *The Foreigner*, but neither stands up well under extended comparison with Conrad's work. By contrast, American humor—which had a long history of being able to hold its own in the world market-place—began to explore new ways of pulling naive legs and giving pretension the raspberry.

In short, American humor moved to Chicago, where Eugene Field functioned as a spiritual father to those humorists associated with the infamous Whitechapel Club: George Ade, Opie Read and Finley Peter Dunne. Field, of course, is best remembered for his sentimental chest-nuts like "Little Boy Blue" and such orthodox children's classics as "The Gingham Dog and the Calico Cat," but that is rather like "remembering" Walt Whitman for "O Captain, My Captain." There was a dark, debunk-ing streak in Field that, in retrospect, is more important, more delicious and infinitely more contemporary. As Walter Blair and Hamlin Hill point out in *America's Humor*, Fields' "outrageous burlesques of the New England Primer . . . gleefully mocked children's do-good readers."[9] Two examples of his "sick" humor will suffice:

> This is a gun. Is the Gun Loaded? I do not know. Let us Find out. Put the Gun on the table and you, Susie, blow down one barrel, while you, Charlie, blow down the other. Bang! Yes, it was loaded. Run quick Jennie, and pick up Susie's head and Charlie's lower jaw before the Nasty Blood gets over the New carpet.[10]

> The Cat is asleep on the Rug. Step on her Tail and See if She will Wake up. Oh, no; She will not wake. She is a heavy Sleeper. Perhaps if you Were to saw her Tail off with the carving knife you might Attract her attention.[11]

Granted, Southwestern humorists enjoyed making finicky readers wince. As their manifesto would have it, a good joke maimed people; a great joke killed them. Field put an urban, sophisticated spin on the humor of cruelty. His mutilations were parodic, more dependent on the well-turned phrase than the bare-knuckled fist.

What Field dabbled with in the *Denver Tribune*, George Ade mined systematically in Chicago. His first fable was written in 1897, and by 1899 he had enough for his first collection, *Fables in Slang*. *More Fables in Slang* (1900) followed in something of the way in which Hollywood would later have Abbott and Costello meet the Wolf Man or Gidget go

Hawaiian. By 1920 there were eight more collections of Ade's "fables," along with many others that never slipped between hard covers. Critics are sharply divided about the terms and the significance of Ade's enormous appeal, but one thing is clear: Ade struck a posture we have not yet fully exhausted, no matter how many "fables" James Thurber & Co. added, no matter how many Bronx cheers the hicks endured.

In the beginning, of course, it was the sophisticate who was on the receiving end of tall tales, whoppers and leg-pulls. Benjamin Franklin knew full well that America was synonymous with possibility, and that bigness and swagger could flourish here in ways that a cramped, aristocratic Europe could never hope to match. Exaggeration is as much a part of our national inheritance as are democracy and our capacity for Dream. So, when England claimed that the colonies could not provide even *one* pair of stockings for each inhabitant from the wool produced in America, Franklin wrote back with eighteenth-century eloquence and a tongue firmly planted in his cheek. It seems that American sheep are creatures of a very different wool: "Dear Sir [Franklin began], do not let us suffer ourselves to be amuse'd with such groundless objections. The very Tails of the American sheep are so laden with Wooll, that each has a little Car or Waggon on four little wheels, to support & keep it from trailing on the ground. Would they chauk their Ships, would they fill their Beds, would they even litter their Horses with Wooll, if it were not both plenty and cheap?"[12]

And naturally, Franklin—being Franklin—did not stop there. It is the nature of the tall tale to *keep* stretching. Nobody pulls a patsy's leg just one time. Christopher Newman in Henry James's *The American* "had sat with Western humorists in knots round cast-iron stoves, and seen 'tall' stories grow taller without toppling over, and his own imagination had learned the trick of piling up consistent wonders."[13] Franklin knew that trick to his bones in 1765, nearly a century before the Southwestern humorists made it their stock-in-trade.

Moreover, if Franklin could sucker the English into believing that our sheep were, indeed, a special breed, he could get them to swallow even bigger "consistent wonders":

> And yet all this is a certainly true, as the Account said to be from Quebec, in all the Papers of last week, that the inhabitants of Canada are making Preparations for a Cod and Whale Fishery this "Summer in the upper Lakes." Ignorant people may object that the upper lakes are fresh, and that Cod and Whale are Salt Water Fish: But let them know, Sir, that Cod, like other fish attack'd by their Enemies, fly into any Water where they can be safest; that Whales, when they have a mind to eat Cod, pursue them wherever they fly: and that the grand leap of the Whale in that Chase up the Fall of Niagra is esteemed, by all who have seen it, as one of the finest Spectacles in Nature.[14]

Comic exaggerations of this sort begin by gilding the lily at its stem and then working slowly upward. Colonists ribbed their antagonists across the ocean, city dandies who stumbled into a rustic setting were bombarded with misinformation and tenderfeet soon learned that "fair game" referred as much to them as to the furry animals they encountered on the trail. In short, pulling down vanity has a special appeal in wide-open democratic countries and while the foolish braggart has a long history weaving back to Plautus and early Roman comedy, the incarnation he takes in America is that of the windbag, usually a pedantic scholar or a prissy man of the cloth. We call him the *alazon*, the man who says more than he knows. His fate is to be foiled and generally befuddled by the *eiron*, the man who knows more than he says. American literature has kept its *eirons* in the campfire and played its comic cards close to the vest. Indeed, the appeal of comic deflation, of giving the blowhard his come-uppance, seems inexhaustable, whether the country bumpkin is Will Rogers or Herb Shriner or the triumvirate who man the booth during ABC's "Monday Night Football."

The last phenomenon is worth exploring in some depth. No doubt there is a Rip Van Winkle aspect to our annual winter hibernation in front of the tv set and, no doubt, it has something to do with the eternal boyhood of the American male, but even literary sociology of this sort cannot adequately explain the chemistry that has made Howard Cosell, Don Meredith and Frank Gifford *more* than sportscasters. Cosell's jaw-breaking vocabulary and self-congratulatory erudition, his pompous demeanor and comic blather make him the *alazon* incarnate. In the national imagination—which is always directional—he stands for the East, which our age equates with New York City and Jewishness. By contrast, Don Meredith (known affectionately—and "down home"—as Dandy Don) is the tight-lipped *eiron*. His is a Western spirit. Thus, "Monday Night Football" pits "book larnin'" against country wisdom, the man of statistics and fact against the man of experience and feeling. Frank Gifford, of course, mediates between the two, bristling with the credibility that can, and does, sell everything from soda pop to safety razors. For those who tune in to see a football game, Gifford provides the play-by-play: who has the ball, on what yard line and where they must reach for a first down. Meanwhile, Cosell and Meredith keep the rest of the prime time audience entertained. They also remind scholars with an itch to keep things tidy and moving forward in straight, chronological lines that the more American humor changes, the more it remains, essentially, the same.

In the case of George Ade and his fables, *slang* turned the tables on the rube, exposing all that was limited, and delimiting, about his world. As Lee Coyle points out, Ade's fables reveal "the loneliness of the farm, the destruction of the village, the emptiness of the city, the inadequacy of traditional values, the tedium of life without laughter, the lust for status and culture, the national distrust of ideas and acceptance of prosperity as an ultimate value."[15] If Southwestern humorists gradually narrowed the space allotted to pompous narrators and allowed folk creations increasingly longer stretches in the vernacular, Ade tests out how far one might go if a street savvy voice held all the cards and surveyed the landscape, darkly.[16] Here, for example, is a typical Ade fable taken from E. B. White and Katharine S. White's famous anthology, *A Subtreasury of American Humor*:

> Now it happens that in America a man who goes up hanging to a balloon is a Professor.
> One day a Professor, preparing to make a Grand Ascension, was sorely pestered by Spectators of the Yellow-Hammer Variety, who fell over the Stay-Ropes or crowded up close to the Balloon to ask foolish questions. They wanted to know how fur up he Calkilated to go and was he Afeerd and how often he did it. The Professor answered them in the Surly Manner peculiar to Showmen accustomed to meet a Web-Foot Population. . . .[17]

"The Professor Who Wanted to be Alone" reverses the usual situation in which a city slicker peppers the rural natives with ridiculous questions. But more than that, Ade inverts the language ("how fur up he Calkilated to go and was he Afeerd") that rolled so easily off the Phunny Phellows' tongues. For Ade, ignorance was neither bliss nor especially funny; rather, fractured spelling and rural coinage were the stuff of which "Yellow-Hammers" were made.

Mark Twain's death ended an era that had achieved its fullest stature in *Adventures of Huckleberry Finn*, a work which allowed Huck to narrate his own story—unframed, uninterrupted and with his full-throated, poetic power. To be sure, Twain remained a public figure until his death, but it was Ade whom the public read and chuckled over. Put another way: The age of modern American humor had begun and while there would always be a residue of the boast-and-swagger school (one thinks of, say, Muhammed Ali during his heyday) to remind us of Mike Fink, conditions at ground zero, at the quotidian level of daily experience, had changed radically.

For the modern humorist, braggadocio remained a given, but its terms were transposed to a more appropriate key. Not only had the locale shifted from the keelboat or Western campfire to the city street, but what a comic persona crowed about was more often ineptitude rather than prowess, weakness rather than strength, crippling inferiority rather than swaggering confidence. Moreover, the cast of comic writers— who they were, where they came from and, most important of all, where they went—bore little resemblance to the platform humorists of the late nineteenth century. Now, writers tended to move East, first to Chicago and then to New York: George Ade, Franklin P. Adams, Don Marquis and, after the First World War, a Robert Benchley bumbling in from New England or a James Thurber arriving a bit later from Columbus, Ohio. While the *serious* writers of the Lost Generation fled America for Paris, the wags got jobs on the big American newspapers and began to move American humor into the twentieth century. The result, as Carl Van Doren pointed out in the 1920s, was a clustering of "town wits" who gave New York City something of the flavor that, say, Addison and Steele provided for eighteenth-century London.[18]

The differences, however, are a measure of what distinguishes eighteenth-century *wit* from twentieth-century insanity. Modernist literature is, at one and the same time, an attitude and a technique. Its stomping ground is the City—whether it be T. S. Eliot's London or James Joyce's Dublin or Marcel Proust's Paris. And something of the same thing can be said about modern humorists; city rhythms—subways and clatter, crowded thoroughfares and sheer noise—are reflected in the what and how they wrote. In this sense, the very title of Fran Liebowitz's first collection—*Metropolitan Life* (1978)—continues a tradition that George Ade and his Whitechapel compatriots began.

But that said, let me hasten to add that modern American humorists and the Modernist giants share more than an affection for the city life. S. J. Perelman, for example, made no secret of his debt to James Joyce's *Ulysses*; for him, the thick novel was comic art of the highest water, a place to do post-graduate study in word play at its wildest and puns at their funniest. James Thurber, whose failing eyesight must have made him feel a kindred spirit with the similarly afflicted Joyce, wrote one of his first *New Yorker* sketches ("More Authors Cover the Snyder Trial") in styles that parodied those of James Joyce and Gertrude Stein. As is often the case, respect—even reverence—lurked just behind the send-up.

Modernist literature, of course, comes armed with heavy-water manifestoes—usually in the form of pronouncements about what makes this or that movement avant-garde, daring and, most of all, NEW—that would make respectable humorists blush. I belabor this point because Harold W. Ross was the unlikeliest of candidates to found a magazine that would place the best modern American humorists between slick covers and draft the "manifest" under which the *New Yorker* would prosper. He was self-taught, unpolished, ill at ease and, more often than not, the butt of the jokes by his best writers. In a world where quick, literary wits were the measure of all things, Ross once asked, apparently with a stright face, if Moby Dick was the whale or the man. Although the portraits of Ross handed down to us, from Dale Kramer's *Ross and the New Yorker* (1951) through James Thurber's *The Years with Ross* (1959) and Brendan Gill's *Here at the New Yorker* (1975), suggest that Ross, like beauty, can only be found in the eye of the beholder, there is wide agreement about what he accomplished. His devotion to Fowler's *Dictionary of Modern English Usage* and his unflagging insistence that every paragraph, every sentence—indeed, every word—be correct, precise and polished has served American humor well. Moreover, his instincts about what an urban magazine should look like and *be* were exactly right. If December 1910 is the date when human character changed, I would submit that February 25, 1925—when the first issue of the *New Yorker* (with a drawing of Eustace Tilley, the New York City dandy, adorning its cover) rolled off the presses—is the date when the "character" of American humor changed.

Granted, Ross's *raison d'être* was simpler than those we associate with Ezra Pound or Ford Maddox Ford or Wyndham Lewis, but his famous prospectus was just as clear about its sense of mission: the *New Yorker* would turn up its nose at the "old lady in Dubuque" and its readers "will be kept apprised of what is going on in the public and semi-public smart gathering places—the clubs, hotels, cafes, supper clubs, cabarets and other resorts."[19] It is a short step from Ross's lips to the ears-and-eyes of "The Talk of the Town," a feature that still persists at nearly the same quality as in the halcyon days when E. B. White and James Thurber contributed to it.

Ross also imagined a magazine that would "not deal in scandal for the sake of scandal nor sensation for the sake of sensation. Its integrity [Ross insisted] will be above suspicion."[20] Luckily for us, the zanies Ross collected upset his even-tempered plans. *New Yorker* cartoonists like Peter Arno, Charles Addams and Saul Steinberg gave the magazine a character that was as irreverent as it probably was neurotic, and it was these features—rather than the ones Ross dreamed about—that accounted for the *New Yorker*'s phenomenal success. The magazine's best humorists followed suit. Robert Benchley is especially important, not only because James Thurber used to worry that the piece he was sweating over had probably been written earlier, and better, by Robert Benchley, but because Benchley understood that modern humorists fatten on modern trouble. His Little Man, like Charlie Chaplin's Little Tramp, is a man confounded, and defeated, by all the traps twentieth-century life set. For example, the necktie: "I pull and yank [Benchley begins], take the collar off and rearrange the tie, try gentle tactics, followed suddenly by a deceptive upward jerk, but this gets me nothing. The knot stays loosely off-center . . . After two minutes of this mad wrenching one of three things happens—the tie rips, the collar tears, or I strangle to death in a horrid manner with eyes bulging and temples distended, a ghastly caricature of my real self."[21] Even the Little Man's daydreams are fraught with nightmarish peril: "I haven't been at a fight for more than three minutes before I begin indulging in one of my favorite nightmares. This consists of imagining that I myself am up in the ring facing the better of the two men."[22] Woody Allen's career tests the thesis that successive generations must rediscover their own versions of the "little man"—in his case, a bemused, bespectacled countenance terrorized by rabbis, teachers, bullies and nearly any woman. He is our version of Everyman: timid, weak, unheroic, but, nonetheless, harboring fantasies of sexual conquest and large, public Success. In a word, Allen is the *schlemiel* we recognize in the mirror, albeit one most easily spotted on Manhattan's chic upper West Side.

Allen's collections—*Getting Even* (1972), *Without Feathers* (1975), and, most recently, *Side Effects* (1980)—continue those traditions of *New Yorker* humor we associate with Benchley, Perelman, Thurber and White. Modern life, rather than the banana peels of slapstick, is what his characters slip on. The difference, of course, is that Allen begins in an age where modernity is an established, widespread fact, a condition that generates syllabi, lectures and heaps of paperback anthologies. The vague ticks that caused, say, James Thurber so much *angst* have become thoroughly domesticated, subjects for banal talk at cocktail parties. So, Allen has done in his sketches what *New Yorker* cartoonists increasingly do in their cartoons—namely, turn the clichés of modern life back upon their "sophisticated" speakers. He is preoccupied, for example, with the fate of modern man, that endangered species he defines as "any person born after Nietzsche's edict that 'God is dead,' but before the hit recording 'I Wanna Hold Your Hand.' "[23] I emphasize the philosophical aspects of Allen's humor, partly because Allen belabors them in his books and films (existentialism is, to Allen, what words beginning with "k" are to Neil Simon's "The Sunshine Boys"—dependable material), partly because I was struck by the painstaking rigor a scholar brought to bear recently on Mark Twain's reading habits.[24] Apparently, this scholar has proved beyond a shadow's doubt what every serious reader of Twain already knew—namely, that Twain owned, and read, large numbers of books, and that he perpetrated the mythos of the rustic, homespun spinner of tall tales and dispenser of low-falutin' wisdom so as not to put off any segment of the population with enough ready cash to buy one of his books or to crowd into one of his lectures. This same indefatigable scholar would, no doubt, be able to prove the opposite about Woody Allen—namely, that he reads dust jackets and reviews, rather than Real Books, and that he perpetrates the mythos of the sensitive New York egghead so he will remain the darling of those who also make it a point to keep up with the dust jackets and the book reviews.

The result, of course, is that those who regard *Rolling Stone* or *Crawdaddy* as intellectual journals or who think that "Saturday Night Live'" is *soooo* funny will have a tough time with Allen's brand of modern humor. His playfulness about Ideas and parodic romps depend on a "familiarity with"—if not an *understanding* of—the originals. For example, what is one to make of the following passage if names like Sartre and Camus draw a blank?

Now Cloquet stepped closer to Brisseau's sleeping hulk and again cocked the pistol. A feeling of nausea swept over him as he contemplated the implications of his action. This was an existential nausea, caused by his intense awareness of the contingency of life, and could not be relieved with an ordinary Alka-Seltzer. What was required was an Existential Alka-Seltzer—a product sold in many Left Bank drugstores. It was an enormous pill, the size of an automobile hubcap, that, dissolved in water, took away the queasy feeling induced by too much awareness of life. Cloquet had also found it helpful after eating Mexican food.[25]

The selection is from *Side Effects*, but Allen used the same rapid-fire juxtapositions in earlier collections. Indeed, sharply alternating rhythms are Allen's stylistic trademark; highbrow ideas and gritty urban details are forced to share floor space in the same paragraph, and often on opposing sides of a semicolon. In "Remembering Needleman," for example, we are told that Sandor Needleman "differentiated between existence and Existence, and knew that one was preferable, but could never remember which . . . 'God is silent,' he was fond of saying, 'now if we can only get Man to shut up.' "[26] It is the same gear-switching Allen has been giving us since his salad days as a stand-up comic in Greenwich Village, when he would grab the mike, turn reflective and ask: "Can we actually 'know' the universe? My God, it's hard enough finding your way around in Chinatown."

Philip Roth—who once boasted that he is much funnier than Lenny Bruce ever was—may not be a *humorist*, properly speaking, but a savagely comic novel like *Portnoy's Complaint* (1969) suggests yet another direction that the modernity of modern American humor might take. It was only when Roth realized, in his words, that "this morbid preoccupation with punishment and guilt was all so *funny*" that *Portnoy's Complaint* became possible. And, of course, the Modernist writer most responsible for liberating Roth's imagination was Franz Kafka: "I was strongly influenced [Roth claims] by a sit-down comic named Franz Kafka and the very funny bit he does called 'The Metamorphosis' . . . there is certainly a personal element in the book [*Portnoy's Complaint*], but not until I had got hold of guilt, you see, as a comic idea, did I begin to feel myself lifting free and clear of my last book, and my old concerns."[27]

Granted, Kafka is a late addition to the long list of Modernist writers who opened new windows for modern American humorists. Forty years ago, Peter De Vries, the comic novelist, published an article in *Poetry* entitled "James Thurber: The Comic Prufrock."[28] In it, De Vries makes a case for Thurber's affinity with Modernist poets, linking Thurber's man on the flying trapeze with Eliot's J. Alfred Prufrock. Needless to say, Thurber was pleased by the extended comparison and, in short order, De Vries was writing for the *New Yorker*. Even more important, T. S. Eliot found the juxtaposition satisfying: His correspondence with Groucho Marx may be more widely known, but the fact of the matter is that Eliot called Thurber "his favorite humorist" and he is quoted in *Time* magazine (1951) as saying: "[Thurber's writing] is a form of humor which is also a way of saying something serious. There is criticism of life at the bottom of it. It is serious and even somber. Unlike so much of humor, it is not merely a criticism of manners—that is, of the superficial aspects of society at a given moment—but something more profound . . . They [Thurber's works] will be a document of the age they belong to."[29] According to Burton Bernstein, Thurber's biographer, Thurber felt that "this was the best estimate of his work ever."[30] And small wonder, for Eliot was a critic of wide learning and enormous influence. But he was also a poet and that fact figures prominently in Thurber's sharp departure from his usual habit of protesting (perhaps a bit too much) about literary criticism. And while I think a case could be made for the common ground of a clean, uncluttered style that writers like Ernest Hemingway and E. B. White shared, I would also insist that Modernist poets played a larger role in the shaping of modern American humor than has been acknowledged.

S. J. Perelman is an instructive case. There is no doubt that he knew his *Ulysses*, but the obsession with foreign phrases, with exotic coinages, with complicated verbal structures suggests an analogue to the poetry of Wallace Stevens. In a forthcoming study of humor in American poetry, Ronald Wallace rightly concentrates on Stevens' view of language as "a living entity, capable of adopting a comic role" and, as proof, he cites a letter Stevens wrote explaining what lies behind his title "The Comedian as the Letter C": "I ought to confess that by the letter C I meant the sound of the letter C; what was in my mind was to play on that sound throughout the poem. While the sound of that letter has more or less variety, and includes, for instance, K and S, all its shades may be said to have a comic aspect. Consequently, the letter C is a comedian. . . ."[31] Long before Neil Simon's Jewish vaudevillians held forth about *k* as a funny letter ("Pickles is funny. *L* is not funny. 'Lettuce' is not funny.") a dandified WASP had insisted on much the same thing.

Moreover, Wallace shows how this penchant for language to surprise us pops up in an extraordinary number of Stevens' poems. In "Snow and Stars," for example. He quotes the following passage, and then proceeds to explicate it in terms of "humor":

> The grackles sing avant the spring
> Most spiss—oh! Yes, most spissantly.
> They sing right puisantly.

Grackles are rather cacophanous, unromantic birds, and when the word "spissantly" (derived from the fifteenth-century word "spissitude," meaning thickness, compactness) slips out, Stevens is momentarily taken aback: "Oh!" Can he use such a lyrical word in this context, the interjection seems to ask? Grackles do show up in the spring, but they are black raucous birds. Can they sing "spissantly?" Persuaded by the word itself, Stevens not only *uses* it but then goes on to *underline* it with a companion word, "puisantly."

Perelman, I submit, allows language to take over the premises in much the same way. He is at his best on the printed page, where language holds still long enough for comic effects to build. Here is an example token from "The Idol's Eye":

> The following morning the *Maid of Hull*, a frigate of the line mounting thirty-six guns, out of Bath and into bed in a twinkling, dropped downstream on the tide, bound out for Bombay, object matrimony. On her as passenger went my great-grandfather, an extra pair of nankeen pants his only baggage and a dirk in his throat ready for use. Fifty-three days later in Poona, he was heading for the interior of one of the Northern States. Living almost entirely on cameo brooches and the few ptarmigan which fell to the ptrigger of his pflowling-piece, he at last sighted the towers of Ishpeming, the Holy City of the Surds and Cosines, fanatic Mohammedan warrior sects.[32]

"Ptarmigan" are grouse of the northern hemisphere, having winter plumage chiefly pure white and with feathered toes. Granted, the word is not quite the same thing as Stevens' "spissantly," but, for Perelman, the *pt-* combination sets into motion some very funny stuff. Perelman searched out words of this ilk, combing telephone directories for odd names and the dictionary for curious words. In both writers the elegant, the baroque, takes on an energy— a *raison d'être* of its own. And while it is certainly true that modern American humorists, as a group, were no strangers to revision, to the multiple drafts that came with the territory of what Thurber once described as "light pieces running from a thousand to two thousand words,"[33] Perelman was probably the fussiest of the lot. He composed like a "poet," with the full attention to ear and eye that the term implies.

All of which brings me to Don Marquis, a humorist who turned the agonies of "poetic composition" into subject matter. Eugene Field's columns and George Ade's sketches gave him a direction ("I wanted to do something like that," Marquis once reminisced), but it was his invention of archy and mehitabel that provided him with a way of getting there. Marquis arrived in New York in 1909 and for more than a dozen years he wrote regular columns for the *New York Sun* and the *Tribune*. Deadlines were a fact of daily life, along with the anxiety that what went smoothly enough on Monday morning might turn slogging and sour by Thursday afternoon. The short line and jagged right-hand margin of *vers libre* was, for Marquis, a perfect solution. He could parody Modernist poetry on one hand, and shovel in home-spun social commentary with the other.

Archy, a poet of the lower-case and a cockroach's body, announced himself in 1927, fifteen years after Franz Kafka wrote his disturbing, tragi-comic tale "Die Verwandlung," or as we know it in the 1937 English translation: *The Metamorphosis*. To be sure, Marquis had E. E. Cummings and other Modernist poets with typographical affectations in mind, but there is a sense in which the *Zeitgeist* operates even when the "facts" of literary history and demonstratable "influence" do not. What we see clearly, however, in *archy and mehitabel* is the old wine of American humor poured into new Modernist bottles. The framing narrator provides the context and the point-of-view stability demands, but it is archy's voice—his "poetry"—that occupies center stage:

> We came into our room earlier than usual in the morning, and discovered a gigantic cockroach jumping about upon the keys.
>
> He did not see us, and we watched him. He would climb painfully upon the framework of the machine and cast himself with all his force upon a key, head downward, and his weight and the impact of the blow were just sufficient to operate the machine, one slow letter after another. He could not work the capital letters, and he had a great deal of difficulty operating the mechanism that shifts the paper so that a fresh line may be started. We never saw a cockroach work so hard or perspire so freely in all our lives before. After about an hour of this frightfully difficult literary labor he fell to the floor exhausted . . .
>
> this is what we found·
>> expression is the need of my soul
>> i was once a vers libre bard
>> but i died and my soul went into the body of a
>> cockroach
>> it has given me a new outlook upon life
>> i see things from the under side now[34]

In spots, archy seems a precursor of John Berryman's *Dream Songs* and the comic Henry who takes his readers and / or the literary establishment to task:

> boss i am dissappinted in
> some of your readers they
> are always asking how does
> archy work the shift so as to get a
> new line or how does archy do
> this or that they
> are always interested in technical
> details when the main question is

whether the stuff is
literature or not
i wish you would leave
that book of george moores on
the floor[35]

Granted, archy's poetry ain't "literature" (indeed, that is Marquis's parodic point), but the hard labor modern American humor requires is a cockroach of a very different color.

In describing archy's perspiration, Marquis writes the allegory of the modern American humorist. As Virginia Woolf knew full well: "On or about December 1910, human character changed." To render that new reality from the "under side," as archy puts it, to see American culture steady and whole and in good humor, required new allegiances, new techniques, new perspectives. It also required that modern American humorists cross the border into Modernism and close the gap between High Culture and Low. And that is precisely what our best modern American humorists did.

Notes

1. Virginia Woolf, "Mr. Bennett and Mrs. Brown," included in *The Captain's Dust-Bed and Other Essays* (New York: Harcourt Brace Jovanovich, 1950), p. 96.

2. Irving Howe, *Literary Modernism* (New York: Fawcett, 1967), p. 15.

3. Joseph Conrad, Preface to *The Nigger of the "Narcissus"* (Garden City: Doubleday, Page & Co., 1924), p. xiv.

4. Mark Twain, *The Mysterious Stranger*, included in Justin Kaplan, ed. *Great Short Works of Mark Twain* (New York: Harper & Row, 1967), p. 366.

5. James Thurber, *The Thurber Carnival* (New York: Harper & Row, 1945), p. 174.

6. *The Thurber Carnival*, p. 174.

7. David Ross Locke (Petroleum V. Nasby), "Shows Why He Should Not Be Drafted," included in Walter Blair, ed. *Native American Humor* (New York: Chandler Publishing Co., 1960), p. 410.

8. *Native American Humor*, p. 104.

9. Walter Blair and Hamlin Hill, *America's Humor* (New York: Oxford University Press, 1978), p. 383.

10. Included in *America's Humor*, p. 383.

11. Included in *America's Humor*, p. 383.

12. From "To the Editor of [a] Newspaper" (20 May 1765), included in Larzer Ziff, ed. *Benjamin Franklin: Selected Writings* (New York: Holt, Rinehart & Winston, 1959), p. 225.

13. Henry James, *The American* (New York: Norton Critical Edition, 1978), p. 97.

14. *Benjamin Franklin: Selected Writings*, p. 225

15. Lee Coyle, *George Ade* (New York: Twayne, 1964), p. 4.

16. For a full discussion of narrative structures and Southwestern humor, see

Kenneth Lynn's *Mark Twain and Southwestern Humor* (Boston: Little, Brown & Co., 1960).

17. George Ade, "The Professor Who Wanted to Be Alone," included in E. B. White and Katharine S. White, eds., *A Subtreasury of American Humor* (New York: Capricorn Books, 1962), pp. 109–10.

18. Carl Van Doren, "Day In and Day Out," *Century*, 107 (December 1923), p. 308.

19. As cited in *America's Humor*, p. 425.

20. As cited in *America's Humor*, p. 425.

21. Robert Benchley, "The Four-in-Hand Outrage," included in *Inside Benchley* (New York: Harper & Brothers, 1942), p. 287.

22. Nathaniel Benchley, ed., *The Benchley Roundup* (New York: Harper & Row, 1954), p. 303.

23. Woody Allen, *Side Effects* (New York: Random House, 1980), p. 81.

24. Alan Gribben, *Mark Twain's Library: A Reconstruction*. 2 vols. (Boston: G. K. Hall, 1980).

25. Woody Allen, "The Condemned," included in *Side Effects*, p. 81.

26. *Side Effects*, p. 6.

27. Philip Roth, *Reading Myself and Others* (New York: Farrar, Straus & Giroux, 1975), p. 22.

28. Peter De Vries, "James Thurber: The Comic Prufrock," *Poetry*, December 1943.

29. As cited in *Time*, 9 July 1951.

30. Burton Bernstein, *Thurber: A Biography* (New York: Dodd, Mead & Co., 1975), p. 361.

31. Ronald Wallace, *God Be With the Clown: Humor in American Poetry* (University of Missouri Press, 1984). Wallace reconsiders major American poets such as Walt Whitman, Emily Dickinson, Robert Frost and Wallace Stevens from the perspective of American humor.

32. S. J. Perelman, "The Idol's Eye," included in *The Most of S. J. Perleman* (New York: Simon & Schuster, 1958), p. 33.

33. *The Thurber Carnival*, p. 173.

34. Don Marquis, *archy and mehitabel* (New York: Doubleday, Doran & Co., 1927), p. 2.

35. *archy and mehitabel*, p. 5.

A Laughter of Their Own:
Women's Humor in the United States   Emily Toth*

Nelt Chawgo, a handsome bachelor, thinks himself invulnerable—until the day he is deceived by dashing Angerose Wilds. She promises marriage, then abandons him. Nelt, heartbroken, is also condemned

*This essay was written specifically for publication in this volume and is included here by permission of the author.

by nearly everyone: he is a "ruined feller"—a "young he-hussy."[1] After all, "young wimmen must sow their wild oats," while young men must see to their own "manly modesty" (p. 306). But Samantha Allen, Marietta Holley's mouthpiece in "A Male Magdalene" (1906), defends Nelt. Could a "he-belle" help it, she asks, if Angerose turned his weak mind with flatteries? (p. 315) The seducer should bear the blame— and finally Angerose does confess to ruining the innocent youth. She will marry Nelt after all, she decides, and make an honest man of him.

Marietta Holley makes her comic points through role reversal— the same technique Joanna Russ uses in 1972, listing heroic plots for female characters:

> Two strong women battle for supremacy in the early West. A young woman in Minnesota finds her womanhood by killing a bear.

As Russ wittily points out, these plots do not work. They are historically improbable, culturally implausible, or both.[2] But Russ' targets, like Holley's, are not her own hapless characters. Nor, like so many satirists, do Holley and Russ attack their readers. Rather, their target is the target of most humorous writing by women: the social roles which imprison us all.

Women humorists, like other women writers, have not yet been given their due. In Marietta Holley's day, for instance, a *Critic* reviewer wrote that Holley "has entertained as large an audience, I should say, as has been entertained by the humor of Mark Twain."[3] Over an unusually long career (1873–1914), Holley published twenty-one very popular novels, many of them about the most pressing social issue in post-Civil War America: women's rights. She even outlived Twain. Still, literary historians, as Susan Koppelman will show in a forthcoming study, routinely leave out virtually all women (and minority) writers of the past,[4] and tend to give fuller coverage only to women of their own era—so that American women's humor appears to begin with Dorothy Parker.[5] In fact, American women's humor begins with the "first" American poet in English: Anne Bradstreet.

Like most women writers, Bradstreet chose women's subjects: home, children. Her humor is gentle—except on one subject. Anne Bradstreet knew, over three centuries before Joanna Russ, that women writers would not be taken seriously by the dominant sex. Either the women would be told to return to their proper domestic role:

> I am obnoxious to each carping tongue
> That says my hand a needle better fits.

Or women's cleverness would be disparaged in no uncertain terms:

If what I do prove well, it won't advance,
They'll say it's stolen, or else it was by chance.[6]

Perhaps because she desperately wanted to be judged fairly, Anne Bradstreet followed the humane humor rule—one of the distinguishing characteristics of most women's humor. Unlike such satirists as Swift and
Juvenal, who build their humor on attacking women for their physical
imperfections, Bradstreet and her successors do not satirize what cannot
be helped.[7]

Women writers have not produced savage criticisms of male bodies—
but they have criticized the *choices* both sexes make: affectations, hypocrisies, irrationalities. Often, in fact, what women writers really criticize
are traditional social norms themselves—and the foolish choices made
by those who do not think or criticize their own society.[8]

Sarah Kemble Knight's diary (1704–1705), for instance, is a com-
pendium of social criticism. Knight laughs at men who show less sense
than their horses, or who support public punishment for a man who
kisses his wife where others might see them. She enjoys describing guests
at an inn who argue all night about the origin of the word "Narra-
gansett," until the rum they are drinking makes further speech impossible.[9] Similarly, during the American Revolution, Mercy Otis Warren
laughed at enemy Tories in poems and plays full of gory incidents. In
1776, she even poked fun at General Gage's army of occupation in Boston
—and she called her play *The Blockheads.*

But female humorists have rarely ventured, as Knight and Warren
did, into the public (male) world of commerce, politics, and diplomacy.
Rather, they have directed their satire toward the irrationalities of life
at home. In *A New Home—Who'll Follow?* (1839), for instance, Caroline Kirkland suggests that *no one* should. The rigors of backwoods
Michigan life, she says, are made far worse by the sticky fingers of her
neighbors, who borrow her broom, thread, and scissors—and, ultimately,
even her cat and her husband's pantaloons.[10] Likewise, Frances Berry
Whitcher, who wrote as "The Widow Bedott," satirized her neighbors in
western New York State for their peculiar dialect and their habit of
talking much and saying little. But somehow the neighbors discovered
she was "The Widow"—and forced her out of town. She died two years
later, in 1852, having remarked that it is "a very serious thing to be a
funny woman."[11] Kirkland, Whitcher, and "Fanny Fern" (Sara Willis
Parton, who criticized the deplorable smoking habits of men in "Tabitha
Tompkins' Soliloquy") all follow the humane humor rule: they mock
people for their choices.[12] They support better living standards, sensible
conversation, clean air—in short, all that makes a home livable, especially
for women.

Marietta Holley, born in upstate New York, was twelve years old
when Elizabeth Cady Stanton, Susan B. Anthony, Lucretia Mott, and the

others met in Seneca Falls in 1848 and wrote their "Declaration of Principles" ("We hold these truths to be self-evident: that all men and women are created equal . . ."). Between 1848 and 1920, the year women's suffrage was finally ratified, women and sympathetic men kept up an unceasing battle for the vote. Throughout her career, Marietta Holley used her wit to support The Cause—and to ask pointed questions about marriage, women's rights, and the real differences between the sexes. In 1873, she published her first Samantha book: *My Opinions and Betsey Bobbet's*, "by Josiah Allen's wife." In all the books, Samantha Allen is the crackerbox philosopher, the wise innocent, the supporter of "megumness" (mediumness, or moderation). In the first book, Samantha's dialogues with her neighbor Betsey, who opposes women's rights, show the gap between high-minded descriptions of women's "calling"—"to soothe lacerations, to be a sort of poultice to the noble manly breast when it is torn with the cares of life"—and the reality. "Am I a poultice, Betsy Bobbet, do I look like one?" Samantha asks—as she irons, stirs preserves, makes maple sugar, bakes, and worries. "What has my sect done, that they have got to be lacerator soothers, when they have got everything else under the sun to do?" Samantha wonders.[13]

Women, Holley notes in other books, are indeed the protected sex— "protected" from having a say in church, in the ballot box, and even over their own clothing, which legally belongs to their husbands. Samantha wonders about the wives of Old Testament prophets ("Miss Daniel, Miss Zekiel, Miss Hosey")—who most likely had to work twice as hard, while their men wandered around in goatskins and took off on "prophesying trips."[14] Holley shows that the rules are made by men— but that it is actually women who do the work of the world, especially its most down-to-earth, practical work. Samantha insists on calling the Meeting House "she" and referring to "our Revolutionary foremothers"— and she asks her husband Josiah to explain something: when do terms like "men" include women, and when don't they? *Laymen*, Josiah says without any apparent opinion, always means women "when it is used in a punishin' and condemnatory sense, or in the case of work." But what about power and salaries? Well, in that case, "or anything else difficult," the word *laymen* "always means men."

Marietta Holley was too shy to speak at suffrage mettings; she was a storyteller rather than an activist. But her sly questions— are men the most logical beings? are women really ladies?—form the core of some of the greatest examples of comic irony produced by the suffrage movement. Alice Duer Miller, for instance, took on the contention that voting would destroy women's mental and moral health, because of the brutal creatures they might meet at the polls (the "men-are-incorrigible-brutes" argument still used by right-wingers today). In "A Consistent Anti to Her Son" (1915), Miller writes:

You must not go to the polls, Willie,
Never go to the polls,
They're dark and dreadful places
Where many lose their souls;
They smirch, degrade and coarsen
Terrible things they do
To quiet, elderly women—
What would they do to you?[15]

What is really being criticized, of course, is the double standard: that one sex is to be sheltered, and judged, and kept from power—while the other, regardless of its behavior, runs the world.

The value of being a "lady" was also satirized by suffragists—notably by Sojourner Truth, a former slave who saw the irony in the idea of female weakness expressed at a women's rights convention in 1851: "That man over there says women need to be helped into carriages and lifted over ditches, and to have the best place everywhere. Nobody ever helps me into carriages or over puddles, or gives me the best place—and ain't I a woman?"[16]

The struggle for women's rights did, in fact, do what its opponents feared: it turned women away from being deferential ladies (if they ever were) and toward being social critics. Women were not always creatures of sentiment, nor were men always citadels of reason—as Anna Howard Shaw, President of the National American Woman Suffrage Association, often told her audiences. Dr. Shaw used to relish describing a Democratic convention she had observed. Men were carrying pictures around the room—screaming, shouting, singing the "Hown Dawg" song. Men jumped on their seats, threw hats in the air, and shouted, "What's the matter with Champ Clark?"—while other men tossed hats and shouted, "He's all right!!!!!" But all this, Shaw noted slyly, had "no hysteria about it—just patriotic loyalty, splendid manly devotion to principle." Still, women at conventions, she pointed out, never knocked off each other's bonnets, nor shouted, "She's all right!" Instead, Shaw reported, "I have actually seen women stand up and wave their handkerchiefs. I have even seen them take hold of hands and sing, 'Blest be the tie that binds.' "[17]

Women humorists from Anne Bradstreet through Anna Howard Shaw were all, in some way, angry: about the limited roles they were given, about the pious platitudes droned at them to justify their submission, about the outright false statements about women's "nature." But their responses were not truly an attack on men, not a "so's your old man" response. Theirs was an attack on patriarchal norms—on hypocrisy, on irresponsibility—in the name of a higher norm. Women humorists were not seeking domination—but equality.

By the late nineteenth and early twentieth centuries, the humorous appeals of poets and orators had crept more and more into the work of fiction writers. Anne Warner, for instance, is best-known for her Susan Clegg stories, in which Susan—an opinionated busybody—gossips, and Mrs. Lathrop interjects an occasional, "Yes?" and "What then?" Susan Clegg spices her apparent ramblings with sharp observations. When the mother of a baby runs off with another man, Susan points out that everyone said, "How could she be so cruel as to leave it!" And then when the woman returns for her child: "How could she be so cruel as to take it!" The point as Susan sees it is that "When a woman branches out, every one's ready to go for her."[18] As for marriage, Susan Clegg tells Mrs. Lathrop that many things look different "comin' down from the altar from what they did goin' up" (p. 472)—a point Anne Warner makes even more strongly in "The New Woman and the Old" (1914), one of the most devastating satires on bourgeois marriage ever to appear in American literature.

The old-style woman, Emily Reed's mother, refuses to acknowledge that marriage is anything but the perfect future for her daughter. Then Emily's suitor describes her duties: she will be his only housekeeper, teach every one of the younger classes at his school, clean the entire school while he goes to Germany to study—and be all that marriage handbooks say a wife should be: pious, domestic, submissive. Emily complains to her mother, who gives a bald, totally unself-conscious picture of the hallowed Victorian marriage: all women work until midnight; all women suffer in drudgery; and "all men are selfish . . . Your father ate all the giblets up to the day he died." Emily protests that she doesn't want to be a slave—to which her mother replies, "But you can't be married without being a slave . . . The thing is to be married."[19] Emily decides that it is not her thing at all.

Some of the happiest characters in Mary E. Wilkins Freeman's and Sarah Orne Jewett's writings are, in fact, spinsters. The heroines of such stories as Freeman's "A New England Nun" and Jewett's "The Flight of Betsey Lane" are not conventionally pretty, nor young, nor romantically-inclined. Rather, they are resouceful and free. Betsey Lane gleefully hitchhikes to Philadelphia, though at sixty-nine she has never been more than a few miles from her New England home. Freeman's "New England nun," Louisa, finds all the adventure she ever wants by staying home—creating a tidy, smiling domestic world, a miniature art form reflecting everything she wants her life to be. Literary critics, too often judging characters by traditional norms (and therefore assuming that spinsters must be unfulfilled), have often missed the satire in Freeman and Jewett, whose targets for humor are those who insist on behaving in conventional, unthinking ways: shocked parishioners, gossipy creatures of both sexes, neighborhood carping tongues. Jewett's and Freeman's characters do not return to "normal." Rather, they create new norms. (Freeman also shows that rigid sex roles limit men—for in

"A Kitchen Colonel," her seventy-eight-year-old hero loves to muddle around in the kitchen, and is unfazed by the hecklings of his neighbor. The hero's self-sacrifices, in fact, enable his grand-daughter to marry the man she chooses—and in the end the hero cries, with that mixture of laughter and tears that marks Freeman's particular brand of humor.)[20]

Kate Chopin's humor is also social criticism, but in a more black-humorous vein—notably in "The Storm" (written in 1898) and "The Story of an Hour" (published in 1894). Both stories concern women who are only outwardly pleased with their marriages. The wife in "The Storm" takes refuge with a former sweet-heart during a thunderstorm—and the storm outside reawakens old desires, until both are swept away with renewed passion. Afterwards she has a particular glow when she greets her husband and son—while her lover writes to his wife that she is welcome to stay on vacation for another month. "So the storm passed, and everyone was happy," the story concludes.[21] The wife in Chopin's "The Story of an Hour" is also happily married, but since she has a heart condition, people are very careful when they give her the news: her husband has been in a fatal train wreck. At first she is sad, but then she watches the budding trees and thinks, "Free! Body and soul free!" She loved her husband—but loves self-assertion more. Then the door opens—and it is her husband, who was far from the scene of the accident. The wife cannot be shielded from the shock—and so, "When the doctors came they said she had died of heart disease—of joy that kills."[22]

Kate Chopin specializes in withholding information from her characters, and withholding judgment from her readers.[23] But her best writings are satiric: she shocks and delights her audience by confounding traditional expectations—particularly the view that marriage must mean self-sacrifice for a woman. The fulfilled woman is the woman alone—laughing after her illicit tempest with a man not her husband, or exulting in her room when she thinks herself freed.

Edith Wharton, on the other hand, seems to have had no particular vision of liberation for women (though she did recognize that in the highest levels of American society capitalism could be deadly). Still, in *The Custom of the Country* (1913), her finest comedy of manners, Edith Wharton shows that an unscrupulous woman can beat the system —as does Undine Spragg, who escapes her dull Midwestern town to make a killing in New York. Undine greedily marries into the old New York aristocracy, and then into the old French aristocracy, and finally into the *nouveau riche* Americans-in-France aristocracy—always pursuing the American dream, always trying to upgrade herself. As one character comments, Undine Spragg is the monstrously perfect result of the system—in which marriage is supposed to be women's only source of identity. She is neither likeable, nor intellectual (she sees the classic French theater as a bunch of people mooning about in bath towels), but she is the perfect vehicle for satire as practiced by American women writers. She *chooses* to be ridiculous, and her success exposes the shallowness of her society's norms.

"Edie was a lady," Dorothy Parker said of Edith Wharton—but Dorothy Parker was not. She was perhaps the first woman writer since Marietta Holley who could truly be called a humorist—that is, a writer whose main focus was on humor, rather than a writer who used humor as one of many literary techniques. Parker is, of course, best-known for her withering one-liners. "You know that woman speaks eighteen languages?" she said about one acquaintance. "And she can't say 'No' in any of them." To a man nervous about his first extramarital affair, Dorothy Parker said soothingly, "Oh, don't worry. I'm sure it won't be the last."[24] And of *The House at Pooh Corner*, a book she reviewed for the *New Yorker*'s "Constant Reader" column, Parker summarized her disgust: "Tonstant Weader Fwowed Up."[25]

Parker's funny-but-deadly poems include meditations on suicide: "Razors pain you . . . Nooses give . . . Gas smells awful . . . You might as well live."[26] Her voice is breezy, worldly, and very cynical: "I shudder at the thought of men . . . I'm due to fall in love again."[27] Her poems expect deception out of love, and her clever turns of phrase offer satire, not hope:

> By the time you swear you're his,
> Shivering and sighing,
> And he vows his passion is
> Infinite, undying—
> Lady, make a note of this:
> One of you is lying.[28]

Similarly, Parker's short stories suggest that woman's lot is not a particularly happy one. Unlike nineteenth-century heroines, her characters are not made contented through creating well-ordered solitary lives. In fact they are quite incompetent in the household: one husband, surveying the bed his wife has just made, demands: "What is this? Some undergraduate prank?"[29]

Some Parker short stories have a unique blending of humor and resentment that no other writer has ever managed—particularly in such soliloquys as "The Waltz," a young woman's cynical musings while dancing with a young man. Though she has said she would adore waltzing with him, she thinks the truth: "Being struck dead would look like a day in the country, compared to struggling out a dance with this boy."[30] Grimly, she wishes he would at least leave her shins as he found them—but at the same time she tells him his "little step" is "perfectly lovely," but just a "tiny bit tricky to follow." At the end she wonders if the dance has lasted thirty-five years, or maybe a hundred thousand—then tells him she would "adore to" dance another waltz with him. Parker shows that the young woman has no alternative—for how can she dare say what she considers saying: "It's so nice to meet a man who isn't a scaredy-cat about catching my beri-beri"? Women are expected to please men. Parker's target is neither the clumsy young man nor the bruised young woman, but the social roles they are locked into.

Human vulnerability makes much of Parker's humor poignant as well as amusing. In the short stories, she is merciless toward unthinking, self-styled do-gooders ("Arrangement in Black and White," "Clothe the Naked"). She hates the rich ("From the Diary of a New York Lady," "The Custard Heart"). But her finest subject is the gap between women and men: *she* hangs on his every word, *he* forgets what he has said; *she* waits for him to phone, *he* cannot understand why she is upset; *he* would like to tell her about his day, *she* would like to tell him about hers—but each figures the other would not be interested anyway.

Dorothy Parker emancipated women writers from the need to be nice, to hide their anger. Though her wit was often at her own expense, she nevertheless said what she thought. In fact, she paved the way for a new openness in humor—for housewives, for feminists, and for women who are both. Indeed, by the 1940s two distinct streams of American women's humor had emerged. The first, derived largely from the nineteenth-century domestic tradition, focussed on the humorous aspects of women's sphere: children, family chores, home-making. But only a decade after Marietta Holley's last Samantha book, Dorothy Parker had already pioneered in the new stream of women's humor: finding irony, humane humor, and radical criticism of patriarchal norms almost entirely in the world beyond the home. Parker's humor leads most directly to the feminist humor of such writers as Erica Jong, Toni Cade Bambara, Alix Kates Shulman, and Rita Mae Brown—while the domestic stream has produced Betty MacDonald, Phyllis McGinley, Peg Bracken, and Erma Bombeck.

Though Betty MacDonald in *The Egg and I* (1945) and Phyllis McGinley in *Sixpence in Her Shoe* (1964) promote a grin-and-bear-it attitude toward the tribulations of housework, much of their humor seems either hateful (MacDonald) or patronizing (McGinley) in the 1980s. MacDonald makes housekeeping, even on a chicken ranch, seem trivial and dull; McGinley glorifies the many roles a housewife can play (chauffeur, gardener, cook, nurse) and says that any woman who does not find all these jobs creative and fulfilling has only herself to blame. But like Jean Kerr, author of *Please Don't Eat the Daisies* (1957), and Shirley Jackson, author of *Life Among the Savages* (1953) and *Raising Demons* (1957), McGinley was not a full-time housewife.

The domestic humorists before Peg Bracken were, in fact, telling *other* women to stay in their place—but Bracken in *The I Hate to Cook Book* (1960) said, with humor, what Betty Friedan showed seriously in *The Feminine Mystique* (1963): the home is too small a world. Not every woman is totally fulfilled with chauffering, gardening, cooking, nursing—and Bracken was among the first to say openly that cooking, in particular, is often a detestable activity. The *I Hate to Cook Book* taps what most women humorists have found: the mingling of satisfaction and resentment, of anger and amusement, that creates an ironic perspective on the "normal" world. *The I Hate to Cook Book* revels in tricks: garnishes to disguise failures, and ways to con the family into thinking something canned is original. Bracken even provides sample remarks for convincing a husband that frozen-and-heated rolls are really home-baked. "Admittedly," she writes, "this is underhanded, but then, marriage is sometimes a rough game."[31] Her goal is not to train the ideal, spotless homemaker. Rather, Bracken criticizes the norm, by showing how a woman can ignore much of it, fake the rest, and go on to the important things in her life.

Likewise, Erma Bombeck tells strong truths cloaked in humor. She analyzes traditional images of women—and demolishes them. As early as 1967, Bombeck was writing that the housewife could not win. If she complained, she was neurotic; if she did not, she was stupid. If she stayed home with children, she was an overprotective "boring clod." If she worked outside, she was selfish, and "her children will write dirty words in nice places."[32] Nor can Supermom ("Super Mom!") be an appropriate replacement for the housewife. In *The Grass Is Always Greener Over the Septic Tank* (1976), Bombeck portrays a super mother who does everything right: bakes her own bread, delivers puppies, even waxes her garden hose. But the neighbors hardly praise her. Instead, they whisper snidely—until the super mother begins to change. She buys deodorants not on sale, she secretly cooks TV dinners, and when she hears that her child is using toothpaste with fluoride on the side, the reformed super mother says, "Who cares?" Bombeck concludes: "She was one of us."[33] To be "one of us" in Erma Bombeck's world means not fitting the old mold, the nineteenth-century norm of the all-nurturing, all-perfect angel in the house. Bombeck recognizes that Super Mom can be a super sucker, no more appreciated than women whose children send Mother's Day cards to Colonel Sanders. Erma Bombeck is not the housewife's tranquillizer. Rather, she speaks the unspeakable, and says with humor what other feminists, such as Marilyn French (in *The Women's Room*), say with rage.

Erma Bombeck is the bridge between the housewife stream of humor and the new feminist stream—which is perhaps best represented by Erica Jong, whose adolescent ideal was Dorothy Parker. In her poems and novels, especially *Fear of Flying* (1973), Jong debunks myths and shatters taboos—particularly about menstruation, female masturbation, and lust. Jong uses words traditionally forbidden to women: the ultimate romantic fantasy, in which there is no mumbling, no fumbling, no outside world intruding, is called "the zipless fuck." *Flying's* heroine Isadora Wing dreams of the zipless fuck while adventuring around Europe in a parody of *The Odyssey*. She mocks the portentous and wrong-headed psychoanalytical descriptions of WOMAN, and she yearns for sexual excitement and literary success, love and laughter—but on female terms. At the end of her quest, Isadora does something no male hero ever did: she has her period. In the bathtub, Isadora gazes at the mighty artifact: "the Tampax string fishing the water like a Hemingway hero."[34]

Erica Jong traces the roots of new feminist humor to Dorothy Parker—but also to Sylvia Plath, whose novel *The Bell Jar* (1963) is one of the first pieces of women's writing to look directly at the male anatomy. When the medical student Buddy insists on undressing in front of the heroine, what she sees reminds her most of "turkey neck and turkey gizzards."[35] Again, what is being mocked is *not* Buddy's anatomy—as men have mocked the female body. Rather, Plath is mocking the norm: the belief that viewing the genitals of the opposite sex is an instant turn-on. That may be true for men—but not for women.

Most new feminist humorists of the 1970s and 1980s lack the morbid edge of Plath's writing, however. Instead, they have chosen exuberance, adventure, sex and love and laughter—and breaking many taboos simply by ignoring them.

In the literature of the 1970s, tampax insertion becomes a comical rite of passage for young women, especially in such novels as Lois Gould's *Such Good Friends* (1970) and Alix Kates Shulman's *Memoirs of an Ex-Prom Queen* (1972).[36] It is easily the equivalent of winning the big game, and in Judy Blume's *Are You There God? It's Me, Margaret* (1970), three teenagers vie to see who will have the first period. One even tries to make a deal with God, offering to be good around the house if He will give her some breasts. The heroine does finally get "it," then stops her mother from showing her how to us napkins ("Teenage Softies"): "Mom, I've been practicing in my room for two months!"[37] Thus we have a happy, if unconventional, ending: girl gets napkin.

The nineteenth-century domestic writers praised the same virtues—generosity, practicality, neatness—but could not write about menstruation or lust, nor use four-letter words. Nor could they describe the special treat Alix Kates Shulman's protagonist in *Memoirs of an Ex-Prom Queen* has, when she discovers her "joy button" (clitoris) and the pleasures of masturbation. Nor could they print what Shulman describes in "A Story of a Girl and Her Dog" (1975): the day a dog licks a young girl, Lucky, in a most sensitive place—and Lucky revels in the feeling. That is the day of Lucky's "brightening."[38]

New feminist humorists are insistently honest, especially about the first sexual experience—in which, for women, the earth rarely moves, nor is ecstatic and simultaneous communion achieved. Lisa Alther's heroine in *Kinflicks* (1976), for instance, has her first experience in a fallout shelter, with a greasy motorcyclist fresh from a den of iniquity called The Bloody Bucket. His condomed penis is "the size and shape of a small salami, lime green and glowing fluorescently." The heroine waits for the cosmic joy romances have promised, but instead hears herself saying, "You mean that's *it?*"[39]

These feminist humorists are keen observers, preferring independence to snivelling and appreciating irony and role reversal. Gail Parent's *David Meyer Is a Mother* (1976), for instance, satirizes norms for men— in that David Meyer begins life as a conscienceless exploiter of women, but ends up begging his roommate to have a baby, so *he* will be fulfilled. In between, David learns that the sexual revolution has begun, and he is fighting on the losing side. Women take him out, and then neglect to call; his boss expects him to sleep with her to keep his job. In the end, he is delighted to withdraw to the sanctity of Home—the nineteenth-century haven in a heartless world becomes the most attractive place for this late twentieth-century man to be.

Sexual harassment is also a target for satire in E. M. (Esther) Broner's *Her Mothers* (1975), in which a mother attends a conference of scholars, and asks five of the men why they are attending. All have high-minded, altruistic or political motivations. The Indian wants to "buy guns" for his people ("and to fuck women"), the Black man wants to "make contacts for my people" ("and to fuck me some women"), the Jewish man wants to represent "the Jew as Eternal Immigrant" ("and to fuck some women"). Finally, the heroine meets her mentor, a charming, aging, respected friend who tells her his purpose. He wants to reacquaint himself with old friends and "fuck some women."[40] Esther Broner uses satire because it is indirect, a way to attack hypocrisy. Much of new feminist humor has been devoted to attacking hypocrisy—but more recent writers have gone beyond criticizing the foibles of society, and the other sex. Writers of feminist humor are now proposing alternatives.

Alternative worlds for women, like that in Bertha Harris' *Lover* (1976), are not an invention of the 1970s. As early as 1915, Charlotte Perkins Gilman described a women's utopia in *Herland*—a model country stumbled upon by three contemporary American men who immediately say to themselves: "This is a *civilized* country . . . . There must be men."[41] Instead, the explorers find a civilization consisting entirely of women, and run along reasonable lines that make our world seem humorous, bizarre, and certainly irrational. Herlanders laugh at one explorer's constant attempts to show himself to be "a man, a real man"; they cannot understand why the frantic explorers find it so upsetting to be treated exactly the way the women treat each other. *Herland*, of course, questions the ways of the real world in which Gilman lived. Romantic love, one explorer learns, is really just "caveman tradition" (p. 93). Herlanders find sex distinctions amusing, especially the ambiguous use of "man" (pp. 60, 137), and they clearly prove one of the explorers wrong when he claims: "Women cannot co-operate—it's against nature" (p. 67).

Newer writers like Toni Cade Bambara have put into practice the values expressed in *Herland*. In Bambara's story "Raymond's Run" (1971), for instance, young Squeaky is the fastest runner on the block. She wins her big race—but she also revels in having her retarded brother share her victory, and in making friends with her strongest competitor. Squeaky's triumph celebrates physical fitness, health, and joyful activity for women—but also supports traditionally feminine values: concern for others, co-operation, and sincerity—being "honest and worthy of respect . . . you know . . . like being people."[42] "Being people" in a woman's world is what many recent feminist humorists are really writing about— as Bambara says in "Medley" (1977): "I arranged my priorities long ago when I jumped into my woman stride."[43]

Alice Walker's mother-character in "Everyday Use" (1973) has also hit her woman stride. She is big-boned and strong and proud of it: "My fat keeps me hot in zero weather."[44] Mama also has an amused love for both her daughters: the nervous, crippled, stay-at-home (Maggie), and the brisk, militant adventurer, sporting an Afro and a new African name (Wangero). Walker pokes some fun at Wangero—not for her ideas, but for her pretensions. But it is Maggie who stays with Mama, with "a real smile, not scared," and they sit "just enjoying, until it was time to go in the house and go to bed" (p. 88). The ending has women's warmth.

A true heroine, feminist humorists are saying today, has warmth and spunk and vitality the characteristics of Molly Bolt in Rita Mae Brown's *Rubyfruit Jungle* (1973). Molly grows up poor, unloved, but full of ideas; her first childhood business is selling (for 5¢) the chance to see "the strangest dick in the world"—property of her chum "Broccoli" Detwiler, who seems to enjoy the notoriety.[45] Because she is bright and ambitious and curious, Molly soon learns that love is not confined to the opposite gender. She creates herself as she grows up lesbian, laughing at pretensions that do not hurt others—and fighting those that do. She threatens to expose the hypocrisy of her smarmy teachers, caught in an adulterous rendezvous; she objects to the idea that getting married is "something you have to do, like dying" (p. 36). The only norms she accepts are those she has chosen. When she goes to the big city to seek her fortune, she meets many desperately alienated people: a woman whose fantasy is to be admired at a Times Square urinal, a man who imagines himself with stupendous breasts. A rich grapefruit freak pays Molly $100 to throw fruit at him, his path to sexual ecstasy. But *Rubyfruit Jungle* is also about reconciliation: combining love and work, bringing together mother and daughter, mixing laughter and tenderness. Being people.

There is no canon of women's humor in America, though there are two excellent anthologies: Martha Hensley Bruère and Mary Ritter Beard's *Laughing Their Way: Women's Humor in America* (1934) and Gloria Kaufman and Mary Kay Blakely's *Pulling Our Own Strings: Feminist Humor and Satire* (1980).

A comprehensive survey of American women's humor would include many writers not mentioned here—among them Harriet Beecher Stowe, Zora Neal Hurston, Flannery O'Connor, Ellen Goodman, Nora Ephron, Nikki Giovanni. Creators of one-liners would be included, such as Florynce Kennedy for "A woman without a man is like a fish without a bicycle." Very little has been written about female stand-up comedians or cartoonists.[46] And since women's humor characteristically criticizes and subverts patriarchal norms, it is not always amusing to the other sex—which may account for its absence from many humor anthologies.[47] What does seem clear is that women's humor—as a weapon, and as communion—is not apt to wither away. Pretensions and hypocrisies are still with us—and so is the anger that they create.

But women's humor has gone beyond the stage of imitating men's humor (pure mockery), and beyond attacking traditional humor (parody, role reversal), to the third stage: creating new norms, a new culture.[48] In the future, American female wits may create more poems like Hisaye Yamamoto's 1949 combination of a Japanese form (*haiku*) with French *élan* and down-to-earth American needs:

> It is morning, and lo!
> I lie awake, comme il faut,
> sighing for some dough.[49]

The gap between what *is* and what *should be* still exists, as it did when Alice Duer Miller wrote "Feminism," just before women got the vote:

> "Mother, what is a Feminist?"
> "A Feminist, my daughter,
> Is any woman now who cares
> To think about her own affairs
> As men don't think she oughter."[50]

What women's humor is, ultimately, is women's seeing what they oughter: being equal, being people, being smart. Women humorists, like Marietta Holley's Samantha, will continue to have one irrepressible trait in common: "I could stop my tongue—but I couldn't stop my Thinker."[51]

Notes

1. Marietta Holley, "A Male Magdalene," in *Samantha versus Josiah* (New York: Funk and Wagnalls, 1906), p. 304. Other references to this edition will be made by page number in the text.

2. Joanna Russ, "What Can a Heroine Do? or Why Women Can't Write," in *Images of Women in Fiction: Feminist Perspectives*, ed. Susan Koppelman Cornillon (Bowling Green: Popular Press, 1972), p. 3.

3. Patricia Williams, "The Crackerbox Philosopher as Feminist: The Novels of Marietta Holley," *American Humor: An Interdisciplinary Newsletter*, 7 (Spring 1980), 16.

4. Susan Koppelman, Introduction to *The Other Woman: Stories of Two Women and a Man* (New York: Feminist Press, 1984).

5. See, for instance, Enid Veron's 1976 anthology, *Humor in America* (New York: Harcourt Brace Jovanovich), which purports to survey the history of American humor—yet the only female humorists included are Flannery O'Connor (a short story); Dorothy Parker (two pages of short poems); and Judith Viorst (a minor contemporary poet, given three pages). Parker's significance is further diminished by the inclusion of Alexander Woollcott's snide sketch, "Our Mrs. Parker."

6. Anne Bradstreet, "The Prologue to the Tenth Muse," in *Salt and Bitter and Good: Three Centuries of English and American Women Poets*, ed. Cora Kaplan (New York and London: Paddington, 1975), p. 29.

7. For the long history of misogynist humor, see Katharine Rogers, *The Troublesome Helpmate: A History of Misogyny in Literature* (Seattle: University of Washington Press, 1966).

8. Women's humor as an attack on patriarchal norms is discussed further in Judy Little's *Comedy and the Woman Writer: Woolf, Spark, and Feminism* (Lincoln: University of Nebraska, 1983).

9. Sarah Kemble Knight, "The Journal of Madam Knight," in *The American Tradition in Literature*, ed. Sculley Bradley et al., 4th ed. (New York: Grosset & Dunlap, 1974), I, 148.

10. Caroline Kirkland, "Borrowing in a New Settlement," from *A New Home—Who'll Follow?* in *Laughing Their Way: Women's Humor in America*, ed. Martha Bensley Bruère and Mary Ritter Beard (New York: Macmillan, 1934), pp. 5–6.

11. Frances Berry Whitcher, "The Widow Bedott," in *Laughing Their Way: Women's Humor in America*, pp. 6–8.

12. Fanny Fern, "Tabitha Tompkins' Soliloquy," in *Laughing Their Way: Women's Humor in America*, pp. 10–12.

13. Quoted in *Laughing Their Way: Women's Humor in America*, p. 53.

14. My discussion of Holley derives from Jane Curry, "Samantha 'Rastles' the Woman Question," *Journal of Popular Culture*, 8 (Spring 1975), 805–24. *Samantha Rastles the Woman Question* is also the title of Jane Curry's forthcoming book on Holley, to be published by the University of Illinois Press.

15. Alice Duer Miller, "A Consistent Anti to Her Son," in *Pulling Our Own Strings: Feminist Humor and Satire*, ed. Gloria Kaufman and Mary Kay Blakely (Bloomington: Indiana University Press, 1980), p. 85.

16. Eleanor Flexner, *Century of Struggle: The Woman's Rights Movement in the United States* (New York: Atheneum, 1968), p. 90.

17. Aileen S. Kraditor, *The Ideas of the Woman Suffrage Movement, 1890–1920* (New York: Doubleday Anchor, 1965), p. 90.

18. Anne Warner, "Miss Clegg's Adopted," *Century*, 46 (1904), 471. Further reference to this story will be by page number in the text.

19. Anne Warner (French), "The New Woman and the Old," in *The Experience of the American Woman*, ed. Barbara H. Solomon (New York: New American Library, 1978), pp. 126–27.

20. Mary E. Wilkins, "A New England Nun" (pp. 1–17) and "A Kitchen Colonel" (pp. 427–47), both in *A New England Nun and Other Stories* (New York: Harper & Brothers, 1891). Mary E. Wilkins took Charles Freeman's name when she married him in 1902, at the age of fifty. Thereafter, her writing never achieved the quality of her earlier work, and in particular, she lost most of her humor. It was an unhappy marriage, finally ending in divorce.

21. Kate Chopin, "The Storm," in *The Complete Works of Kate Chopin*, ed. Per Seyersted (Baton Rouge: Louisiana State University Press, 1969), p. 596.

22. "The Story of an Hour," in *The Complete Works of Kate Chopin*, pp. 352–54.

23. "The Storm" was not published during Chopin's lifetime; "The Story of an Hour" was rejected by a magazine editor as unethical. See Per Seyersted, *Kate Chopin: A Critical Biography* (Oslo: Universitetsforlaget and Baton Rouge: Louisiana State University Press, 1969), p. 68.

24. To date, the most comprehensive source of Parker anecdotes is John Keats, *You Might as Well Live: The Life and Times of Dorothy Parker* (New York: Simon & Schuster, 1970). Marion Meade is at work on a new and more sympathetic biography of Parker.

25. *The Portable Dorothy Parker* (New York: Viking, 1973), p. 518.

26. "Résumé," in *The Portable Dorothy Parker*, p. 99.

27. "Symptom Recital," in *The Portable Dorothy Parker*, p. 112.

28. "Unfortunate Coincidence," in *The Portable Dorothy Parker*, p. 96.

29. "Mrs. Hofstadter on Josephine Street," in *The Portable Dorothy Parker*, p. 157.

30. "The Waltz," in *The Portable Dorothy Parker*, pp. 47–51.

31. Peg Bracken, *The I Hate to Cook Book* (Greenwich, Conn.: Fawcett Crest, 1960), pp. 24–25.

32. Erma Bombeck, *At Wit's End* (Greenwich, Conn.: Fawcett Crest, 1967), p. 219.

33. Erma Bombeck, *The Grass Is Always Greener Over the Septic Tank* (Greenwich, Conn.: Fawcett Crest, 1976), p. 207.

34. Erica Jong, *Fear of Flying* (New York: New American Library, 1973), p. 310.

35. Sylvia Plath, *The Bell Jar* (New York: Harper & Row, 1971), p. 75.

36. The humor involved in tampax-insertion scenes is analyzed in Janice Delaney, Mary Jane Lupton and Emily Toth, *The Curse: A Cultural History of Menstruation* (New York: Dutton, 1976), esp. pp. 151–54.

37. Judy Blume, *Are You There God? It's Me, Margaret* (New York: Dell, 1970), p. 148.

38. Alix Kates Shulman, "A Story of a Girl and Her Dog," in *Rediscovery: 300 Years of Stories By and About Women*, ed. Betzy Dinesen (New York: Avon, 1982), p. 24.

39. Lisa Alther, *Kinflicks* (New York: Knopf, 1976), pp. 126–27.

40. E. M. Broner, *Her Mothers* (New York: Berkeley, 1975), pp. 185–86.

41. Charlotte Perkins Gilman, *Herland* (New York: Pantheon, 1979), p. 11. Other references to this edition will be made by page number in the text.

42. Toni Cade Bambara, "Raymond's Run," in *Gorilla My Love* (New York: Random House, 1972), p. 32.

43. Toni Cade Bambara, "Medley," in *Midnight Birds*, ed. Mary Helen Washington (New York: Doubleday Anchor, 1980), p. 268.

44. Alice Walker, "Everyday Use," in *Black-Eyed Susans*, ed. Mary Helen Washington (New York: Doubleday Anchor, 1975), p. 79. Further reference to this story will be made by page number in the text. "Everyday Use" will be reprinted in the forthcoming anthology *Between Mothers & Daughters: Stories Across a Generation*, ed. Susan Koppelman (New York: Feminist Press, in press).

45. Rita Mae Brown, *Rubyfruit Jungle* (New York: Bantam, 1973), p. 5. Further reference to this edition will be made by page number in the text.

46. For some discussion of stand-up comics, see my "Female Wits," *Massachusetts Review*, 22 (Winter 1981), 783–93.

47. In a recent article, Nancy Walker quotes some reasons given for omitting Marietta Holley from humor histories, despite her great importance in the nineteenth century. In *Native American Humor* (1947), James Aswell writes that Holley "most particularly... didn't amuse me." In *America's Humor: From Poor Richard to Doonesbury* (1978), Walter Blair and Hamlin Hill say that Holley "could never have become as popular today as she did during her lifetime." Most peculiar is C. Carroll Hollis' comment in Louis D. Rubin's *Comic Imagination in American Literature* (1973). According to Hollis, Marietta Holley's work is "of interest to historians, not citizens." Nancy Walker's study is "Wit, Sentimentality, and the Image of Women in the Nineteenth Century," *American Studies*, 20 (Fall 1981), 5–22.

Jane Curry's recent successes in performing Marietta Holley's stories show that there is still a large, appreciative audience for Holley's wit and wisdom.

48. The three stages in women's literature are discussed in Elaine Showalter, *A Literature of Their Own: British Women Novelists from Brontë to Lessing* (Princeton: Princeton University Press, 1977).

49. Hisaye Yamamoto, "Seventeen Syllables," in *The Third Woman: Minority Women Writers of the United States*, ed. Dexter Fisher (Boston: Houghton Mifflin, 1980), p. 486. Originally published in 1949.

50. Alice Duer Miller, "Feminism," in *Laughing Their Way: Women's Humor in America*, p. 222.

51. "The Miraculous Light," in *Samantha versus Josiah*, p. 223.

POSTSCRIPT

The Future of American Humor:
Through a Glass Eye, Darkly

Hamlin Hill*

Since 1980, the study of American humor has reached its maturity. While an occasional eyebrow rises to question its academic respectability and justification, such "eyes" are in an increasing minority.

Presses publish books on the subject without hesitation. Among more esoteric subjects belong John Allen Paulos' *Mathematics and Humor*, Conrad Hyers' *The Comic Vision and the Christian Faith*, David Hassler's *Comic Tones in Science Fiction*, Paul McGhee's *Children's Humor*, and Norman Holland's *Laughing: A Psychology of Humor*, all suggesting the invasion of the study into disciplines other than the literary one.[1] More traditional were Walter Blair and Raven McDavid's *The Mirth of a Nation*, Neil Schmitz's *Of Huck and Alice, Humorous Writing in American Literature*, Kenny Williams and Bernard Duffey's anthology *Chicago's Public Wits*, and Ron Wallace's forthcoming study of humor in American poetry, *God Be With the Clown*, all of which exploited more literary areas of investigation. Stanley Trachtenberg's *American Humorists, 1800–1950* contained two volumes of research materials by various contributors, giving the subject the weighty dignity of an encyclopedia.[2] David E. E. Sloane is currently overseeing a volume for Greenwood Press with contributions about *American Humor Magazines and Comic Newspapers*.

Conferences, workshops, and seminars on the topic have proliferated: the National Endowment for the Humanities sponsored its third seminar for college teachers at the University of New Mexico in the summer of 1981; the Western Humor and Irony Membership produced its first of many proposed annual conferences at Arizona State University, from 1–3 April 1982, with a resulting record of the proceedings that ran to a whopping 412 pages. The Third International Conference on Humor took place at the end of August, 1982, in Washington, D. C.,

*This essay was written specifically for publication in this volume and is included here by permission of the author.

with Number Four scheduled for Tel Aviv, Israel, in June, 1984. In April, 1983, a conference on "Humor in Health Care" took place in Portland, Oregon. There was even a First Festival of Radical Humor on the New York University campus in April, 1982 which, according to James Wolcott's report, sounded like a Marx Brothers movie with the parts played by the street people of Berkeley.[3] Nor were such gatherings limited to the United States. In December, 1982, the Spanish American Studies Association organized its annual meeting on the subject of humor; and in May, 1983, the United States Information Agency and the Council for International Exchange of Scholars sponsored a two-week workshop in Bangalore, India, on American humor for Indian college teachers.

If the workhorse of the discipline, *American Humor: An Interdisciplinary Newsletter*, appeared in mortal financial difficulties in 1983, *Studies in American Humor* revived with handsome support from Southwest Texas State University. Both *American Quarterly* and the *Jahrbuch für Amerikastudien* (Würzburg, Germany) scheduled special issues devoted to American humor.

The dilemma of attempting to look forward from here lies not in the ill health or the endangered state of the discipline, but rather in the embarrassment of riches which it currently enjoys. Perhaps the best division—still—is to separate professional humor from its high-browed twin, though that distinction is becoming increasingly artificial.

I

> Though your wife ran away with a sailor that day,
> And took with her your trifle of money;
> Bless your heart, they don't mind—they're
>   exceedingly kind—
> They don't blame you—as long as you're funny.
>   W. S. Gilbert, *Yeoman of the Guard* (1888)

Professional humorists—the ones in it for the immediate success, the quick laugh, and the fast buck—have been sabotaging the standards of literary critics in the United States for at least a hundred and fifty years. Until recently, the critics' revenge has been ostracism of their work. Like Gilbert's Jack Point in *Yeoman of the Guard*, such humorists have suffered from the various charges of being jesters and clowns, meretricious and venal. Several of them, like Mark Twain or Woody Allen, have risen from the popular to the "serious" level, and required reappraisals. But the unlucky ones who remain popular have usually remained unrecognized. For example, there has not been enough study of Max Shulman or H. Allen Smith or Jean Shepherd or William Price Fox, all of whom deserve critical analysis, as do other writers with mass comic appeal.

Technology now allows us to store and retrieve the products of the popular culture media—cassettes and discs, films and records give us access to live performances, television shows, and movies so that the genius of non-literary humorists is preserved. If too little of Ernie Kovacs' material survives, the same is not true for the generation of comedians who followed him and learned from him. The names are too familiar to require cataloging, but the critical analysis is almost non-existent. Norman Lear, Carl Reiner, and Mel Brooks have raised television scripts and movie plots to high comic art, deserving of serious appraisal.

We live in an age of parody; *Newsweek* made the phenomenon the cover story for its issue of April 21, 1983, focusing on a narrow sliver of it, the rage for lampoons of self-help books. But the predilection is more widespread than that one example: the movies *Superman* and *Annie* parody the comic strip; *Blazing Saddles* parodies the format of the Western; in *The Great American Novel*, Philip Roth parodies the prose style of earlier American writers. Joseph Papp's production of *Pirates of Penzance* parodies Gilbert and Sullivan. What explains the situation?

The authors of the *Newsweek* story, David Gelman and George Hackett, say that "most humorists agree that there is a continued need for parody, perhaps of a more sophisticated kind, in the age of dense-pack missile-bearing plans and supply-side recessions." And they quote Michael O'Donoghue, script writer for "Saturday Night Live" and editor of *The National Lampoon*, as proposing that such comedy reflects "a violent, desperate time. Humor is a release of tension, and you react to what is happening around you. The world is ready to nuke itself out. . . . Dick Van Dyke and Donna Reed just don't cut it anymore."[4] If such theories sound more appropriate to Dada than to *The Official Preppy Handbook*, and suspiciously pretentious, they nevertheless help in a way to explain the craze which ranges throughout almost all popular-culture humor.

Parody is the emotional opposite of satire. It lacks satire's indignation and anger; it exaggerates the model it is based upon without wishing to reform it. It mocks, where satire ridicules; it teases, where satire taunts. In a perverse sense, then, parody is satire that has lost its spirit, its will to fight, and has become futilitarian in its resignation. Or, theoretically, it flourishes in periods of tranquility, while satire reigns in periods of turmoil. In either case, parody equates with complacency, and students of American humor would do well to contemplate what its current popularity says culturally about the national funny-bone.

The unlimited wealth of primary materials is there to make such judgments. But too few students of our discipline appear to be examining them. It is necessary, perhaps, to ignore esthetic yardsticks when measuring popular humor, and use historical, psychological, and sociological ones instead. (Why, for instance, after the first shock reaction to *Holocaust*, did "Holocaust jokes" circulate widely in both the United States and West Germany?) Perhaps the alliance of popular culture studies with the study of humor will produce the kind of analysis now so surprisingly absent from scholarship in our discipline.

II

> Mirth is the Mail of Anguish—
> In which it Cautious Arm,
> Lest anybody spy the blood
> And "you're hurt" exclaim!
>
> Emily Dickinson, #165

If studies of popular humor are yet to be written, the deluge of criticism about "serious" novelists is equally imbalanced. The study and analysis of the postmodern comic novel is an avalanche, and one in which the seriousness has almost buried the humor. Barth and Barthelme, Pynchon and Hawkes, anyone named Wright except for Orville and Wilbur, the entire range of "fabulators," black humorists, apocalyptic novelists, and fictional nihilists have been scrutinized, discussed, and interpreted to the point of critical biopsy.

It is unfortunate, though, that the criticism seems unable to account satisfactorily for the humor of this school of writers. Its philosophical premises, its nightmare vision, its renunciation of order and logic, and its "wasteland" technique have all provided scholars with fertile (and by now, perhaps, overdone) subjects for discussion. But its humor? Why we laugh at the metaphysics of postmodernism still eludes definition, so far as I know.

Everyone (even Michael O'Donoghue, quoted above) knows that "humor is a release of tension," in at least one of its modes. That explains why we laugh at current highbrow fiction. But it does not explain what we laugh at, or how modern novelists so gauge our responses that they produce laughter instead of tears. Why don't we care more about characters with whom we empathize? Why do potentially tragic situations become pratfalls to modern readers? What, in the mind of the audience or the manipulation of the artist, creates a world that seems hopeless, helpless, but nevertheless funny? When someone confronts that issue—not in a single short work, but in the general tone of modern literature—that critic will have focused on the humor of our most fashionable novelists rather than upon their threadbare pessimism.

Serious literature consists (fortunately) of more than post-modern novelists, of course. Drama, habitually neglected by students of American humor, is a medium which combines the script with the visual comic impact of the actors and actresses whom we associate with specific plays. *My Fair Lady, Annie, Cats, Fiddler on the Roof,* the list goes on and on; and each is a combination of playwrighting skill and acting

timing and audience susceptibility which deserves some academic consideration. For that matter, why has Cole Porter never received his
appropriate recognition as one of our major comic playwrights?

There is enormous additional ground to cover in the field of comic
poetry, even after Ronald Wallace's book. The tone of much contemporary poetry is at least wistfully wry if not outright funny. And it
begs for analysis.

III

By forever, I mean thirty years.
Mark Twain, *Mark Twain in Eruption*

The study of Mark Twain shows no signs of abating—after considerably more than thirty years. Both the Iowa / California edition of his
works and the Mark Twain Papers series have scheduled volumes as far
in the future as the end of the twentieth century. And given their rate
of progress so far, that may well be an exceedingly optimistic timetable.
There will, it seems fairly certain, be at least one more generation of
scholars working on these editions—if not generations yet unborn. Text-
ual critics, annotators, bibliographers have enough to occupy them for
decades.

On the other hand, there is a serious question as to whether the
commitment to the work on the two Mark Twain editions is not in fact
a detriment to the study of Mark Twain. At least one generation of
Mark Twain students (the one that gathered in Iowa City in the summer
of 1963 to plan the edition) has worked for two decades on a set of the
standard works, only eight volumes of which have actually been published. Many of these original editors have either retired or died without enjoying the pleasure of seeing their assigned volumes even started
on the publication process. One has to wonder how many works of
scholarship and criticism were aborted by twenty-year commitments to
editorial work.

Fortunately, a younger generation of students of Mark Twain is
immune to that frustrating temptation. To name only a few, Alan Gribben, David E. E. Sloane, Stanley Brodwin, Neil Schmitz, and Susan K.
Harris have contributed significant recent studies. Gribben recently assessed some of the gaps in Mark Twain scholarship;[5] and I attempted
the same enumeration much earlier.[6] Almost all of these suggestions still
need extensive investigation. And in spite of the resistance of conserva-
tives, the need for a full-fledged psychological study of Mark Twain
remains the most crying one. In a decade when the word "radical" has
moss gathering around it, we still need radical interpretations of Mark
Twain. He is encased in a PR mystique which tends to inhibit honest
evaluation. In the next decade or so, possibly, we will enjoy a more
sophisticated look at Mark Twain than we have had so far.

Undoubtedly the sesquicentennial of Mark Twain's birth, in 1985, also the hundredth anniversary of the publication of *Adventures of Huckleberry Finn*, will provide a watershed. Already, conferences are being planned at Pennsylvania State University for April, 1984, and at Elmira College for the Fall of 1985. A collection of *Adventures of Huckleberry Finn: Centenary Essays*, edited by Robert Sattelmeyer and J. Donald Crowley, is in press at the University of Missouri. And James Nagel, editor of *Studies in American Fiction*, has announced a special Mark Twain issue for the Autumn 1985 number. The Iowa / California Edition hopes to have its definitive *Huck Finn* published in 1985, and Harper & Row plans to reissue the old Chandler facsimile of the first edition with an updated introduction and bibliography. These are just the first swells of what will surely become a tidal wave of re-examination and reappraisal.

Twain is a magnetic legend, a national shrine that transcends geography, and a distillation to the entire world of everything American. He deserves better than anyone has yet given him.

IV

Where it will all end, knows God.
David Gelman and George Hackett,
"Making Fun For Profit," *Newsweek*,
25 April 1983

Although the unexplored territory for the study of American humor is vast, probably even God would not want to be too definite about the direction our humor will take. Humor, like litmus paper, responds to external stimuli; so that to predict its future is very close to forecasting the course of history, politics, economics, sociology, and mass psychology combined. So, why not?

A pattern has become obvious in the recent past: humorists who begin their careers as frivolous become increasingly sober and gloomy. Woody Allen and Steve Martin (not to mention Twain, Thurber, and Perelman) have turned relatively "serious" in their most recent products. Do popularity and longevity breed comic contempt? We might add the "exhaustion" of Barth and the silence of Salinger and Kesey to the formula, and conclude that the comic voice, like some man-made element, appears to have a shorter and shorter half-life. (Whatever happened, except perhaps for Lily Tomlin, Arte Johnson, and Goldie Hawn, to the cast of "Rowan and Martin's Laugh-In"?) The Three B's of comic journalism—Baker, Bombeck, and Buchwald—sound increasingly tired and jaded.

Possibly, then, no major, sustained comic voice will arise and endure between now and the end of the century, to take a place with Franklin,

Twain, Thurber and possibly Woody Allen. The postmodernists have become too cryptic, involuted and opaque to maintain the comic spirit. They are, like Hemingway's gut-shot jackel in *The Green Hills of Africa*, gnawing at their own entrails. The "black humor" phenomenon of the 1960s and 1970s has dissipated by diluting itself in the popular culture mainstream; no one seems to be a strong inheritor of its legacy.

If there are no contenders for the humorous voice of the last decade and a half of the twentieth century, that absence does not signal the decline or fall of American humor. There would appear to be more and more voices, rather than fewer and fewer. Perhaps the United States has become so multi-faceted that it is unrealistic to expect a single author to represent our humor. But the cliques and the in-groups have representatives galore, from the drug-culture vestiges like Cheech and Chong to the Valley Girl nonsense of Southern California. Such humor triggers a predictable set of adjectives: wacky, zany, frivolous, irreverent—and, apparently, imperishable.

On January 1, 1967, Paul West commented in *Book Week* that "fantasy is the refusal of a world that is impossible, in the sense of being intolerable, in favor of a world that is impossible in the sense of being preposterous." That distinction is a useful one. "Intolerable" (black, realistic) humor appears to be on the wane, while "preposterous" fantasy waxes, healthy and robust.

Perhaps we are dancing the night before the battle of Waterloo; but, predictably, we *are* dancing. Perhaps we are laughing less at ourselves than we once did (an insight that foreigners to American culture frequently assert), but we are laughing. However "sick" and fatalistic we may be, the funny bone is still functioning—and may well be the only salvation for us all.

Notes

1. Paulos (Chicago: University of Chicago Press, 1980); Hyers (New York: Pilgrim Press, 1981); Hassler (Westport, Conn.: Greenwood Press, 1982); McGhee (New York: John Wiley and Sons, 1982); Holland (Ithaca, N.Y.: Cornell University Press, 1982).

2. Blair and McDavid (Minneapolis: University of Minnesota Press, 1983); Schmitz (Minneapolis: University of Minnesota Press, 1983); Williams and Duffey (Baton Rouge: Louisiana State University Press, 1983); Wallace (Columbia: University of Missouri Press, 1984); Trachtenberg (Detroit: Gale Research Co., 1982).

3. James Wolcott, "You're Under Arrest, Jane Everywoman," *Harper's*, July 1982, pp. 67–70.

4. David Gelman and George Hackett, "Making Fun for Profit," *Newsweek*, 25 April 1983, p. 70.

5. Alan Gribben, "Removing Mark Twain's Mask," *ESQ*, 26 (1980), 167–71.

6. Hamlin Hill, "Who Killed Mark Twain?" *American Literary Realism*, 7 (1974), 121–24.

INDEX